# GUANTANAMO BAY AND THE JUDICIAL-MORAL TREATMENT OF THE OTHER

# Guantanamo Bay and the Judicial-Moral Treatment of the Other

## ☞ Edited by Clark Butler ☜

PUBLISHED IN COOPERATION WITH THE
INSTITUTE FOR HUMAN RIGHTS,
INDIANA UNIVERSITY-PURDUE UNIVERSITY FORT WAYNE

PURDUE UNIVERSITY PRESS
WEST LAFAYETTE, INDIANA

Copyright 2007 by Purdue University.
All rights reserved.

Printed in the United States of America.

**Library of Congress Cataloging-in-Publication Data**
Guantanamo Bay and the judicial-moral treatment of the other / edited by Clark Butler.
   p. cm.
   Includes bibliographical references and index.
   ISBN-13: 978-1-55753-427-9 (alk. paper) 1. War on Terrorism, 2001--Moral and ethical aspects. 2. Terrorism--Investigation--Moral and ethical aspects. 3. Detention of persons--Cuba--Guantánamo Bay Naval Base. 4. Prisoners of war--Legal status, laws, etc.--Cuba--Guantánamo Bay Naval Base. 5. Prisoners of war--Government policy--United States. 6. Aliens--Government policy--United States. 7. Human rights--Government policy--United States. I. Butler, Clark, 1944-
  HV6432.G825 2007
  174'.42--dc22

                                                            2006026145

## Contents

INTRODUCTION: SOFT AMERICAN EMPIRE VERSUS PLAYING THE
   U.N.-E.U. CARD / Clark Butler     1

### PART 1: GUANTANAMO BAY

BREAKING THE TRADITION: THE CASE FOR THE 640 DETAINEES
   IN GUANTANAMO / David Rudenstine     15

AMERICAN TREATMENT OF DETAINEES AND THE
   U.S. SUPREME COURT / William Durland

SECURITY, CIVIL LIBERTIES, AND HUMAN RIGHTS:
   FINDING A BALANCE / Jennifer Casseldine-Bracht

TERRORISM, A NEW CHALLENGE FOR INTERNATIONAL
   HUMANITARIAN LAW / Anisseh Van Engleland-Nourai     66

ON THE JUDICIAL TREATMENT OF GUANTANAMO
   DETAINEES WITHIN THE CONTEXT OF
   INTERNATIONAL LAW / Saby Goshray     80

### PART 2: THE JUDICIAL TREATMENT OF THE OTHER

GHANDI'S ALTERNATIVE TO THE ALIEN
   OTHER / Richard Johnson     119

THE CLOSED SOCIETY VERSUS THE RIGHTS
   TO EMIGRATE AND IMMIGRATE / W. L. McBride     132

JUST AND FAVORABLE REMUNERATION: A NEGLECTED
  HUMAN RIGHT / Milton Fisk                              146

MORAL RIGHTS, MORAL RESPONSIBILITY, AND THE FAILURE OF
  MORAL KNOWLEDGE / Dallas Willard                       161

CONTRIBUTORS                                             179

INDEX                                                    183

The Editor wishes to express appreciation to the Office of Research and External Support at the Indiana University-Purdue University Fort Wayne Campus for its funding of the December 2004 conference on which this volume is based.

# GUANTANAMO BAY AND THE JUDICIAL-MORAL TREATMENT OF THE OTHER

# Introduction

## On Soft American Empire versus Playing the UN-EU Card

### ⌒ CLARK BUTLER ⌒

A few years ago many of us, after the fall of the Soviet Union, took seriously the idea of soft American empire. World security was vital, and a world empire of the willing, with foundations in world capitalism and entrepreneurship, and in worldwide democracy after the fall of the Soviet Union, seemed an attractive use of American power. America, after forgoing its first chance to strike out for American world empire after World War II, was now suddenly in the era of the second chance. There was certainly no other world superpower to do the job.

But the success of soft American empire always depended on details of execution as much as, or even more than, on considerations of grand strategy. Successful execution in Kosovo or Afghanistan always risked being followed by failure due to poor, uninformed execution in Iraq or elsewhere. The United States, by its presidential form of government, tends to be more prone to failure of foreign policy than countries with parliamentary democracy. Presidential democracy in fact tends to be a contradiction in terms. Because the roles of chief of state and head of government are combined in the same person, to criticize policies of the head of government is, unlike criticism of the prime minister in Britain, to throw mud on the flag. Because the chief of state is the symbol of the nation, the very idea of a loyal opposition and of a democratically vigilant citizenry is undermined. To criticize a president who wraps himself in the flag is to be disloyal to the nation. The nation rallies around the president. This allows misguided policy to be pursued out of false presidential pride long beyond the point where its possible flaws become apparent to those not under the aura of presidential power. Even if the spell is broken, there is no possibility of early parliamentary elections to find a new head of government. This may be considered the most fundamental flaw of the United States Constitution.

A presidentially protracted failure of execution could be a military failure in urban guerrilla warfare, but it could also reflect a moral failure on the American home front. Purely military success might not withstand a moral failure of the United States to lead the world by practicing the fundamental values it had claimed to uphold. To many today, Guantanamo Bay and Abu Graib seem to symbolize this danger. The concern is that Abu Graib may not be merely traceable to regrettable occasional oversights by military recruiting officers overly eager to meet their quotas, allowing a few bad apples into the armed forces. It may in fact be traceable to a larger crisis of moral education in the United States, in the American family, in the country's elementary and secondary schools, and even in its universities.

Despite the periodic desecration of Jewish and Muslim cemeteries on the European continent, Europe, with the help of the Council of Europe and the European Court for Human Rights, has more nearly solved the general problem of moral education as human rights education, the problem of establishing a universal moral minimum. It has done so by subordinating itself to the United Nations Universal Declaration of Human Rights throughout all levels of education and domestic law. Moral education presupposes a consensus on values, and the hesitancy with which such a consensus occurs in the United States pushes public schools, which are locally rather than nationally regulated, to leave moral education in the hands of family and church. The United States is averse to the idea of placing its Constitution, like those of the European Union, under the higher authority of the Universal Declaration. This makes the attainment of a universal moral minimum more difficult to achieve than in Europe, which has the additional advantage of national ministries of education.

Still, the United States may have something to learn from studying Europe's use of the Universal Declaration. The recent adoption, now more or less official in the United States, of the language of diversity shows that local control of schools need not impede the universal penetration of new ideas, especially when federal funding is involved. Yet the apparently socialist character both of European economies and of some Articles in the Universal Declaration dissuades the United States from taking its lead from the Declaration. The United States is seemingly dissuaded by fear that doing much of anything under the auspices of the United Nations implies an unacceptable surrender of American sovereignty to the international organization.

Yet we must recall that the 1948 Universal Declaration of Human Rights was derived from Franklin Delano Roosevelt's 1942 Four Freedoms Speech. Roosevelt placed freedom of belief and freedom of worship first in rank among human rights. Only afterwards, in Roosevelt's hierarchy, came freedom from fear and the more socialistic freedom from want, for he who wills the end must ultimately will the means.

Americans, without distortion of the now canonical document, are free to interpret the Universal Declaration so that freedom of thought—what they themselves cherish as freedom of speech—is the only logically necessary human right. That right is a necessary as a condition of the very possibility of universal dialogical rationality. Such rationality, by opening up the field of possible respondents as widely as possible, is required by the maximum vindication of anyone's belief in the course of truth-directed human discussion. The more socialistic rights in the Declaration then become noncategorical, hypothetical rights. Their validity must be tested empirically by social science to establish whether and how, locally or universally, they support the one necessary right. For example, how does a particular system of universal health care enhance or undermine, locally and universally, the universal exercise of freedom of thought? Until social science speaks with one voice on this matter, libertarians and socialists can agree to disagree in advancing the discussion. Libertarians heuristically may adopt socialist assumptions if they choose to participate in European discussions, and socialists may adopt for the sake of argument more libertarian assumptions if they choose to take part in some American discussion circles. In the meantime, universal moral education can proceed with a broad consensus on civil rights, especially dialogical freedom of thought, agreeing only to embrace whatever universal free inquiry ends up requiring in the way of publicly guaranteed material resources for the implementation of such rights.

I have suggested the possibility that a failure of American empire might in part be a moral failure. The essays in this volume largely point to such a failure and call for a sustained new initiative in moral reeducation. A "them versus us" mentality has led many Americans to suppose that, despite their financial indebtedness, they enjoy a consumer paradise that is the envy of the rest of the world. Others allegedly dearly want what Americans have, and in the defense of what Americans have it takes unnumbered foreign lives to equal the value of one American life. But the remedy of a human rights–based universal moral minimum might not be in place in time to forestall failure of the strategy of soft American empire, an empire of equals in which some are simply more equal than others.

The danger always exists that a provincial, faith-based, theologically driven morality may fail to reinforce the cosmopolitan universal moral minimum, but rather may eclipse it. But let us grant that provincialism may only be a grave risk, perhaps not a death sentence, on soft American empire. Yet precisely because of the risk, it is crucial that the United States, or any nation in its position, have a contingency plan in place in case of such failure.

Let us call the current course of U.S. world policy, including the proclaimed policy of preemptive strike, plan A. Not knowing the future, the United States needs to prepare for the contingency of failure in Iraq, or if not in today's Iraq then in some other Iraq of tomorrow. Even while many strongly hope for success of plan A, especially because for better or worse we have already embarked upon it, there has to be a plan B held in reserve. Two international coordinated centers of decision-making must enter into our thinking when we consider plan B. They are the United Nations and the European Union.

Many Americans are reluctant to place the destiny of the United States in the hands of the United Nations. But that has really never been the question. The United Nations is not a sovereign agency to which American sovereignty can be lost, and the European Union is only beginning to show promise of becoming a sovereign superpower capable of earning the respect of the American superpower. When Europe advocates peaceful solutions, Americans can always point to Europe's limited capacity to wage war. To have that capacity and still refrain from using it would increase the authority of Europe's voice in the world, though at the price of compromising the depth of its current social service paradise.

The United States today suffers from the lack of a dialogue partner whose power it can respect as roughly equal to its own. The Soviet Union was such a power, though Soviet values, like those of China today, were further removed from American values than those of the European Union. Because it has not yet integrated still-sovereign national defense systems into a true European defense, the European Union is not yet an equal dialogue power. Plan A, the idea of soft American empire—an informal world empire whose destiny would be that of a federation of equals based on universal capitalist and democratic values—must not be rejected out of hand. Yet it is in America's interest to keep in reserve plan B as a contingency plan, not to dismiss Western Europe as old Europe, but to realize that so-called Old Europe is in fact spearheading new Europe through the Franco-German alliance. With 450 million people and greater collective wealth than the United States, the European Union has superpower capacity. Potentially it is the equal of the United States, though it is not so in fact. What the member states of the European Union spend collectively on defense can approach the ballpark of what the United States spends, though it is not yet a coherently integrated effort.

A number of European countries, notably Germany, are pacifist. Europeans need to realize that the purpose of an integrated European defense is not to make war, but to lend weight to European judgment in dialogue with the American partner. At present the United States welcomes allies who follow its lead, but shuns the idea of equal dialogue partners. Yet experience teaches that dialogue between equally empowered voices has the greatest heuristic value, and leads to the most reasonable result. The American monologue solely with itself since 1989 can be a recipe for insanity.

Yet, in suggesting that the United States hold the European Union in reserve as a possible future equal dialogue partner, Europe itself would have to do its part. Western Europe offers subsidies and social services to its populations of which many Americans can only dream. But the degree to which these services would need to be curtailed were Europe to become an equal dialogue partner and make a greater investment to an integrated defense is often exaggerated. The challenge to Europe in defense is not primarily budgetary. The challenge lies in the sacrifice of the very idea of a sovereign national defense as the last and greatest bastion of national sovereignty. The challenge is to implement the primacy of Strasbourg over Brussels.

For the present we may call plan B "playing the European card," but it can also be called playing the United Nations card. Although immediately Europe is the most promising dialogue partner for America, the multi-lateral possibility within the United Nations of someday including other strong democratic voices from Russia, China, India, or elsewhere should not be excluded. Neoconservative Americans are still deeply skeptical of playing this card. Yet if United States moral leadership were sufficiently damaged by a combination of ill-conceived preemptive strikes, unresponsiveness to global warming, and other such factors, the United Nations—initially based on a new special relationship between America and the European Union—might become the best remaining hope. This would not necessarily be the end of the neoconservative option for America. If a moral failure or a failure of intelligence leads the United States to take plan B seriously, a subsequent failure of even plan B cannot be excluded, and it might oblige America to return to and rethink the neo-conservative plan A of soft American empire. Any call upon Europe to step up to the plate may remain unanswered. European students, who pay little tuition and who receive subsidized room and board, consider themselves more often privileged rather than spoiled, decadent, or dependent beneficiaries of a vast American neocolonial protectorate from the Atlantic to the Urals.

A failure of either plan leads us to rethink the other. So though some neoconservatives may not be speaking as loudly now as a couple of years ago, and though their voices are not prominent in this volume, we ourselves must still hold them in reserve for a possible future with which to threaten Europe with decline into irrelevance. For some the fact that neoconservatism is still being held in reserve will be just the incentive needed to make plan B work. In either case, the neoconservative hypothesis must continue to be taken seriously. This remains true today, though plan A may turn out not to be the only alternative to plan B.

The idea for this volume began with a vote by philosophy students in an American department of philosophy in December 2003 to examine Guantanamo Bay and the Judicial Treatment of Aliens in an international conference. Quite clearly, it was already at that time an issue weighing heavily on their conscience. As Guantanamo in the months after continued to be a moving target, we broadened the theme to include more than the treatment of aliens by the United States. Other times in history and other places in the world could provide enlightening parallels.

Treatment of the foreigner in contemporary human rights law has roots in the biblical concept of hospitality, since the Hebrews perceived that they had been slaves in the land of Egypt. But the *justification* for hospitality, as contrasted to its historical *cause*, need not be merely that we do not ourselves wish to be the oppressor because we were once oppressed. It may also be that the stranger comes to us as a messenger, with something to teach.

Yet foreigners are given visas and admitted to a country selectively for numerous reasons: to reunite families, to provide political exile, to promote tourism, to offer study opportunities, to promote foreign trade, to contribute to international scientific cooperation, to allow opportunity for economic refugees—but also to be prisoners of war or captured mercenaries. Once foreigners are in the country, they may be considered dialogue partners, but they may also be viewed as a menace. They may be subjected to surveillance, regulations, judicial proceedings, punishment, torture, economic exploitation, or expulsion. There are obvious conflicts between the diverse roles played by the foreigner. It is difficult for prisoners to be dialogue partners. Interrogation is not dialogue, and the value of the information it yields may be different from that of dialogue. It is difficult to argue that all strangers on one's soil should be primarily dialogue partners. The most that can be said is that they should be, as much as possible, dialogue partners, as much as is consistent with the respect for the human right to security that conditions any ideal dialogue situation.

The essays in this volume fall into two parts: Guantanamo Bay and, more generally, the judicial treatment of aliens. The essays on Guantanamo Bay are critical of American policy and practice there. Yet one principle of discussion in the public domain is that all who are concerned—or who believe they are concerned—should be invited to the table, but that no one is obliged to enter the discussion. Contributions to discussion made under duress are simply not credible. Neoconservatives were never excluded here. But they never came to the table. Some of them may have been waiting for the lessons of the Iraqi War to be more conclusive. A few may have suspected they would be sidelined as token representatives of a position dwarfed by a majority of more liberal contributors. A widely circulated call for participants may have missed some because they are in think tanks or other organizations that do not regularly receive information about certain university-based academic ventures, due to not having the familiar university academic appointments.

Yet the purpose of this volume is to advance public discussion. Not wishing to publish a political tract, we must make a sincere effort to take up the point of view of absent dialogue partners as we develop our positions. There is a sense in which the dominant consensus viewpoint within a polity is always right. When Rousseau said that the majority is always right, the most reasonable way to interpret him is to suppose that the dominant view represents a *target theory* which all who do not place themselves outside the discussion circle of the larger national society must provisionally and respectfully adopt as a point of departure for the sake of argument. The path to the truth for anyone in that larger circle, sharing in its general will, is indirect, leading through serious consideration of the majority view, but also allowing the possibility of its eventual self-refutation.

So when a publicly influential part of the whole discussion circle is missing in a volume on Guantanamo Bay, the range of discussants who have signaled their presence must strive to compensate and become the whole. No right to absolute security is even possible for mortal human beings, and no state dedicated exclusively to an alleged human right to such security is truly committed to human rights. The degree of insecurity which governments ought to protect us against is only the degree that eliminates wide-ranging freedom of thought, narrowing thought precisely to little but the thought of our own insecurity. Nonetheless, our contributors, as they revised their essays, were encouraged to give attention to the *human right to security* alongside the civil-liberties concerns which were largely paramount with them.

In my introductory comments above I have followed my own advice by heuristically adopting the perspective that is underrepresented here, but which in the wider public has been more influential. The neoconservative movement in American political thought is complex. A few short years ago many of us were tempted by one important tendency in it. The reflections I have shared have been a thought experiment that purposively avoids disparaging dismissal of the neoconservative idea from which contributors to which volume have distanced themselves.

In the first contribution, David Rudenstine, dean of the Benjamin J. Cardozo School of Law at Yeshiva University, argues why in the end Guantanamo Bay was always likely to lead to a new constitutional correction of Executive privilege in the United States. The June 2006 Supreme Court decision that invoked international law along with the Constitution to condemn practices in Guantanamo Bay (including proposed special military tribunals) has now confirmed his thesis.[1]

William Durland is, like Rudenstine, a trained constitutional lawyer who also subdues a seething underlying passion aroused by Guantanamo by cool legal analysis. He is legal director of the Center on Law and Human Rights, Colorado Springs. We are led to wonder whether national security is more threatened than protected by emulating tactics better known, and more often expected, among America's enemies. Political realism, a realistic appreciation of real evil in our enemies, is in order, but does it really require getting down in the mud and fighting on the enemy's terms? Rudenstine and Durland both appeal to the American people and its judicial institutions to instigate the constitutional corrective, which has now taken place. Implicitly, they call for collective moral reeducation throughout America to prevent future Guantanamos from occurring.

The third respondent to events surrounding Guantanamo, Jennifer Casseldine-Bracht, is a research associate at the Indiana-Purdue Fort Wayne Campus (IPFW) Institute for Human Rights. She is informed by international human rights law but writes as a political philosopher and civil libertarian rather than as an attorney. She makes the case that respect of international law enhances rather than threatens national security. She traces neglect of constitutional protection for civil rights to causes lying in the current but possibly reversible political context in the United States.

Anniseh Van Engeland-Nourai, with French citizenship and education and Iranian roots, is a protection and assistance delegate on the staff of the International Red Cross in Geneva. She uses her legal training to argue that existing international humanitarian law, beginning with the Geneva Conventions, is sufficient to deal with the threat of terrorism without the ad hoc invention of new international law based on concepts such as that of "enemy combatants" falling into a crack without human rights protection. A crack in such protection widens into a chasm that jeopardizes and strictly annuls the human rights norms of us all, for human rights are either universal or nonexistent.

The Marquis de Lafayette was no terrorist or suicide bomber. But we are reminded, in reading Van Engeland-Nourai, that Lafayette, coming to America by his own means, not as a paid mercenary but as an ideologically committed fighter for the American revolutionary cause, could only have been considered an "enemy combatant" by Great Britain, if such a concept had then been identified. It is odd that America owes its own independence in part to a man who assumed a role now decried by America itself as depriving the role-taker of any claim to the basic rights on which the young North American republic took its stand. In so doing Lafayette contributed to the later official and decisive declaration of war by France on America's colonial rulers.

Saby Ghoshray, vice president for Development at the World Compliance Corporation, was born in India and educated in the United States. He focuses principally on the American military tribunals improvised to replace civil courts in which the accused would normally be tried if they did not fall under the Geneva Conventions. He finds including the very different roles of accuser, investigator, incarcerator, prosecutor, judge, and executioner—all played by independent protagonists in the classical procedure of justice as originally modeled on tragic theater—in a single agency to be a travesty on justice. The example of the internment camps for Japanese Americans in World War II has been insufficient to inoculate this country from a recurrence of something suspiciously similar. Ghoshray's faith in the United States, now confirmed by the Supreme Court, is likewise a faith that, through the thicket of court appeals and with varying outcomes, the idea of justice will emerge reinforced by the conscious correction of current deviations.

It is sometimes said that every important learning experience has to occur twice to truly sink in. Napoleon, like Germany in the twentieth century, had to be defeated twice; after Vietnam, the United States may need to learn the same lesson a second time in Iraq. And so Guantanamo's lesson may penetrate America's conscience more deeply the second time around than the first time, during the internment of the Japanese.

Part 2 of this volume ranges more widely than Guantanamo. It addresses the central question of moral education in America, a question that Guantanamo raises. It explores a root moral malaise that seems to have made events like Guantanamo and Abu Graib possible. Richard Johnson, founding director of the Peace and Conflict Studies Certificate Program at the Indiana-Purdue Fort Wayne Campus, draws on Gandhi in addressing the American reflex—in part born of dreamlike even if credit-based consumer affluence—of falling into the "us versus them" dichotomy, which he views as the fallacy of the *alien other*. This is the fallacy which the philosopher Hegel addressed in his central call for *negation of the negation*, i.e., negation of our contradictory negation of the other dialogical selves in the very relationships which make us the selves we are. It is said that in Islam three female witnesses are needed to counter one male witness. In the light of bombing tactics since World War II, how many non-American deaths are needed to equal one American death?

We may be told that the world policeman requires, for the sake of the security of all, more security than is enjoyed by those he protects. But the very notion of a world policeman, abstracted and absolutized apart from any legitimating constitutional world federal democracy, and indeed from any world political authority at all, is a contradiction in terms. Gandhi, like Hegel in the West, teaches us that the other is never truly alien, and is destined to be included in one inclusive moral community with us.

William McBride, Distinguished Professor of Philosophy at Purdue University, West Lafayette, also takes up the Hegelian theme of the *inclusion of the other*. Appealing to Karl Popper's distinction between a human rights–based open society and the closed society, he concurs with Herbert Marcuse and others who deny the conventional belief that the closed society is either in decline or is restricted to societies other than our own Western or, more particularly, American society. He sees ominous signs since 9/11 of a resurgence of the closed society of "us versus them" in the United States. Guantanamo Bay is symptomatic. In opposition to this tendency, he upholds the recognized human right to emigrate from one's own land and, hence, to enjoy favorable immigration policies elsewhere in the world.

Immigration is a key means of protecting the basic human right of freedom of thought for individuals oppressed by local provincialisms. At least in the middle term, it is an essential tool in the fight against world poverty and inequality. Economic refugees are often decried as a *local* problem for affluent and not so affluent local workers, and indeed they are. But, taking a larger perspective, they are part of the solution to the *global* problems of poverty and extremes of economic inequality. They will remain part of the solution to that larger problem until greater economic parity achieved between regions of the world demotivates economically motivated immigration.

McBride rightly reminds us that neither immigration nor emigration is a strict human right comparable to freedom of thought, since both presuppose the very idea of the more or less closed sovereign nation-state or multinational state in a relation of exclusion to other such states. Humanity once existed without local state frontiers and logically may so exist again. At that point, the free flow of services, as well as of ideas and goods, may be better protected as a human right than it is currently by rights of immigration and emigration, which are inherently limited by local state sovereignty.

Milton Fisk, a professor emeritus of philosophy at Indiana University, Bloomington, also focuses on contemporary exclusion of the other, not by limitations on immigration, but by the lack of a living wage, from which both non-immigrating populations and economic refugees suffer. One long-term key to fighting terrorism, we know, lies in giving more of the foot soldiers of terrorism, with Guantanamos following in their wake, a stake in life, a living wage. Fisk sees the wage contract today from a Marxist perspective as purely formal, negotiated on an unequal playing field in which employers dictate the terms. The practice denies reciprocity, solidarity. It denies universal community between persons who realize that human rights require respect for one another's full agenda in life, and not merely for his or her immediate need to subsist. The ideal of a universal living wage becomes a goal for a world labor movement, even if it demands temporary sacrifices by local labor movements. Reversible local compromises in the world labor market may occur on the road to a universal living wage. The poor try to reduce their poverty by immigration or by local militancy at home while still remaining poor. Affluent workers in the West enjoy less affluence than yesterday, or a stagnant living wage through imported cheap labor and outsourcing.

The World Trade Organization, we know, is dedicated to increased trade, economic growth, and global wealth. But Fisk builds a convincing case for a world labor movement struggle to assign to the WTO the revised goal of growth and increased global wealth *contingent on* a universal living wage. China, with an economy growing 10 percent a year, may not be ready to price a living wage into the products it exports, but western Europe was similarly unready in the nineteenth century. Yet the wealth China finally accumulates may make a world consensus on the matter easier in the future. Even then, a living wage may require cessation of the inhumane use of locally concentrated wealth to frustrate a living wage in remaining poor countries by farm subsidies and other such means. France, for all its much vaunted history as champion of the Third World, today still patently convicts itself in this regard of inauthenticity.

Dallas Willard, a professor of philosophy at the University of Southern California, takes the longest view in addressing the moral root causes of Guantanamo and judicial exclusion of the other in the established twentieth-century academic tradition in moral philosophy. He records the decline of the very concept of ethical knowledge in Western philosophy in centers of higher learning in the past hundred years. He notes that the Victorian age did not question such knowledge, however quaint, provincial, or condescending such "knowledge" may sometimes seem to us today. Academic philosophy in the English-speaking world retreated from cognitively grounded normative ethics into meta-ethics and normative relativism, with a deleterious effect on Western society in general, with its increasing tendency to the self-righteous complacent egoism of the fortunate. Secular ethics teachers typically no longer teach right and wrong, either because they believe it does not exist or because they hold it is impossible or too difficult to discover. The minority that would continue such teaching is viewed as naïve.

Willard's essay is a fitting conclusion to this volume because it highlights the crying need for a counteroffensive in academic ethics. Indeed, since the United Nations Universal Declaration of Human Rights, the possibility of a real countermovement has arisen: a restoration of normative ethics now conceived as the ethics of universally constructing and then respecting objectively grounded individual human rights, beginning with dialogical freedom of thought.[2]

## Notes

1. *Hamdan v. Rumsfeld*, No. 05-184, U.S. Supreme Court, June 29, 2006.
2. Clark Butler, *Human Rights Ethics* (forthcoming).

PART 1

GUANTANAMO BAY

# American Preeminence, Separation of Power and Human Rights

## *The Guantanamo Detainee Case*

⌐ DAVID RUDENSTINE ⌐

In June 2004, the United States Supreme Court once again validated Alexis de Tocqueville's well-known observation that "[s]carcely any political question arises in the United States that is not resolved, sooner or later, into a judicial question."[1] It did so by deciding three cases[2] arising out of the wars in Afghanistan and Iraq as well as the more open-ended war against terrorism. I propose to discuss one of these three cases in some detail. I will argue that the outcome in the case constituted a major departure from past decisions, which emphasized the importance of judicial deference towards the Executive branch during times of crisis. I will speculate about the Court's own attitude towards its decision to break with tradition and the reasons that may have persuaded it to do so. I will opine about the significance of the break, and then end with general observations about America's power, accountability, and commitment to human rights.

### THE GUANTANAMO CASE: *RASUL V. BUSH*

On June 28, 2004, the Supreme Court decided a narrow, legalistic, tedious question, but in so doing it completely upended President Bush's plan for imprisoning alleged enemy combatants and terrorists, checked the president's drive for unprecedented power, reaffirmed the importance of separation of powers, and put the Court on a course to have a significant voice in future cases involving national security.

The case arose from petitions for writs of habeas corpus filed by David Hicks and Mamdouh Habib, two Australian citizens, and Fawzi Khalid Abdullah Fahad Al Odah and eleven other Kuwaiti citizens, who were captured in Afghanistan in early 2002 during hostilities between United States and the Taliban. Some time later, they, along with about 640 other non-Americans—all captured abroad—were imprisoned at the naval base at Guantanamo Bay (where now in 2006 more than 700 remain).[3] The base, which the United States occupies pursuant to a 1903 lease agreement executed with the Republic of Cuba following the Spanish-American War, comprises about 45 square miles of land and water along the southeast coast of Cuba. The habeas petitions claimed that the detainees faced indefinite imprisonment without an opportunity to prove their innocence, asserted that they were not combatants against the United States and had not engaged in any terrorist acts, requested that they be informed of the charges against them and that they be allowed to meet with their families and counsel, and asked that they be given access to the courts or some other impartial tribunal so that they could prove their innocence.

The narrow legal question presented in *Rasul v. Bush* was whether the federal habeas statute grants the federal courts jurisdiction to review the detention of aliens in Guantanamo. The government made several arguments claiming the federal courts lacked jurisdiction: The president has power as the commander in chief to detain indefinitely those captured in Afghanistan, Congress had specifically authorized the indefinite imprisonment of these individuals, and Congress had withheld from the federal courts jurisdiction over habeas petitions filed by individuals imprisoned at Guantanamo. The detainees, who pressed the federal courts to exercise jurisdiction, responded in kind: As commander in chief, the president lacked the power to detain indefinitely the Guantanamo 640, Congress had not given the Executive the power to detain these individuals indefinitely, and the statute defining habeas jurisdiction did authorize federal courts to review the habeas petitions filed by the detainees.

By a vote of 6 to 3, the Court ruled in favor of the detainees: as written, the habeas statute granted the federal courts jurisdiction to review the detainees' habeas petitions. In reaching that result, the Court said nothing about what should happen next. It left until another time and another case what process should be followed to determine whether the government could continue to imprison the 640 detainees.[4] As the Court stated: "[w]hether and what further proceedings may become necessary after respondents make their response to the merits of petitioners' claims are matters that we need not address now."[5]

On its face, the Court's opinion in *Rasul* was no trumpet of liberty, no ringing endorsement of the importance of due process, no memorable restatement of the significant linkage between having a vital democracy and a strong separation of powers doctrine. There are no lofty phrases and no uplifting sentences. Instead the opinion is written in the narrowest and the most cautious of terms, and went no further in offering guidance to the lower courts than was absolutely necessary to decide the legal question before it.

But the opinion, dry as sand, masks the significance and vibrancy of the decision. Until the Court decided *Rasul,* the Bush administration assumed that it could imprison indefinitely, and without any judicial interference whatsoever, those captured in a combat zone and suspected of being enemy combatants or terrorists, so long as it detained these individuals outside the United States. The Court in *Rasul* torpedoed that assumption. It did so by asserting that the courts have jurisdiction over the petitions filed by the Guantanamo detainees and by leaving the ultimate reach of federal court jurisdiction in habeas cases uncertain.

The Court created this uncertainty by including within its opinion statements that support both a contracted and expanded definition of habeas jurisdiction. The contracted conception of federal court jurisdiction in habeas cases is based on statements in the opinion that make two related points. First, the Court emphasized the special and exceptional control the United States exercises over the naval base at Guantanamo Bay: "By the express terms of its agreements with Cuba, the United States exercises 'complete jurisdiction and control' over the Guantanamo Bay naval base, and may continue to exercise such control permanently if it so chooses." Second, the Court asserted that the application of the habeas statute "to persons detained at the base is consistent with the historical reach" of the writ to "so-called exempt jurisdictions," "all other dominions under the sovereign's control," and a territory that was "under the subjection of the Crown." The Court emphasized that later British cases "confirmed that the reach of the writ depended not on formal notions of territorial sovereignty, but rather on the practical question of 'the exact extent and nature of the jurisdiction or dominion exercised by the Crown.'" Combined, these two points suggest that the Court was signaling that although the federal court had habeas jurisdiction outside of the United States, it was quite limited—perhaps only to Guantanamo.

The expanded conception of habeas jurisdiction rests on other statements that make jurisdiction dependent upon courts having jurisdiction over the secretary of defense, the ultimate custodian of alleged enemy combatants and terrorists imprisoned under the authority of the United States military.

The statements provide: "No party questions the District Court's jurisdiction over petitioners' custodians. . . . Section 2241 by its terms, requires nothing more." If those statements measure the scope of jurisdiction that federal courts will have, then the federal courts will have jurisdiction no matter where on the planet those detained are imprisoned so long as Pentagon officials in Washington control the imprisonment. These were the statements that Justice Scalia pounced on when he charged in his dissent that the majority was extending the reach of habeas statute "to the four corners of the earth." This "breathtaking" decision, Scalia wrote, permits "an alien captured in a foreign theater of active combat to bring a [habeas] petition against the Secretary of Defense," thus "forcing the courts to oversee one aspect of the Executive's conduct of a foreign war."

The uncertainty created by the opinion over the reach of habeas jurisdiction was no accident. If the Court intended habeas jurisdiction to reach to the four corners of the globe, there was no reason for it to emphasize the special circumstances surrounding Guantanamo or to recount the historical reach of the writ in Britain. And if the court intended habeas jurisdiction to be limited to Guantanamo or other narrowly defined areas that had a special connection to the United States, the Court would not have suggested that jurisdiction existed so long as a court had jurisdiction over the custodians.

But why would the Court create this uncertainty? Although one can only speculate as to the reasons underlying the uncertainty created by the Court's opinion, what seems likely is that the Court was trying to shape a doctrine that respected two important concerns. First, it wanted to preserve its capacity to review the possibility of indefinite confinement of aliens who are suspected of being enemy combatants or terrorists and who are imprisoned some place other than Guantanamo. Second, the Court wanted to retain discretion in future cases so that it could respect the commander in chief's need for unfettered authority over detainees imprisoned on the battlefield or nearby, and for some period of time after capture. To be responsive to both concerns, the Court needed to eschew rigid rules so that it could define the future scope of jurisdiction in light of these competing concerns.

The outcome in *Rasul* was certainly a boon for the detainees. Although the parties are once again in the courts fighting over the nature of the hearing to be provided, the detainees will at least now be given some process. But the outcome was more significant than that. In *Rasul*, the president insisted on the power to imprison indefinitely and without trial those captured in a combat zone. This was an extreme claim, and in rejecting it, the Court upheld the nation's traditional commitment to due process and to separation of powers. The president has the power to imprison alleged enemy combatants and terrorists, but not indefinitely, and not without some mechanism of review, at least not in the absence of specific congressional authorization.

The Court's decision in *Rasul* is equally significant in another, more general respect. When placed in historical perspective, the Court's decision in *Rasul* constitutes a sharp break with the Court's well-established pattern of deferring to the Executive branch in national security cases. This pattern of deference makes *Rasul* possibly a pivotal case that opens the way for the Court to check the Executive branch in national security matters. But before considering the significance of *Rasul*, let's first review the tradition. Three examples drawn from the twentieth century illustrate the tradition.

## WORLD WAR I CASES

The political controversy within the United States surrounding World War I resulted in over 2,000 convictions under the Espionage Act of 1917. Only a handful of these cases reached the Supreme Court in 1919. One of these cases was *Schenck v. United States*.[6] In *Schenck*, the defendants were charged with conspiring to print and circulate a document that would allegedly cause insubordination and obstruction in the military forces and the draft. They were also charged with conspiring to use the mails and actually using the mails to transmit this nasty document "to men who had been called and accepted for military service."

Now what did this document state that these defendants prepared and conspired to circulate? Here I rely upon Justice Oliver Wendell Holmes, who wrote the opinion for the Court in *Schenck*. The document in question was a one-page leaflet with writing on both sides. On its first printed side, it quoted the Thirteenth Amendment to the Constitution, which prohibits slavery and involuntary servitude. It "intimated"—Holmes's word—that "conscription was despotism in its worst form and a monstrous wrong against humanity in the interest of Wall Street's chosen few." The heading on the second side stated, "Assert Your Rights," and among other things it stated: "If you do not assert and support your rights, you are helping to deny and disparage rights which it is the solemn duty of all citizens and residents of the United States to retain."

Holmes wrote for a unanimous Court in affirming the convictions. In doing so he wrote the following words:

> We admit that in many places and in ordinary times the defendants in saying all that was said in the circular would have been within their constitutional rights. But the character of every act depends upon the circumstances in which it is done. The most stringent protection of free speech

would not protect a man in falsely shouting fire in a theater and causing a panic. The question in every case is whether the words used are used in such circumstances and are of such a nature as to create a clear and present danger that they will bring about the substantive evils that Congress has the power to prevent. It is a question of proximity and degree. When a nation is at war many things that might be said in time of peace are such a hindrance to its effort that their utterance will not be endured so long as men fight and that no Court could regard them as protected by any constitutional right.[7]

Holmes concluded by remarking that if the "tendency" of the speech was to cause disruption or obstruction, it did not matter that the speech in question failed to cause any disruption or obstruction. Eventually *Schenck* and its companion cases became known as the "bad tendency" cases. In *Schenck*, the defendants were convicted because they prepared and circulated a written document. The speech in question did not advocate criminal conduct, and there was no evidence or even a claim that the speech in question constituted incitement. And there was no evidence that the speech in question had any negative consequences for the military or the draft. Nonetheless, and even in the face of Holmes's statement that the conviction for speech could be upheld only if it created "a clear and present danger," the conviction was upheld on the ground that the "tendency"—again, Holmes's word—of the speech (as well as the intent of the speakers) was to cause disruption and obstruction. At the foxhole level, *Schenck* and its companion cases, which have long since been repudiated, might be viewed as merely the first expressions by the Supreme Court to define First Amendment law. Indeed, even Holmes, joined by Brandeis, distanced himself from these three cases only months later in 1919,[8] and set forth a new and different statement of First Amendment law in a dissent in *Abrams v. United States*.[9] But I think that view is too crabbed. Although these cases raised important free speech issues, the Court's statement of where the boundary separating an individual's freedom of speech from the government's power to criminalize speech was in my view also a statement of the Court's willingness to defer to the assertion of power by the Executive and Congress during a time of crisis.

## JAPANESE INTERNMENT

My second example illustrating the tradition of judicial deference to the Executive during a time of crisis is the internment of persons of Japanese ancestry during World War II. On February 19, 1942, about ten weeks after the Japanese attack on Pearl Harbor, President Roosevelt signed Executive Order 9066. This order was allegedly designed to protect the United States from espionage and sabotage, and provided that the army might designate "military areas" in the United States "from which any or all persons may be excluded, and with respect to which the right of any person to enter, remain in, or leave shall be subject to whatever restrictions" the "Military Commander may impose in his discretion."[10]

Over the next eight months, 120,000 individuals of Japanese descent were forced to leave their homes in California, Washington, Oregon, and Arizona.[11] According to Supreme Court Justice Murphy, "not one person of Japanese ancestry" who was removed and detained "was accused or convicted of espionage or sabotage after Pearl Harbor while they were still free."[12] About two-thirds of the individuals interned were U.S. citizens, representing almost 90 percent of all Japanese Americans. No criminal charges were brought against these individuals. They were not given any kind of hearing that might have resulted in their release. They were not informed about how long they would be detained.

In 1944, the Supreme Court decided the case of Fred Korematsu,[13] who had challenged his conviction for violating the military exclusion order imposed on persons of Japanese ancestry, and by a vote of 6 to 3, the court upheld Korematsu's conviction. Justice Hugo Black wrote the majority opinion, and the degree of deference toward the military and the president is best illustrated by quoting Justice Black's own words.

After noting that the case involved a racial classification, which made it "immediately suspect" and subject to the "most rigid scrutiny," Justice Black made plain that the Constitution did not forbid all racial classifications, and that those warranted by "pressing public necessity" were acceptable. Using those considerations as his guide, Justice Black then proceeded to identify the pressing public necessity that warranted the exclusion, which boiled down to this: The exclusion order was necessary because "of the presence of an unascertained number of disloyal members of the group, most of whom we have no doubt were loyal to this country," and because the military claimed that it was "impossible to bring about an immediate segregation of the disloyal from the loyal." In other words, the Supreme Court accepted the military's claim that it was imperative to remove 112,000 individuals from their homes—even though it believed that the overwhelming majority were loyal to the United States—because the military suspected that some were disloyal and it did not believe it could distinguish those who were disloyal from those who were loyal.

Justice Murphy wrote a strong dissent in which he emphasized that he was unpersuaded that any public danger was so "immediate, imminent, and impending" as to justify the military exclusion and internment policy. He also pointed out that the British government, through individualized tribunals, examined 74,000 German and Austrian aliens to determine "whether each individual enemy alien was a real enemy of the Allies or only a 'friendly enemy.'"[14] The result of those hearings, which were conducted in a six-month period after the outbreak of the war, was that only 2,000 individuals were ultimately interned.[15]

*Korematsu* is particularly poignant in illustrating judicial deference. Justice Black makes his deference plain on the face of his opinion, and Justice Murphy's dissent sets off Justice Black's opinion in sharp relief. Because the British, who were bombed by the Germans and who faced German land forces stationed only thirty miles across the English Channel, responded to their internal threat with greater subtlety and fairness, the Supreme Court's acceptance of the more brutal and unfair American response only makes the Court's deference seem even more extreme. Of course, *Korematsu* has, as one leading commentator opined, "come to live in infamy."[16] Not only have the academic commentators condemned it, but also Congress enacted a law in 1988 apologizing for the World War II exclusion and internment policy and provided reparations.

### AMERICAN COMMUNIST PARTY

My third and last illustration of the strong judicial tradition of deference to the Executive during a time of crisis is rooted in the McCarthy period of the early 1950s. In 1951, the Supreme Court was confronted with a case in which the leaders of the American Communist Party were convicted of violating the Smith Act of 1940, which among other things made it a federal felony to advocate, advise, or teach the duty of overthrowing any government in the United States by force or violence, or to organize a group or society to do the same, or to conspire to do the same.[17] The trial in this case lasted nine months and resulted in a 16,000-page record. The intermediate reviewing court, the Court of Appeals, had concluded that the evidence supported several findings, including that the Communist Party is a disciplined and deceptive organization; it is rigidly controlled; the party tolerates no dissension from policy established by the leadership; and that it aimed to overthrow the government by force and violence. The Supreme Court accepted these factual findings and limited its review of the case to whether the conviction, based on the facts as found, violated the defendants' rights under the First Amendment.

There was no doubt that the government could enact laws to punish those who sought to overthrow the government by force or violence. That was not the issue. The issue was whether the government could make criminal the defendants' speech that advocated the overthrowing the government by force and violence, the organization of a political party to encourage the same, and conspiracy to organize a political party to do the same. In considering this issue, it was agreed that there was no evidence of any kind that the defendants were advocating that the government be overthrown now or at any time in the future. Nor was there any evidence that the defendants had taken any steps or had planned to take any steps, or had conspired to take any steps to effectuate their goal. So the issue was one of the substance of their ideology and the peaceful advocacy of an ideology.

In a 6-to-2 opinion, the Supreme Court sustained the conviction. In reaching this result, the Court confronted a choice between *either* shaping a legal rule urged by many, including the defendants, that allowed the government to prosecute speech only when the advocacy was directed to inciting or producing imminent lawless action *or* endorsing a legal rule recommended by the government that permitted the government to criminalize speech when the speech presented no threat whatsoever. The Court chose the latter approach. The Court wrote that the government need not wait until "the putsch is about to be executed, the plans have been laid and the signal is awaited." A combination of the ideology along with the conspiracy "creates the danger" sufficient to justify criminalization.

As in the first two examples, the Court exercised substantial discretion in shaping the applicable legal rule, and as in the two other examples it adopted a legal rule that granted the Executive branch substantial authority to assure order and security in the name of a current crisis, by fashioning new criminal tools that resulted in the loss of traditional liberty.

In each of these three examples it is now thought that the Executive had greatly exaggerated the national security danger and that the members of the Supreme Court, as well as others, had deferred to the Executive branch because of unsubstantiated security fears. Indeed, each incident is now widely considered an embarrassment to our underlying national commitment to the separation of powers, which protects democratic values and individual liberty.

### THE EXCEPTION: THE PENTAGON PAPERS CASE

There has been only one exception to this pattern of judicial deference during a time of war or national crisis.[18] In 1971, the government sought a prior restraint against the *New York Times* to bar it from publishing excerpts from the Pentagon Papers, a 7,000-page classified study of America's involvement in Vietnam spanning the period from the end of World War II to 1968. In support of its request for a prior restraint the government maintained that the threatened disclosures would reveal war plans, compromise intelligence operations, and undermine efforts to negotiate a settlement. The Nixon administration argued that the Court should accept its allegations as true because it had primary responsibility for national security and the courts lacked the expertise to assess national security considerations. After sixteen days of frenetic litigation, the Supreme Court denied the government the injunction it sought, which had the effect of permitting the *New York Times* (as well as the *Washington Post*, which had begun to publish excerpts from the top-secret report after the *Times* had been initially enjoined) to continue to publish reports from the secret study. Although the government had predicted serious and irreparable harm to the national security if the classified study were made public, there is no evidence that the public disclosure of the Pentagon Papers injured the national security. Because of the hectic nature of the litigation—the Supreme Court heard oral argument on a Saturday morning and made its decision the following Wednesday—there was no majority opinion. Instead a short *per curiam* opinion merely stated that the government had failed to sustain the "heavy" evidentiary burden it had in a prior restraint case. But even in this free press case involving the nation's preeminent newspapers, the doctrine of deference had its adherents. Listen to the dissenting opinion by the highly respected Associate Justice John Harlan (joined by Chief Justice Warren Burger and Associate Justice Harry Blackmun):

> It is plain to me that the scope of the judicial function in passing upon the activities of the Executive Branch of the Government in the field of foreign affairs is very narrowly restricted. This view is, I think, dictated by the concept of separation of powers upon which our constitutional system rests. I agree that, in performance of its duty to protect the values of the First Amendment against political pressures, the judiciary must review the initial Executive determination to the point of satisfying itself that the subject matter of the dispute does lie within the proper compass of the President's foreign relations power. Moreover, the judiciary may properly insist that the determination that disclosure of the subject matter would irreparably impair the national security be made by the head of the Executive Department concerned after actual personal consideration by that officer. But in my judgment the judiciary may not properly go beyond these two inquiries and re-determine for itself the probable impact of disclosure on the national security.[19]

Obviously, if Justice Harlan had had his way, the Pentagon Papers case would have come out the other way, and the *Times* and the *Post* would have been enjoined from publishing further excerpts from the top-secret history. But his view did not carry the day, and the government was denied the preliminary injunction it sought.

## WHY DID THE COURT BREAK WITH THIS TRADITION IN *RASUL* AND FOLLOW THE PENTAGON PAPERS CASE?

Given this background one might well have expected the Court to show great deference to President Bush and decide that the federal courts lacked habeas jurisdiction over the petitions that had been filed. After all, to the extent that the Pentagon Papers case exercised any pull on the Court, the pull could be discounted on the ground that it involved a unique claim for a prior restraint and it did so against the nation's two most prominent newspapers. In contrast, the petitioners in *Rasul* were outsiders who had arguably taken up arms against U.S. soldiers. Moreover, there is the overlay that the government needs more power to detain potential adversaries than before because we are engaged in a different kind of war, a war against terrorism. The opposing army in this war is not a traditional army. It is a faceless and un-uniformed army; it does not seek to conquer either land or resources; it lacks a hierarchical structure; and it is not based in any one nation-state but instead spread across several countries, in which it lives in the seams of society. So two questions arise. How confident was the Court as it broke new ground? And why did the Court break new ground?

### Confidence

Let's first focus on the majority's confidence—or more to the point, its lack thereof—as it asserted that the federal courts had jurisdiction over the petitioners' habeas petitions. I have already said that the majority opinion was dry as sand and no trumpet of liberty. It was, as I said, tedious and technical. There are no rhetorical flourishes in Justice Stevens's majority opinion in *Rasul*, as there are in Justice O'Connor's majority opinion in *Hamdi*, also decided that day and granting Hamdi, a detained United States citizen, a hearing that would allow him an opportunity to challenge the charges against him. Thus, consider Justice O'Connor's statement that it is "during our most challenging and uncertain moments that our Nation's commitment to due process is most severely tested; and it is in those times that we must preserve our commitment at home to the principles for which we fight abroad."[20] Or listen to her claim that was widely quoted in the press at the time: "We have long since made clear that a state of war is not a blank check for the President when it comes to the rights of the Nation's citizens."[21]

The difference between Stevens's and O'Connor's opinions is striking. And that difference cannot be explained because the court in *Rasul* is assessing the rights of enemy aliens during wartime. Thus, consider a few lines from Justice Black's dissent in an earlier case involving the treatment of aliens during wartime. In *Johnson v. Eisentrager*,[22] which was decided in 1950 and which the government claimed should control in *Rasul*, the Supreme Court concluded that the federal courts lacked jurisdiction over the habeas petitions filed by 21 German citizens who had been captured by U.S. forces in China, tried and convicted of war crimes by an American military commission headquartered in Nanking, and incarcerated in the Landsberg Prison in occupied Germany. With that in mind, consider the rhetoric of Black's final paragraph in his opinion:

> Conquest by the United States, unlike conquest by many other nations, does not mean tyranny. For our people "choose to maintain their greatness by justice rather than violence." Our constitutional principles are such that their mandate of equal justice under law should be applied as well when we occupy lands across the sea as when our flags flew only over thirteen colonies. Our nation proclaims a belief in the dignity of human beings as such, no matter what their nationality or where they happen to live. Habeas corpus, as an instrument to protect against illegal imprisonment, is written into the Constitution. Its use by courts cannot in my judgment be constitutionally abridged by Executive or by Congress. I would hold that our courts can exercise it whenever any United States official illegally imprisons any person in any land we govern. Courts should not for any reason abdicate this, the loftiest power with which the Constitution had endowed them.[23]

The absence of quotable lines in *Rasul* also has nothing to do with Justice Stevens's capacity to pen such lines. On the very same day that his opinion for the Court in *Rasul* was announced, his dissenting opinion in *Padilla*—another case involving a detained citizen and raising technical jurisdiction questions as were raised in *Rasul*—was also released. Here is how he concluded that dissent:

> At stake in this case is nothing less than the essence of a free society. Even more important than the method of selecting the people's rulers and their successors is the character of the constraints imposed on the executive by the rule of law. Unconstrained Executive detention for the purpose of investigating and preventing subversive activity is the hallmark of the Star Chamber. Access to counsel for the purpose of protecting the citizen from official mistakes and mistreatment is the hallmark of due process.
>
> Executive detention of subversive citizens, like detention of enemy soldiers to keep them off the battlefield, may sometimes be justified to prevent persons from launching or becoming missiles of destruction. It may not, however, be justified by the naked interest in using unlawful procedures to extract information. *Incommunicado* detention for months on end is such a procedure. Whether the information so procured is more or less reliable than that acquired by more extreme forms of torture is no consequence. For if this Nation is to remain true to the ideals symbolized by its flag, it must not wield the tools of tyrants even to resist an assault by the forces of tyranny.[24]

While it is only my speculation, I think that the absence of any rhetorical flourish in Rasul was deliberate and reflected the Court's awareness that it was in fact breaking with tradition, that it was potentially positioning itself to review in the future Executive detention of many individuals captured in this new kind of war against a different adversary who might face indefinite imprisonment, and it did not want the public to perceive it as possibly siding with the detainees as opposed to trying to curtail presidential power. So the stinginess of the language is no accident; it was reflective of the potentially important step that broke with tradition, and the delicate balance the Court tried to maintain as it broke with that tradition.

*REASONS*

Many reasons surely prompted the justices in *Rasul* to reject the president's position, and we are unlikely to know them all with any certainty. I will mention four that seem to me most likely.

First, the mystique surrounding national security and classified information has dissipated substantially in recent years. As a result, Congress, the press, and the public routinely demand information they would not have in the past. The essence of this point was captured by Michael D. McCurry, White House press secretary under President Bill Clinton, who was recently quoted as observing: "Just 10 years ago, you could basically shut off any question on anything by saying, 'That's an intelligence matter and we never discuss it.' Now that just doesn't cut it anymore, and part of the reason is that people are so skeptical of intelligence as a consequence of intelligence failures pre-9/11 and pre-Iraq war."

Second, President Bush sought exceptional power which seemed extreme even to this comparatively conservative and deferential Court. What President Bush sought was unreviewable power to hold detainees in Guantanamo indefinitely.

Third, the Court may have believed, given the failure of Congress to exercise much oversight of the Executive's treatment of those captured and detained at Guantanamo, that it as a co-equal branch of government needed to act to assure a measure of checks and balances in the system.

Fourth, and last, it may be that a majority of the Court has increasing confidence that it has a limited but important role to perform in cases involving national security. If this surmise has any merit to it, it is because the members of the Court have increasing confidence that they are qualified to make some decisions affecting national security that they previously would have shied away from. If this is true, and I hope it is and I think it may be, it is because we are all much more accustomed than ever before to having classified material pertinent to national security in the public press.

### THE MEANING OF *RASUL* FOR THE COURT IN THE YEARS AHEAD

One of the most serious current threats to our democratic values, our traditionally open society, and our liberties during the current war on terrorism is the felt needs of the national security state. Left unchecked, the Executive branch may well take misguided actions as it seeks to assure security. This has been the lesson of the past; there is no reason to believe that the past will not have contemporary analogues. The courts offer a potentially powerful check and reassuring counter-balance to this potential abuse of power. But for years the Supreme Court deferred to the Executive branch and inappropriately diminished its own power in national security cases, thus contributing to an unhealthy imbalance of power and the needless loss of liberty.

The decision in *Rasul* suggests that the Supreme Court, similar to Congress, the press, and the public, may be much less accepting of government representations that courts stay out of certain areas because of national security "do not enter" signs. If this turns out to be true, then *Rasul* will come to be viewed as the moment when the Supreme Court began to correct a harmful and regrettable pattern. Such a development would be a good thing for our freedom and our democratic order.

Will this happen? I was more hopeful, much more hopeful, before the 2004 election. It is not just that President Bush lost in *Rasul*—or *Hamdi*. Rather, from all the evidence available, one can only predict that when he has an opportunity to nominate someone to the Supreme Court, the person nominated will favor a diminished role for the judiciary with regard to reviewing Executive action, especially in the areas of foreign affairs and national security.[25]

Of course, a newly confident Supreme Court that did not shy away from reviewing Executive action in national security cases cannot replace a vigilant Congress that jealously guards its power, especially with regard to making war and securing our nation's security. Such an active and skeptical Congress will have more of a chance to keep a determined president within some bounds, which in turn will be important to preserving separation of powers, which I think is fundamental not only to a democratic order but to individual freedom.

In that regard, there is not much on the public record to cheer about. Both with regard to the Patriot Act and the war resolution regarding Iraq, Congress failed in my view to exercise due diligence and responsibility. Indeed, with regard to the Iraq resolution, rather than retaining the power to declare war and using it only when the president was prepared to actually make war, the Congress gave the president the blank check he requested, just as an earlier Congress had given President Johnson a blank check when it passed the Gulf of Tonkin Resolution.

But even a skeptical and vigilant Congress is not a substitute for a prudent and wise Executive. And all that that means is that the Supreme Court decisions of June 2004 deserve applause and cheers because a Court with a newly defined role in national security matters is an important correction of a highly regrettable tradition, but that it is no substitute for a skeptical Congress and a prudent Executive.

## AMERICAN POWER, DEMOCRATIC VALUES, AND HUMAN RIGHTS

When ratification of the United States Constitution was debated in 1787 and 1788, Alexander Hamilton secured the help of John Jay and James Madison in writing the 85 papers first published in newspapers and later collected and published as *The Federalist*. In the third sentence of the first paragraph of the first paper, Hamilton, perhaps deliberately flattering his audience and enhancing the importance of what was at stake, wrote:

> It has been frequently remarked that it seems to have been reserved to the people of this country, by their conduct and example, to decide the important question, whether societies of men are really capable or not, of establishing good government from reflection and choice, or whether they are forever destined to depend for their political constitutions, on accident and force.

What was true then, may be true today. Since the disintegration of the Soviet Union, the United States possesses unrivaled power in the world. During that relatively short time, and most particularly since 9/11, it has become painfully plain for all to see that the use and abuse of power by the United States has great potential to strengthen and to harm human rights around the globe and that its actions around the globe have a fairly direct and immediate impact on the scope of freedom and security of those who claim the United States as their home. And so, as a lawyer might say, the jury is still out as to how the United States will use its power and authority in the world, and whether in the near term and the long term peace and liberty will be strengthened, whether toleration of differences and the peaceful resolution of disputes will prevail, and whether mutual respect across racial, ethnic, and religious groups and societies will blunt the urge to use force to advance interests.

None of us today know how events will unfold in the months and years ahead. But there is one thing about which I am confident. And that is this: To err is human and to err in the exercise of devastating power holds out great risks for those of us who live in the United States and who feel deep loyalty to the remarkable traditions of this most unusual of countries, as well as for those individuals who live in distant lands and whose lives and families are caught in the cross hairs of America's power. Because of that we must insist that our courts and our Congress perform their critical functions in governing in times of crisis when security is on the line, rather than deferring to the Executive branch. In offering this simple observation I take as my text another passage from *The Federalist*. These few lines are from Number 51, written by James Madison. I am sure they will be familiar to many.

> But what is government itself, but the greatest of all reflections on human nature? If men were angels, no government would be necessary. If angels were to govern men, neither external nor internal controls on government would be necessary. In framing a government which is to be administered by men over men, the great difficulty lies in this: You must first enable the government to control the governed; and in the next place oblige it to control itself.

The United States is now at center stage, and the current reviewers, both in this country and abroad, are sharply divided, with many critics making deadly serious charges. In June 2004, the Supreme Court struck out in a new and potentially important direction in an effort to curtail the power of the commander in chief in wartime. This was a remarkable development of historic potential and importance. But even if the Court uses these decisions as guides in future cases, it bears repetition that the Court in the end cannot substitute for a skeptical and vigilant Congress and a prudent Executive.

Today, the people of the world are watching what the United States does with its power, and they—as well as we—are waiting to see, as Hamilton asked, whether societies are "really capable or not of establishing good government from reflection and choice." Because I am an optimist, I am hopeful. But disciplining and restraining American power in the service of human rights at home and abroad will take much more than hope. It will take a vigorous Legislature, a determined Judiciary, a prudent Executive, and, most importantly, an aroused citizenry that insists, as Hamilton wrote, on "establishing good government from reflection and choice."

## Notes

1. Alexis de Tocqueville, *Democracy in America*, ed. Phillips Bradley (New York: Vintage Books, 1960), vol. 1, p. 290.

2. *Hamdi v. Rumsfeld*, 124 S. Ct. at 2633 (2004); *Rasul v. Bush*, 124 S. Ct. at 2686 (2004); *Rumsfeld v. Padilla*, 124 S. Ct. at 2711 (2004).

3. As of May 15, 2006, the Department of Defense released the names of 759 prisoners (http://www.dod.mil/pubs/foi/detainees/detaineesFOIArelease15May2006.pdf).

4. That other time arose in *Hamdan v. Rumsfeld,* 126 S. Ct. 2749 (2006), in which the Court concluded that the military commission convened by President Bush to try the Guantanamo petitioner "lacks the power to proceed" because its structure and procedures violate both the Uniform Code of Military Justice and the Geneva Convention (idem at 2786).

5. *Rasul v. Bush,* 542 U.S. 466, 485 (2004).

6. *Schenck v. United States,* 249 U.S. at 47 (1919).

7. *Schenk v. United States,* 249 U.S. at 47 (1919).

8. *Abrams v. United States,* 250 U.S. at 616 (1919).

9. Holmes dissenting in *Abrams,* 250 U.S. at 630: "But when men have realized that time has upset many fighting faiths, they may come to believe even more than they believe the very foundations of their own conduct that the ultimate good desired is better reached by free trade in ideas—that the best test of truth is the power of the thought to get itself accepted in the competition of the market, and that truth is the only ground upon which their wishes safely can be carried out. That at any rate is the theory of our Cconstitution. It is an experiment, as all life is an experiment. Every year if not every day we have to wager our salvation upon some prophecy based on imperfect knowledge."

10. Quoted in *Korematsu v. United States,* 323 U.S. at 214, Sullivan casebook at 669.227 (1944) (Roberts, J., dissenting).

11. Geoffrey Stone, Friend of the Court Brief in U.S. at 370 (2003).

12. See Murphy's opinion—Sullivan, page 670, n.4. *Korematsu,* 323 U.S. at 241 (1944) (Murphy, J., dissenting)

13. *Korematsu v. United States,* 323 U.S. at 214 (1944). (exclusion issue). See also *Hirabayashi v. United States,* 320 U.S. at 81 . . . U.S. . . . (1943), sustaining conviction for violation of the curfew imposed on persons of Japanese ancestry.

14. *Korematsu,* 323 U.S. at Sullivan at 670.242 n. 16. (1944) (Murphy, J., dissenting).

15. Sullivan at 670, n. 670. Idem.

16. Kathleen M. Sullivan and Gerald Gunther, *Constitutional Law,* 14th ed. (New York: Foundation Press, 2001), at 669, n. 3.631 n. 4.

17. *Dennis v. United States,* 341 U.S. at 494 (1951).

18. *New York Times Co. v. United States,* 403 U.S. at 713 (1971).

19. *Times v. United States,* 403 U.S. at 756–57 (1971) (Harlan, J., dissenting).

20. *Hamdi v. Rumsfeld,* 124 S. Ct. at 2648 (2004)

21. *Hamdi v. Rumsfeld,* 124 S. Ct. at 2650 (2004)

22. *Johnson v. Eisentrager,* 339 U.S. at 763 (1950).

23. *Johnson,* 339 U.S. at 798.

24. *Padilla,* 124 S. Ct. at 2735 (2004) (Stevens, J., dissenting).

25. From the available evidence, the prediction that President Bush would nominate an individual who favors deference to the Executive has come to pass. In July 2005, Associate Justice Sandra Day O'Connor announced her retirement and President Bush nominated U.S. Appeals Court Judge John Roberts to succeed her. When Chief Justice William H. Rehnquist died in September 2005, President Bush nominated Roberts to succeed him as Chief Justice, and the Senate confirmed. President Bush then nominated U.S. Appeals Court Judge Samuel A. Alito, Jr., to succeed Justice O'Connor, and he was confirmed in January 2006. Justice Roberts was part of the majority in *Hamdan* in the Circuit Court, 415 F. 3d 33 (2005), which was ultimately reversed by the United States Supreme Court. 126 S. Ct. 2749 (2006). As for Justice Alito, he dissented in *Hamdan,* defending President Bush's commission procedures. 126 S. Ct. at 2810.

# American Treatment of Detainees and the U.S. Supreme Court

## ☞ William Durland ☜

The direct cause of World War II was a "dastardly" and "sneak" attack on American soil without warning. The United States adamantly declared that only our enemies—Germany, Italy, and Japan—engaged in preemptive attacks and undeclared wars contrary to international law. Their military regimes had no respect for enemies and seldom afforded prisoners of war rights under the Hague and Geneva Conventions and were more likely to torture and execute them, we were told.

Believers in a linear progression of political evolution from medieval autocracy to modern democracy say the end of that world war was a dramatic step forward to world peace under the rule of law in a community of nations. The new United Nations, revitalized International Court, and the more extensive and enforced international rules of law and war, beginning with the United Nations and Nuremberg Charters, were the core. America lent all its resources to a strong international community, which could objectify and universalize the fundamental moral foundations of due process.

I returned to America from Germany in 1957, completing my military service. It was at law school thereafter that the Mallory case[1] brought these values home for me. It involved detention, physical abuse, confessions, and the absence of arrest and due process, all of them matters that are still very current today. A long-time proposition in American law holds that no involuntary confession may be introduced as evidence against a defendant in a criminal case. A confession is involuntary if it was compelled by physical or psychological force, coercion, or inducement. The reason is the information's inherent untrustworthiness.

Emerging from the Mallory case, in which Mallory was detained in order to extract a confession from him by force, was the McNabb-Mallory Rule.[2] The rule stated that no confession is admissible in a federal court against a defendant if it was obtained during an illegal detention, "that is, while the arrestee was held in violation of the statutory requirement that he be taken promptly before a committing court magistrate."[3]

The judicial rule set a general requirement that "any unnecessary delay" in taking an arrestee before a magistrate would form the basis for exclusion, and unnecessary delay was determined to be six hours from the time of arrest *or* detention, whichever was earlier. The basis for a broader nationwide (not simply federal) constitutional rule gave birth to *Escobedo v. Illinois*[4] and *Miranda v. Arizona*.[5] In *Escobedo*,

> For hours while the accused was being questioned in the station house, repeatedly demanding an opportunity to consult with his previously-retained counsel, and while his attorney in another part of the building was demanding to see his client, the officers prevented any such meeting until their lengthy interrogation had resulted in a confession.[6]

The events of the case were considered a violation of fundamental fairness. A denial of due process was implicit in the refusal of the right to consult with an attorney or to be alerted to an absolute constitutional right to remain silent.[7]

In *Miranda*, it was held that "due process of law requires that before a suspect in custody of the law is questioned by police officers he must be advised" of his rights.[8] Any custodial interrogation of a suspect who has not been apprised of these fundamental constitutional rights will result in such evidence being excluded.[9] *Miranda* expanded the requirements to provide informed notice of everyone's fundamental rights. Today, a concerted effort to de-evolve *Miranda* has set the stage for detention abuses on a grander international scale, affecting citizens and aliens alike. Such abuses, involving detention, torture, refusal of legal representation, admissibility of hearsay evidence, no fair and speedy trial, and the like, have been perpetuated by American power enforcers. The rights are identical; the nationalities and geography are different. We are dealing now with aliens as well as citizens and not only in U.S. detention centers but overseas as well. Similar detentions have occurred on the basis of terrorist charges against foreign nationals outside the U.S.

What happened after 9/11 has been an overextension of security laws, which acts to gut existing laws protecting our freedoms, justice, and peace. In other words, a social contract grounded in the political philosophies of Rousseau, Montesquieu, and Locke has shifted to a Hobbesian contract in which we voluntarily give up much actual freedom to an emerging autocrat for promised security. Similar experiences in occupation security have resulted in Israel's institutionalizing indefinite detention, arrest on suspicion, and collective punishment, which has only brought it more enemies.[10] *Human Rights Watch*, reflecting on the 9/11 terrorist attacks on the World Trade Centers and Pentagon, writes:

> There are people and governments in the world who believe that in the struggle against terrorism, ends always justify the means. But that is also the logic of terrorism. Whatever the response to this outrage, it must not invalidate that logic [i.e., the logic that the enemy's use of the end to justify the means warrants our similarly doing so]. Rather, it must uphold the principles that came under attack yesterday, respecting human life and international law. That is the way to deny the perpetrators of this crime their ultimate victory.[11]

One major instrument of the diminution of the rule of law has been the process by which Bush justified the Iraqi war. First, it was weapons of mass destruction, and then it was an Al Qaeda connection. These allegations would justify a nation in imminent threat of attack defending itself in cooperation with its allies. Clearly, this was not the case. Bush switched his justification to regime change and then added "bringing democracy." These are not legitimate reasons for preemptive strike and occupation.[12] Neither were they offered with any sense of honesty, for Pakistan, Saudi Arabia, and other such U.S. allies have repressive regimes and lack essential democracy, while some possess weapons of mass destruction. The U.S. simply fed into Bin Laden's greatest hopes and, in the process, divested itself of the rule of law in regard to detaining citizens and aliens, and in many other ways. As for Bin Laden, we have given him another prize—the easy availability of U.S. targets in the Middle East that were not there before. In fact, we have reenacted a long attenuated conflict between Christian and Islamic fundamentalists in the rush to build empire.

The Patriot Act[13] is another major legal instrument of the demise of the rule of law for security's sake. An overreactive response granted the national government expansive powers in dealing with aliens and citizens. Racial profiling, scapegoating, indefinite detentions, mistreatment, and refusal to supply information on persons detained were legalized under the Patriot Act. A proposed Patriot Act II would have legalized secret arrests, trials and torture, the elimination of habeas corpus, and fifteen additional crimes punishable with the death penalty. It was scrapped for minor amendments to the act itself in 2006.[14]

Although the Patriot Act technically limits detentions to seven days before the government must charge the defendant with a crime, detainees, once charged and found to be engaged in terrorist activities, can be held for six months. At Guantanamo Bay and in Iraq and Afghanistan, alien detainees have been interned, as have U.S. citizens inside the U.S. as well. Deemed to be by presidential oracle "enemy combatants," they were detained indefinitely. The U.S. government defines an enemy combatant, as distinct from prisoner of war status, as an individual who belongs to or supports the Taliban military, Al Qaeda "terrorist" forces, or associated forces that are engaged in hostilities against the United States or its coalition partners. Persons so identified solely at the discretion of the president or his delegates have been held without being charged with a crime and without legal representation until the "war on terrorism" is ended.[15] Detainees' conversations with their counsel, where counsel was available, at Guantanamo and elsewhere, were not private in spite of the Sixth Amendment. Legal counsel was refused most of the time.

Long before the present detentions took place, the indefinite detention and summary deportation of alien immigrants was a routine matter in immigration law. Then just months before 9/11, the U.S. Supreme Court took a progressive turn and ruled against the government's use of indefinite detention of illegal immigrants when their own homeland refuses to accept them.[16] But 9/11 has again restricted immigration law generally. The landmark cases of Yaser Esam Hamdi and Jose Padilla involve only two of the three citizens and hundreds of alien detainees subjected to human rights violations. Another U.S. citizen who has been detained as a result of these so-called wars is Matthew Lindh.[17] On June 28, 2004, the Supreme Court ruled on these cases as arising as a result of the "war on terrorism."

In addition to the other issues involving the detainees is the procedural one of where, if ever, the detainees will have their day in court, and of whether it will be in a civilian or military tribunal. The case for a military tribunal cites aliens Khalid Sheikh Mohammed and Zacharias Moussaoui as "picture book" examples of why the U.S. judicial system should not be used. However, it was applied to them by "advanced interrogation" techniques in hopes of making them talk.[18] Proponents of the military court idea argue that the civilian court process in Moussaoui's case has been "something like a joke." A federal jury in 2006 returned a verdict of guilty with life imprisonment without any corroborating evidence that the crimes charged were committed. The Bush administration has been advised to educate Americans as to why a tribunal would work while the federal government system would not. Such tribunals have been used against dedicated and dangerous enemy non-combatants, with limited use in extraordinary cases like the one involving Mohammed. It should be noted that the Nuremberg Military Tribunal after World War II was used against non-combatants and combatants who assisted their country's Nazi war effort, but these persons were not detained indefinitely.[19] At Guantanamo Bay, Cuba, the U.S. has held hundreds of persons from more than forty countries without charges or trial, causing severe criticism and a call to action by both political and faith-based organizations.[20] Opponents argue that the military tribunal system is not impartial and provides no appeal to civilian courts, and may not be used when civilian courts are available.

*Hamdi v. Rumsfeld* reached the U.S. Supreme Court on a writ of certiorari from the Fourth Circuit U.S. Court of Appeals. Hamdi was confined in Virginia and South Carolina military jails.[21] The justices were divided: Anthony Kennedy, Stephen Breyer, and Chief Justice William Rehnquist joined Sandra Day O'Connor, who delivered the Court's controlling decision and judgment. Justices David Souter and Ruth Bader Ginsberg disagreed with the first four, who had concluded that Hamdi's detention was authorized. However, these two, along with Thomas, agreed with the four that the case should be remanded to the lower trial court so that Hamdi might have a meaningful opportunity to offer evidence that he was not an enemy combatant.

Justices Antonin Scalia and John Paul Stevens together filed a dissenting opinion, even though they are on opposite ends of the liberal-conservative spectrum. Justice Clarence Thomas alone filed a second partially dissenting opinion, but affirmed O'Connor. Although the reasons are the key to this decision, the numbers were important as well. Thomas held that Bush's acts were not subject to judicial review. Souter and Ginsberg, along with Scalia and Stevens, held views which affirmed Hamdi's constitutional and human rights not to be detained, and the remaining O'Connor four provided the Court's affirmative judgment in a middle-of-the-road decision, but one welcomed as the first U.S. Supreme Court case which declared that indefinite detention is not an absolute right of the Executive to impose.

The Court began by stating that it was called "to consider the legality of the Government's detention of a United States citizen on United States soil as an 'enemy combatant'" and to address the process owed constitutionally to "one who seeks to challenge his classification as such."[22] The U.S. Fourth

Circuit Court of Appeals, a very conservative court when I practiced before it, held that Hamdi's detention was legally authorized and he could not challenge his enemy combatant status. O'Connor and company found that, although the detention was legally authorized by Congress, due process demands that a citizen held in the U.S. as an enemy combatant be given "a fair opportunity" to rebut the factual basis of that detention "before a neutral decision maker."[23] It based its opinion on a congressional resolution that was passed one week after 9/11 authorizing the president to "use all necessary and appropriate force against those nations, organizations, or persons he determines planned, authorized, committed, or aided terrorist attacks" or "harbored such organizations or persons, in order to prevent any future acts of international terrorism against the United States by such nations, organizations or persons."[24] Soon thereafter, Bush renewed the U.S. mission to find Osama Bin Laden, subdue Al Qaeda, and stop the Taliban in Afghanistan from supporting Bin Laden and Al Qaeda. Nothing in the above language specifically gives the president authority to detain persons he determines should be incarcerated indefinitely without notice, arrest, right to counsel, or trial by jury.

The Court gave Hamdi the narrow right to a "meaningful opportunity" before a "neutral decision maker" to contest the factual basis of his detention. Hamdi's argument had to be brought by a writ of habeas corpus by his father, Esam Fouad Hamdi, who had no access to his son since he was taken away in 2001. Since then, Hamdi had been "without access to legal counsel or notice of any charges pending against him ... in violation of the 5th and 14th Amendments to the U.S. Constitution." The petition asked the Court, among other things, to (1) appoint counsel, (2) cease interrogation, (3) declare his detention unconstitutional, (4) schedule an evidentiary hearing, and (5) order his release from "unlawful custody." Hamdi's father maintained that his son went to Afghanistan to do "relief work" and was in the country only two months before 9/11 trapped him there, and that he could not have received any military training.

The Federal District Court appointed a public defender and ordered that the lawyer have access to Hamdi. The Fourth Circuit decided that "appropriate deference" must be given to the government's "security and intelligence" interests, directing the District Court to do so, to consider "the most cautious procedures first" and conduct a "deferential inquiry into Hamdi's status."[25] As an enemy combatant, his detention "would be lawful," the court ruled. The government had moved the lower court to dismiss the habeas corpus petition, attaching a declaration from one Michael Mabbs, a special advisor to the under secretary of defense for policy. Mabbs indicated in writing that he had been involved with detention of enemy combatants who were with Al Qaeda and the Taliban, expressed familiarity with U.S. military policies, and stated that "based on my review of relevant records and reports" he was familiar with Hamdi. He then provided, the court said, "the sole evidentiary support" for the government's detention, which was that Hamdi was part of a Taliban military unit that yielded to the Northern Alliance after he engaged in battle and surrendered to them his rifle. A U.S. military screening team determined he was an enemy combatant. A subsequent interview with Hamdi, he said, confirmed this. No other documents support Mabbs's statements.

The District Court decided the Mabbs declaration was "little more than the government's say so" and criticized its "general and hearsay" nature. The court ordered the government to turn over in detail supporting documents, including copies of statements by Hamdi, notes from interviews, lists of interrogators, and other details. The District Court indicated these materials were necessary for a "meaningful judicial review" and to determine whether due process was satisfied. The government appealed, and the Appellate Court reversed the District Court, stating that because Hamdi was "captured in a zone of active combat in a foreign theater of conflict, . . . no factual inquiry or evidentiary hearing to allow Hamdi to be heard . . . was necessary or proper."[26] The Fourth Circuit concluded that the assertions by Mabbs provided a sufficient basis to conclude that the president constitutionally classified Hamdi under his war powers. The court rejected application of Article 5 of the Geneva Convention as rendering this detention unlawful under international law. U.S. Code Section 4001(a) provides that "[n]o citizen shall be imprisoned or otherwise detained by the United States except pursuant to an act of Congress." But the Appellate Court further determined that no "express congressional authorization of detentions" was required, because "the necessary and appropriate force" clause in the congressional resolution would include detention. The Fourth Circuit denied a rehearing, and the case went to the Supreme Court, which vacated the Fourth Circuit judgment and remanded the case back to the U.S. District Court. The O'Connor opinion agreed that Congress had authorized Hamdi's detention.[27] But Hamdi argued that his detention is "indefinite." The government's position is that it is "indefinite" until the "war" is over. Nevertheless, the Supreme Court affirmed the proposition that because active combat operations are still going on in Afghanistan (as well as in Iraq), his detention is part of the congressional approval of the exercise of "necessary and appropriate force."

Finally, the government argued before the Supreme Court that "further factual explanation is unwarranted and inappropriate in the light of the extraordinary constitutional interests at stake," and that the Court should take "evidence supplied only by the executive to support its own determination" as sufficient. Hamdi's attorney responded that "an individual challenging his detention may not be held at the will of the executive without recourse to some proceeding before a neutral tribunal to determine whether the executive asserted justifications for that detention have bases in fact and warrant in law," disapproving the hearsay nature of Mabbs's declaration and supporting extensive discovery. Anything less, as the District Court previously concluded, would not be "meaningful judicial review." O'Connor's opinion, in reaching its partial support of Hamdi's contentions, agreed and concluded that

> as critical as the government's interest may be in detaining those who actually pose an immediate threat to the national security of the U.S. during ongoing international conflict, history and common sense teach us that an unchecked system of detention causes the potential to become a means of oppression and abuse of others who do not present that sort of threat.... We reaffirm today the fundamental nature of a citizen's right to be free from involuntary confinement by his own government without due process of law.[28]

It added that the greatest temptation exists to disagree with such guarantees if they will inhibit government action. "We therefore hold that a citizen detainee must receive 1) notice of his classification, 2) an opportunity to rebut it, 3) be afforded a neutral and detached judge, and 4) be heard at a meaningful time and in a meaningful manner and represented by counsel." But O'Connor's opinion then recommends shifting the burden of proof in such a trial to the detainee and allows hearsay evidence, a presumption in favor of the government and a military tribunal.

Stevens and Scalia dissented for the following concise reasons: "Where the government accuses a citizen of waging war against it, our constitutional tradition has been to prosecute him in federal court for treason or some other crime.... Where the exigencies of war prevent that, the constitutional suspension clause, Art. 1, §9, Ch. 2, allows Congress to relax the usual protections temporarily." That article guarantees the privilege of the writ of habeas corpus, which may only be suspended in cases of rebellion or invasion. The congressional Authorization for Use of Military Force, "on which the government relies to justify its actions," is, in fact, an implementation of this suspension clause. Scalia logically concludes that no one contends with the fact that the authorization is an implementation of that clause. Therefore, absent suspension, the Executive's assertion of military exigency is not sufficient to allow detention without charge.

The issue here, Scalia writes, is "whether there is a different, special procedure for imprisonment of a citizen accused of wrong doing *by aiding the enemy in wartime.*"[29] He chides O'Connor for saying yes. Scalia says no, but admits there probably is such a procedure *in wartime* with respect to enemy aliens. The remedy for citizens is a trial for treason under Article III, §3, Ch. 1, which establishes a stricter proof requirement by the government—two witnesses corroborating each other—in order to convict. Scalia, with Stevens, concludes that "the executive lacks indefinite wartime detention over citizens . . ." Hamdi should have been released unless criminal proceedings were promptly brought or Congress suspended the writ. Neither took place. He could be handed over to the criminal authorities, who could detain him for criminal prosecution, or else he must be released from indefinite detention.[30]

Thomas dissented, stating that the detention of Hamdi "falls squarely within the federal government's war powers," which cannot be "second guessed by the judicial branch." The government has a "compelling interest" to hold detainees indefinitely. There are no violations at all, but he affirms the O'Connor opinion, as well.

Souter and Ginsberg concurred and dissented in part. They state that 18 U.S.C. 4001(a), which provides that 'no citizen shall be imprisoned or otherwise detained'," bars Hamdi's imprisonment or detention "except pursuant to an act of Congress." No such act has taken place. The government held that this act does not preclude military wartime detentions. In passing the statute, Souter and Ginsberg argued the Congress had in mind to preclude the detention of U.S. citizens in wartime, influenced by the *Korematsu* case.[31] But O'Connor's decision stated that the congressional authorization was adequate for detention of Hamdi while admitting that it does not "support sufficiently to satisfy 4001(a) as read to require a clear statement of authority to detain." Hamdi's treatment, Souter and Ginsberg say, also violated the Third Geneva Convention, which requires that he be treated as a prisoner of war until a "competent tribunal" decides otherwise. "The President is not commander in chief of the country, only of the military." Martial law is justified only by the closing of civilian courts. Hamdi's detention is forbidden by 4001(a) and unauthorized by Congress. He should be released. They do not agree with O'Connor on some matters but join with her to create a majority 7-2 decision to remand the case to the lower court to implement the O'Connor opinion.

On the same day, the Supreme Court decided *Rumsfeld v. Padilla.*[32] Padilla, a U.S. citizen, was brought to New York for detention in federal criminal custody after federal agents apprehended him while executing a material witness warrant issued by the District Court of the Southern District of New

York, as a result of a grand jury investigation of 9/11. Padilla's attorney moved the District Court to vacate the warrant, but the president ordered Secretary of Defense Rumsfeld to designate Padilla as an enemy combatant to be detained in military custody. He was then removed to a naval brig in Charleston, South Carolina, where he has been ever since. A habeas corpus petition was filed alleging Padilla's military detention violated the Constitution, naming the president, the defense secretary, and Melanie Marr, the brig commander. The government defended on the technical grounds that Marr was the only proper respondent and that she, in South Carolina, was outside the New York district (where the case began). Thereafter the New York court lacked jurisdiction over her. The District Court agreed. The Second Circuit Court of Appeals reversed, holding that the secretary was a proper respondent, that the Southern District had jurisdiction, and that the president lacked authority to detain Padilla militarily and must release him.

The Supreme Court addressed the jurisdiction question first, agreeing with the government that the Southern District of New York lacked jurisdiction over Padilla's habeas corpus petition. It would not consider the Second (N.Y.) Circuit Court of Appeals' decision that the president could not detain Padilla. Habeas corpus petitions are directed only to "the person" having authority over the petitioner, that being Marr. Chief Justice Rehnquist delivered the opinion of the Court, in which O'Connor, Kennedy, Scalia, and Thomas joined. Souter, Ginsberg, and Breyer joined Stevens, dissenting again in a 5-4 government verdict. The dissent stated that "the petition for a writ of habeas corpus filed in this case raises questions of profound importance to the Nation" and that "this is an exceptional case that we clearly have jurisdiction to decide."[33]

The New York District Court had appointed an attorney for Padilla. She filed motions on his behalf, seeking his release on constitutional grounds. A hearing was scheduled, but two days earlier the president commanded Rumsfeld to remove him from the jurisdiction where he was being tried by reclassifying him as an enemy combatant. The government then withdrew its general jury subpoena, and the court, upon the government's request, vacated the warrant and the military took custody over him and transferred him to South Carolina. His attorney filed a writ of habeas corpus. The government acknowledged that the Defense Department took custody of Padilla in the Southern District of New York, which should have provided jurisdiction.

There is a procedural rule in such cases that "special circumstances" can justify exceptions to the "immediate custody rule." "Since the jurisdiction was proper when the Petition was filed, it cannot be defeated by a later transfer," the Second Circuit held. Rumsfeld was the proper person because he was the custodian who ordered Padilla's transfer before Marr obtained custody in South Carolina. The Supreme Court has "consistently rejected interpretations of the habeas corpus statute that would suffocate the writ in stifling formalisms or hobble its effectiveness with the manacles of arcane and scholastic procedural requirements."[34]

The only remedy left to Padilla was to refile the case against Marr alone, causing his detention to continue. The issue posed by the Padilla and Hamdi cases is: Does the president, on his sole authority, have the right, by simply declaring that a "war on terrorism" exists and that U.S. citizens are "enemy combatants," to detain and interrogate them indefinitely in a military prison without arresting, charging, trying or convicting them of any crime or allowing them to know the grounds for their detention or to exercise their constitutional rights of due process, presumption of innocence, speedy trial by a jury of their peers, legal representation, or freedom from cruel and unusual punishment? We don't think so. Citizens have the above rights under our constitutional law and certainly aliens must be afforded the human rights safeguards of international law as well.

On September 22, 2004, the Bush administration agreed to drop criminal charges and release the U.S.-born Hamdi by deporting him to his family in Saudi Arabia. He was required to renounce U.S. citizenship, be subject to travel restrictions, and may not sue the U.S. for injuries suffered. Padilla, however, remained in custody, not charged but rather "identified" as an unindicted co-conspirator in a Florida terrorist case.[35] On November 23, 2005, the Justice Department indicted Padilla on criminal charges, namely, providing and conspiring to provide material support to terrorists. This came after holding him as a U.S. citizen for three years in solitary confinement and for two years without legal representation. In 2006 the U.S. Supreme Court declared his prior deprivation of rights moot because he is now held in a federal prison awaiting trial there.[36]

In addition to the rights of American citizens, aliens have been detained under our immigration laws in Afghanistan, Iraq, and Guantanamo Bay as enemy combatants, and in some cases, they were tortured and abused as in the Iraqi Abu Ghraib prison.[37] In response to the Supreme Court cases, some alien detainees have been released, notably three British detainees. Moreover, in August 2004, a hearing was held to determine whether 585 detainee aliens should remain classified as "enemy combatants."[38] Lawyers have been critical of the review panels, pointing out that they were stacked against prisoners, who were not allowed lawyers at the preliminary sessions of military reviews to assess their status. The media were allowed to witness the panels but could not disclose the names or ages of detainees. After the *ex parte* screening process, the military tribunals convened in late August 2004 with the selected "show cause" trials, affording the defendants legal counsel before a military court (hardly neutral and perhaps not meaningful). The first rulings at Guantanamo Bay concluded that all detainees were enemy combatants and will not be freed.[39]

A bright light thereafter emerged as a result of the Hamdi decision in that modest changes took place in the treatment of detainees. New abuses, such as those revealed at Abu Ghraib, have surfaced in Guantanamo. Spy charges against Ahmad Al Halabi, a Muslim interpreter at Guantanamo, were recently dropped. On October 21, 2004, a U.S. judge ruled that British detainees must be allowed lawyers, and freed British detainees are seeking $10 million in damages for their three years of Guantanamo detention.[40] The establishment of military tribunals with lawyers present for alien detainees only begins the long process of the restoration of rights, some of which have been guaranteed as a result of *Hamdi*. Violations of the 1949 Geneva Convention have been cited against CIA and Justice Department officials who authorized the transfer of detainees out of Iraq and Afghanistan in October 2004. On November 8, 2004, military trials (also known as "commissions" and "tribunals") for alien detainees were ruled unlawful by a federal judge in the *Hamdan* case.[41] The detainees may be prisoners of war under the Geneva Conventions and entitled to legal protections. The rules governing military trials, which favor the prosecution, the district court judge found invalid. Hearings are a requirement to determine whether those held as "enemy combatants" are POWs. Justice O'Connor's presumptions in favor of the prosecution in the *Hamdi* case could therefore be subsequently challenged. After the Appeals Court overruled *Hamdan* and supported the president's "inherent power," the U.S. Supreme Court in 2006 reversed, ruling that Bush has no such powers authorized by Congress, declaring the "military tribunals" invalid and in violation of the Geneva Conventions, and decided that the principles of the Uniform Code of Military Justice are applicable instead. This constitutes a significant step forward beyond *Hamdi* and *Padilla* but certainly not the last word for detainee human rights.[42]

The abuses of empire-building, violations of the international laws of war, and arbitrary detentions of citizens and aliens domestically in the U.S., at Guantanamo Bay, and in Iraq, Afghanistan, and Pakistan reflect similar methods used by our ally Israel effectively, if not legally or morally, in handling victims of occupation in Palestine, Lebanon and Syria.[43]

The limited legal affirmations expressed by a plurality of the U.S. Supreme Court involving the human rights of its own citizens illustrate the gross dangers, particularly for aliens, which continue to exist. The solution is simple—end the occupations, enforce the rule of international law now, and apply constitutional due process to all "persons" as the Fourteenth Amendment directs, regardless of citizenship. Peace will only truly come when we recognize that human rights take precedence over all other rights and duties. Distinctions between citizens and aliens must fall as an intrusion upon the moral values of the human family, whose ultimate rights to life and liberty are sacred.[44]

But it will be up to the American people to give protection against such transgressions. The 2004 election indicated that they "did not seem to mind that their personal freedom had been taken away ... and do not seem unduly concerned ... with those placed in 'protective custody.'" These words were written by William Shirer in his diary while a reporter in Berlin between 1930 and 1940 covering the rise of Hitler and the changes made in the democratic institutions of that country by Hitler and his party to create the security state that would shortly thereafter begin Nazi adventures in empire-building.[45]

Is it but a pious wish that Americans will wake up to a credible argument that the civil human rights of people take precedence over the security of the state? The social contract under which the United States operates as a nation calls for both freedom and security as the defining characteristics of government. But that does not mean that freedom and security have been equal in stature—that is, in preserving the historical values under the laws of the land as intended by the nation's founders. Historically, security rights have been described as the means for the permanent establishment of inherent higher rights. Any claim that security exists as a higher right runs counter to the fundamental expressions of the nation's founding. As Jefferson wrote:

> We hold these truths to be self-evident, that all persons are created equal, that they are endowed by their Creator with certain unalienable rights, among these life, liberty, and the pursuit of happiness. That to secure these rights, governments are instituted among Men, deriving their just powers from the consent of the governed.[46]

Therefore the purpose of government is to provide security as a means to guarantee these fundamental rights. Those rights are the end; the security, the means. A security that acts to take away those rights violates the U.S. Declaration of Independence and the reason for the existence of the United States in the first place. There is but one way to affirm the principle that these human rights take precedence over state security, and that is to hold inviolate those words of Jefferson and to apply them without hesitation to every conflict arising over the attempt to diminish human rights through the rhetoric and power of the security state. Otherwise we will find ourselves moving towards a "system of government that exercises a dictatorship of the extreme right, usually through the merging of state and business leadership together with belligerent nationalism."[47]

There are other Guantanamos around the world. Terrorism has been a reason and an excuse for locking up thousands of people worldwide, i.e. Diego Garcia Island, Uzbekistan, Egypt, Britain, and Israel. Israel has Facility 1391, a secret military prison on an army intelligence base with about 660 prisoners. No one may visit it. They are not told why they are there and have no access to lawyers. It is used exclusively for foreigners: Jordanians, Lebanese, Syrians, and Iranians. Israel has been a party to the retrograde motions to reestablish a medieval "dungeons and dragons" mentality to our democratic world. Heaven help the "new democracies" in the Middle East if that ideology becomes the norm worldwide.

The U.S. Congress and federal courts are beginning to act, and they should continue to do so, to secure these rights of citizens and other persons guaranteed by the Constitution, the Bill of Rights, and the Fourteenth Amendment. These are the highest moral values of the democracy and cannot be relegated to, subsumed under, or eliminated from a narrower list described as "non-negotiable" political and religious values proposed by political neoconservatives or Christian fundamentalists. For in doing so, the purpose of this nation is dishonored, and so are we. Let us preserve our honor and our historic legal and political philosophy in these trying and intolerant times.[48]

## Notes

1. 254 U.S. 449 (1957). Mallory was held in custody until a confession was physically forced.

2. See generally Edward Cleary, *McCormick on Evidence* (St. Paul, MN: West Publishing, 1972), pp. 337–341. *Merriman-Webster's Collegiate Dictionary*, 10th ed. (Springfield, Mass.: Merriman-Webster, Inc., 1999) defines "detain" as "to hold or keep in, or as if in custody; delay, stop, restrain, especially for political reasons." *Black's Law Dictionary*, 6th ed. (St. Paul, Minn.:West Publishing Co., 1990) defines "detain" as "to arrest, to check, to delay, to hinder, to hold, to restrain from proceeding, to stop, to withhold." Detention is "the act of keeping back, restraining or withdrawing . . ." It "occurs whenever (a) police officer accosts (an) individual and restrains his freedom to walk away . . ." (pp. 449–50).

3. *McNabb v. United States*, 318 U.S. 322 (1943); *Mallory v. United States*, 354 U.S. 449 (1957); Rollin M. Perkins and Ronald N. Boyce, *Criminal Law*, 3rd ed. (Mineola, NY: Foundation Press, 1982), pp. 140–141.

4. 374 U.S. 478 (1964).

5. 384 U.S. 436 (1966). Detention and arrest were not synonymous.

6. Perkins and Boyce, *Criminal Law*, p. 141.

7. Ibid.

8. Ibid.

9. Ibid., p. 142.

10. See generally William Durland, *Immoral Wars, Illegal Laws* (Colorado Springs, CO: The Center on Law and Human Rights, 2004); Wadi Muhaisien (professor, University of Colorado), "One Standard for International Law," *Denver Post*, Dec. 1, 2002.

11. *Human Rights Watch*, Sept. 12, 2001.

12. On February 15, 1848, then-congressman Abraham Lincoln stated his view on the Mexican War: "Allow the President to invade a neighboring nation whenever he shall deem it necessary to repel an invasion, and you allow him to do so *whenever he may choose to say* he deems it necessary for such purposes, and you allow him to make war at pleasure . . . and places our President where kings have always stood" (Geoffrey Stone, *Perilous Times: Free Speech in Wartime* [New York: W.W. Norton & Co., 2004], p. 123).

13. Public Law 107–56, Oct. 26, (2001), 115 Stat. 272. The new law has created an atmosphere of national security over human rights. Terrorism charges against two defendants in a Justice Department prosecution were dismissed "in a case riddled with errors by prosecutors" (*Denver Post*, Sept. 2, 2004). The author was part of an *amicus curie* brief, *Scheidler v. National Organization for Women, Inc.*, 537 U.S. 393 (2003), arguing against RICO racketeering laws being applied to nonviolent protestors. The Supreme Court invalidated that practice. The FBI has been accused of linking pacifist demonstrators to terrorist groups as a result of its undercover surveillance activities, including the American Friends Service Committee, of which the author was a regional director (*Denver Post*, Dec. 2, 2004).

14. A petition for a writ of habeas corpus is a request by an individual asking a judge to determine the legality of his detention by the government. Eliminating it prevents a judge from reviewing the legality of the detention and the release of a detainee unlawfully held. The author's first case in federal court was the successful release of a detainee on a writ of habeas corpus, *Fisher v. Overholser*, H.C. 227–62 (June 25, 1962) and *Cameron v. Fisher*, no. 17364, U.S. District Court of Appeals for the District of Columbia (June 13, 1963).

15. The president claims such powers were authorized by congressional resolution ("Authorization for Use of Military Force," 115 Stat. 224 [2001]; *Denver Post*, Sept. 15, 2004). A prisoner of war is defined in Article 4 of the 1945 Geneva Convention. The Federalist Party passed the Alien and Sedition Acts in 1798, empowering the president to seize, detain, and deport any noncitizen he deemed dangerous to the United States with no right to a hearing, to be informed of the charges against him, or to present evidence on his behalf. All final decisions were made by the president (Stone, *Perilous Times*, p. 31). The act was subsequently repealed.

16. Linda Greenhouse, "High Court Upholds Immigrant Detentions," *New York Times*, April 30, 2003.

17. *United States v. Lindh*, 212 F.Supp. 2d 541 (D.VA, 2002). Attorneys for Lindh asked for a reduction of his sentence upon news of Hamdi's deportation agreement. He was captured in the Afghan war during the period of military hostilities and pled guilty to two felonies, providing service to the Taliban and carrying explosives while doing so. More serious charges were dropped. In *Rasul v. Bush*, 542 U.S. 466 (2004), the Supreme Court ruled that federal courts may hear challenges to the legality of foreign nationals' detentions.

18. Mark Bowden, "The Dark Art of Interrogation," *Atlantic Monthly*, Oct. 2003, pp. 52–76. The Supreme Court decided the issue of the constitutionality of military tribunals during the Civil War. In *ex parte Milligan*, 71 U.S. (4 Wall) (1866) the Court decided that military tribunals were not constitutional even in time of war or insurrection if the civil courts were open. The Court held that "necessity must be actual and present; the invasion real, such as effectively closes the courts and disposes of civil administration." Milligan was a civilian and a citizen.

19. The American public has been quite reticent about such fundamental political abuses of aliens. See also Geneva Convention, Art. 118, 1949, and Hague Convention, Art. 20, July 27, 1949. As in the case of Moussaoui, Hamid Hayat has also been prosecuted on belief or intent only without any evidence of any overt act (see Amy Waldman, "Prophetic Justice," *Atlantic Monthly*, October 2006, p. 82).

20. *ACLU Newsletter*, Spring 2004, pp. 1, 4–5; *Fellowship of Reconciliation Newsletter*, Spring 2004, p. 1. Detainees are also held in Iraq and Israel. The number of estimated detainees in Iraq is between 11,000 and 18,000. In Israel "administrative arrests" are legal, i.e., arrests without trial or any opportunity to respond to accusations if any are revealed. The standard is "dangerous to the public" (Amira Haas, "Nonviolence Frightens the Army," *Ha'aretz*, Nov. 11, 2004).

21. *Hamdi, et al. v. Rumsfeld, Secretary of Defense, et al.*, 542 U.S. 507 (2004). (The following quotations from *Hamdi* in the text are from the above-reported case. The author practiced law before the Fourth Circuit U.S. Court of Appeals involving human rights issues in the past.)

22. Ibid., p. 509.

23. Ibid., p. 533.

24. Joint House Resolution 114. See note 15 above.

25. *Hamdi v. Rumsfeld*, p. 512.

26. Ibid., p. 514.

27. 312 U.S. 1 (1942). The Fourth Circuit cited *ex parte Quirin*, which authorized detention to prevent persons from returning to the field of battle until the end of the war. The U.S. Supreme Court, however, stated that since the Nuremberg Tribunal decision, captivity is merely a "temporary detention, which is devoid of all penal character. He is disarmed, treated humanely and in time ... released." Bush claims the War on Terror goes on and so may detention. Some authorities claim that here is the real error. Terrorism is a criminal act to be punished in civilian criminal courts and not an act of war to be tried before military tribunals. It is a clearly established principle of the law of war that detention lasts no longer than active hostilities.

28. Section III, C,1 of Justice O'Connor's opinion.

29. *Hamdi v. Rumsfeld*, p. 558.

30. Scalia makes reference to Lincoln's unconstitutional suspension of the writ of habeas corpus during the Civil War, rejected by the U.S. Supreme Court in *ex parte Merryman*, 17 F. Cas. 144 (c.d. Md., 1861). Only Congress has such a right.

31. 323 U.S. 214 (1944). In February 1942, at the beginning of World War II, by President Roosevelt's Executive Order No. 9066, 120,000 Japanese U.S. citizens and aliens were removed to concentration camps (the remains of which still exist, one of which I visited in Granada, Colorado). Two-thirds were American citizens. They were detained for the duration with no charges and no notice of where they were going, for how long, and what their conditions were to be. They could only take with them what they could carry. The property they left was stolen or confiscated. "... [t]here was not a single documented act of espionage, sabotage or treasonable activity committed by any citizen of Japanese descent or Japanese national residing on the West Coast." From 1988 to 1998 20,000 descendants were awarded $20,000 each in final compensation (Stone, *Perilous Times*, p. 287). Justice Murphy, dissenting in *Koramatsu v. United States*, 323 U.S. 214 (1944), wrote: "The judicial test of whether the government on a plea of military necessity, can validly deprive

an individual of any of his constitutional rights is whether the deprivation is reasonably related to a public danger that is so 'immediate, imminent, and impending' as not to admit of delay and not to permit the intervention of ordinary constitutional processes to alleviate the danger." He called for "individual investigation and hearings"; moreover he found no need for removal and characterized it as "the legalization of racism" (ibid., pp. 301–02).

32. *Rumsfeld, Secretary of Defense v. Padilla, et al.*, 542 U.S. 426, June 28, 2004. (The following quotations from *Padilla* are from the above-reported case.)

33. Ibid., p. 455.

34. Ibid., p. 461.

35. *The Denver Post*, Oct. 12, 2004.

36. *Padilla v. Hanft* (05-533), *Denver Post*, April 7, 2006, and April 12, 2006.

37. See, for example, Seymour Hersh's series of articles on Abu Ghraib prison abuses, *The New Yorker*, May 17 and 24, 2004. In addition to the prison abuse charges, one reservist has been charged, and perhaps others to follow, in the death of Mullah Habibhllah while in U.S. custody in Iraq from "blunt force" injuries. Investigations are underway by the U.S. military, and photographs have revealed Navy SEALS with Iraqi prisoners who are bloodied, handcuffed, and threatened with a gun (*Denver Post*, Dec. 4, 2004).

38. *Denver Post*, Aug. 4, 2004.

39. *Denver Post*, Aug. 14, 2004. The Red Cross has reported that abuses at Guantanamo Bay have approached the level of torture (*Denver Post*, Dec. 2, 2004). The American Center on Constitutional Rights filed a human rights suit in German courts alleging U.S. officials have condoned torture in Iraq (*Denver Post*, Dec. 1, 2004). Abuse has been occurring since 2002 (*Denver Post*, Dec. 7, 2004).

40. *Denver Post*, Oct. 27, 2004.

41. *Denver Post*, Nov. 9, 2004. *Hamdan v. Rumsfeld*, Civil Action 04-1519 (JR) U.S. Court for the District of Columbia, Nov. 8, 2004.

42. *Hamdan v. Rumsfeld*, No. 05-184, U.S. Supreme Court, June 29, 2006.

43. The Associated Press (and others) have reported Israeli involvement in interrogations of Iraqi detainees at Abu Ghraib prison (*Denver Post*, July 4, 2004). The United States relies on Israeli experience in militarily occupying territories of its neighbors for over thirty-seven years. In fact the roots of Abu Ghraib torture go back fifty years in CIA interrogation training manual instructions and practices (James Hodge and Linda Cooper, "Roots of Abu Ghraib in CIA Techniques," *National Catholic Reporter*, Nov. 5, 2004).

44. This author receives emails from international observers "on the ground" and from conflict resolution organizations of which he is a member, having joined them four times in Iraq and Palestine between 2001 and 2004.

45. William L. Shirer, *The Nightmare Years, 1930–1940*, vol. 2 (Boston: Little, Brown and Company, 1984), pp. 146–156. See also Stone, *Perilous Times*, particularly pp. 552–554.

46. Thomas Jefferson, *The Declaration of Independence*, from Richard Heffner, *A Documentary History of the United States* (New York: Penguin Books, 1991), p. 15.

47. Robert Kennedy, Jr., *Crimes against Nature* (New York: Harper Collins, 2004), p. 193.

48. The ruling in the *Hamdan* case, cited above, requires the president to conform any use of military tribunals or detention practices to existing U.S. constitutional, federal, and international laws, such as the Geneva Conventions and the Uniform Code of Military Justice. The rights of the accused to be present at trial, confront his accusers, and examine all evidence are lacking in Bush's approach as well as the failure to restrict hearsay testimony. Nevertheless, Congress in September 2006 legitimized Bush's secret detention centers in foreign countries administered by the CIA, where torture will be used without any supervision under the "rule of law." Whether all detainees will ever have their day in court remains to be seen in the new American security state.

# Security, Civil Liberties, and Human Rights
## *Finding a Balance*

### ⌒ Jennifer Caseldine-Bracht ⌒

The 9/11 terrorist attacks led Americans to reexamine their commitment to the Geneva Conventions, the Convention Against Torture and Other Cruel, Inhuman, or Degrading Treatment of Prisoners, and even the United States Constitution. We live in a moment in history when we shall be judged by how well we handle the balance between safety and human rights at home and abroad. It seems that respect for international human rights and civil liberties cannot be ensured until we ensure our safety. However, such a two-step approach does not apply in such a simple fashion here. We cannot first simply secure our safety and then secure the civil rights of others and ourselves. Often, respect for civil liberties actually enhances security. In the case of aliens, it is also not clear that ignoring the Geneva Conventions will increase U.S. security. A burden of proof lies on those who hold that security rights need to be upheld at the expense of innocent citizens. I will argue that the best security policies are those that protect the civil rights of aliens and American citizens.

Martin Luther King, Jr. once said, "injustice anywhere is a threat to justice everywhere."[1] So we must ask whether current United States laws and policies are making the world more just or less just. Through the Patriot Act and the Department of Homeland Security's mandates, the United States Constitution has been weakened. In the current climate, a case can also be made that the Geneva Conventions are being ignored.

Let us review a little history. The Geneva Conventions, dating back to 1864, were to provide written universal laws protecting victims of armed conflict. They were to be multilateral and open to all states, allowing for medical personnel to help the wounded. They were due to the vision of Henry Dunant, who was distraught after seeing the suffering caused by the Battle of Solferino. He was committed to the idea that the war injured from both sides should be helped. He worked to establish an international agreement for the protection of medical workers, resulting in the International Committee of the Red Cross (ICRC). He wanted a convention that would recognize the importance of protecting medics who helped during times of conflict. The Swiss government offered to host a conference, at which representatives of twelve states signed the Convention for the Amelioration of the Condition of the Wounded and Sick in Armed Forces in the Field (Convention I). Since then, numerous articles have been added to extend this first nucleus humanitarian right.[2]

The Bush administration has taken exception to the Geneva Conventions due to the unique nature of twenty-first-century terrorism. Human rights groups have called the Bush administration arrogant, stating that Bush cannot pick which international laws he will follow and which he will not. Much of the world is dismayed by a perceived cavalier attitude regarding the Conventions. The Bush administration maintains that the current fight is an exceptional type of war; thus the situation is more complicated than in past wars, so that legitimate reasons exist for bypassing the Conventions. Without rejecting the application of the Conventions in general, the administration argues that Al Qaeda has committed acts horrendous enough to disqualify members from the protections of the Geneva Conventions.

Al Qaeda declared a holy war on the United States and then targeted non-combatants, consequently violating Geneva Convention IV, relative to the Protection of Civilian Persons in Time of War. Additionally, the fact that it does not conduct its operations in accordance with the laws and customs of war does not, according to specific articles of Geneva Convention III, relative to the Treatment of Prisoners of War, justify the Bush administration's position that members of Al Qaeda and the Taliban do not merit prisoner of war (POW) status.[3] It may be said that whether the Bush administration has ignored the Geneva Conventions depends on how these articles are interpreted. But in this case strategic and geopolitical considerations color the interpretation.

The Bush administration has been inconsistent regarding its willingness to adhere to the Geneva Conventions. In February 2002, President Bush declared that the United States would apply the rules of the Geneva Conventions to Taliban soldiers captured during the war in Afghanistan, but would not afford the same recognition to members of the Al Qaeda terrorist network. The administration determined that the Taliban were fighting for the former Afghanistan government, and so the Geneva Conventions would apply. However, the Al Qaeda fighters were viewed as rogue terrorists and thus not entitled to the protections of the Conventions. Yet, in a somewhat twisted logic, the administration said that both the Taliban and Al Qaeda detainees would be treated humanely, as specified by the Geneva Conventions, while not being classified as POWs. It is difficult to understand how the Bush administration could claim that the Geneva Conventions would apply to the Taliban while simultaneously claiming that members of the Taliban should not be treated as POWs. It is unclear how the Bush administration could justify selectively picking and choosing pieces of the Geneva Conventions that would apply to Taliban fighters and still claim to be honoring the Conventions. So far, the administration has only stated that the apparent logical inconsistency is based on the fact that the War on Terror is an unprecedented war.

The geopolitical reasons behind these decisions are illuminating. The Bush administration does not want detainees to be designated as POWs because if they were, there could be no interrogation interviews. Prisoners would only be required to state their name, rank, and serial number. By not designating detainees as POWs, the Bush administration can question the detainees for an indeterminate length of time. Another point for not giving detainees POW status is that it offers the administration greater flexibility, since it has the option of not repatriating the detainees even if "the war" is over.[4]

If anyone peruses the memos addressed to the White House from the White House Council, it becomes apparent that the Bush administration was anticipating trouble justifying why it would not be offering the Taliban protection under the Geneva Conventions. Colin Powell sent a memorandum to Alberto R. Gonzales, the council to the president, and Condoleeza Rice, assistant to the president for national security affairs, on January 26, 2002. In an attachment to the memorandum, this argument was given:

> The Memorandum should note that any determination that Afghanistan is a failed state would be contrary to the official U.S. government position. The United States and the international community have consistently held Afghanistan to its treaty obligations and identified it as a party to the Geneva Conventions. The Memorandum should note that the OLC [Office of Legal Counsel] interpretation does not preclude the President from reaching a different conclusion. It should also note that the OLC

opinion is likely to be rejected by foreign governments and will not be respected in foreign courts or international tribunals which may assert jurisdiction over the subject matter. It should also note that OLC views are not definitive on the factual questions which are central to its legal conclusions.[5]

Even if the Bush administration were honoring the spirit of the Geneva Conventions by stating that all detainees are being treated humanely, a look at another memo is illuminating. In a memorandum from Gonzales to the president dated January 25, 2002, Gonzales is planning a response to complaints from critics, anticipating that other countries will balk at the idea of turning terrorists over to the United States or giving the United States legal assistance if it does not honor its obligation to comply with the Geneva Conventions.

> In the treatment of detainees, the U.S. will continue to be constrained by (i) its commitment to treat the detainees humanely, and *to the extent appropriate and consistent with military necessity* (italics are mine), in a manner consistent with the principles of the GPW, (Geneva Convention in Relation to Prisoners of War) (ii) its applicable treaty obligations, (iii) minimum standards of treatment universally recognized by the nations of the world, and (iv) applicable military regulations regarding the treatment of detainees.[6]

What is military necessity? Does the possibility of extracting *potentially* useful information from a detainee justify inhumane treatment? Gonzales's rationale appears incompatible with international law. Even if the Bush administration can find a loophole in the Geneva Convention to bypass it, does that mean it comes out legally free and clear?

There is also the Convention Against Torture and Other Cruel, Inhuman, or Degrading Treatment to consider. Part 1, Article 1 states:

> For the purposes of this Convention, the term "torture" means any act by which severe pain or suffering, whether physical or mental, is intentionally inflicted on a person for such purposes as obtaining from him or a third person information or a confession, punishing him for an act he or a third person has committed or is having suspected of committing, or intimidating or coercing him or a third party, or for any reason based on discrimination of any kind, when such pain or suffering is inflicted by or at the instigation of or with the consent or acquiescence of a public official or other person acting in an official capacity. It does not include pain or suffering arising only from, inherent in or incidental to lawful sanctions.[7]

Is the United States in compliance with the Convention Against Torture and Other Cruel, Inhuman, or Degrading Treatment? The usually neutral and silent ICRC has felt compelled to break its silence and voice its concerns. It has said that if allegations from some of the detainees are true, then the United States may be guilty of war crimes.

What are some of these allegations? There have been many allegations from many detainees. For example, a letter from Shafiq Rasul and Asif Iqbal to Members of the Senate Armed Service Committee alleged that at Khandahar they were questioned by United States interrogators on their knees, in chains, with guns pointed at their heads and beaten. They were also interrogated in Guantanamo for extended periods of time. The men alleged that it became standard practice to use plastic chairs during the interviews because they were easy to clean off when the detainees relieved themselves during the interrogations. They were not allowed to go to the toilet during interrogations, which could last up to fourteen hours.[8]

Several people who worked at the prison in Guantanamo have reported that prisoners were subjected to harsh treatment. Uncooperative prisoners were stripped to their underwear, with a hand and foot shackled to a bolt in the floor, maximizing the amount of cool air coming from air conditioners (supposedly this was especially difficult for detainees, since most of them have lived in warm climates), playing loud rock music, and using strobe lighting. David Sheffer, a senior State Department human rights official in the Clinton administration and a law professor at George Washington University, said that he believes treating detainees in such a way amounts to satisfying the pain and suffering requirement that is prohibited by the Convention Against Torture.[9]

The Bush administration could be guilty of yet another international law violation, namely the Martens clause. This clause was adopted from a declaration written by Professor Friedrich von Martens, the Russian delegate at the Hague Convention in 1899. It was adopted and included in the preamble of the Hague Convention (II) and states:

> Until a more complete code of the laws of war is issued, the High Contracting Parties think it right to declare that in cases not included in the Regulations adopted by them, populations and belligerents remain under the protection and empire of the principles of international law, as they result from the usages established between civilized nations, from the laws of humanity and the requirements of the public conscience.[10]

Certainly, members of Al Qaeda have not restricted their activities to those that fall within the parameters of laws (or principles) of humanity and the requirements of public conscience. But what about the United States? The Martens Clause is vague. For example, what is "public conscience"? Is it majority opinion? If so, then the United States has detained people in such a way that has outraged the public conscience. If the majority of opinion does not constitute public conscience, then what criteria should be used? The Geneva Conventions utilize the Martens Clause (common Article 63/62/142/158) in order to make the point that even if a party chooses not to honor the Conventions, it is still bound by the principles of humanity.[11] The Martens Clause is important to international law because it embodies its spirit, which is to respect human dignity and minimize the catastrophe of war and conflict.

Even if the Bush administration could make a case for its hit-or-miss compliance with the Geneva Conventions and the Convention Against Torture and Other Cruel, Inhuman, or Degrading Treatment, it has still lost a great deal of public goodwill by undiplomatic comments. For example, one quotation that infuriated many people and probably added fuel to much of the world's frustration with the Bush administration was given by Defense Secretary Donald H. Rumsfeld,

> who, when he was asked in January 2002 why the Geneva Convention did not apply to the detainees, replied that he did not have "the slightest concern" about their treatment after what they had done. The Economist magazine, hardly an anti-American newsweekly, called Rumsfeld's remarks "unworthy of a nation which has cherished the rule of law from its very birth."[12]

Charges that the administration is arrogant and acting above the law have come, in part, from quotations such as this one.

When John Ashcroft resigned as the United States attorney general, President Bush nominated his White House legal counsel, Alberto Gonzales, to be his successor. Gonzales has stated in a memorandum for the president that "this 'new paradigm' of the war on terrorism 'renders obsolete Geneva's strict limitations on questioning of enemy prisoners and renders quaint some of its provisions.'"[13] The defense of that position is that the Geneva Conventions do not apply to members of international terrorist groups or militias. The reasoning is twofold. First, terrorist groups will not follow the rule of law; therefore the United States is under no obligation to follow the laws of war. Secondly, the United States should reward people who do abide by the Geneva Conventions by giving them the same reciprocal special concessions.

One problem with this reasoning is an unstated premise that goes like this: anyone who the Bush administration *believes* is a terrorist is, indeed, a terrorist. Clearly, the fact that the Bush administration *believes* that someone is a member of an international terrorist group or militia does not mean that a person *is* a member of such a group. The Bush administration was sure that Iraq had weapons of mass destruction, too. Also, it was convinced that Portland lawyer Brandon Mayfield was a terrorist. Given errors such as this, it is easy to conceive the possibility that the Bush administration could be making decisions based on either faulty intelligence or a misinterpretation of intelligence.[14]

Secondly, the evidence indicates that the United States has not been made safer by ignoring treaties such as the Geneva Conventions. Once again, there were reasons for the Bush administration's decision to bypass the Geneva Conventions:

> "There was tremendous concern in the interagency process about letting someone go who might come back to haunt us," Mr. White, the former Army secretary, recalled. The desire to release men who might be innocent, he added, "was a fairly small upside, compared to the possible downside of misjudging some guy who then goes out and commits some terrible act."[15]

However, this concern does not justify indefinitely holding potentially innocent people. Does the phrase *inter arma silent leges* (laws are silent amidst arms) apply here? It is ominous to argue that certain laws should be silent during times of war.

The American legal system should be robust enough to stand as it is during times of war. This war on terror has had the utility of bringing certain questions into focus. What rights do American citizens have? What rights do aliens have? Does it matter if a person is captured on American or foreign soil? Does it matter where the person is detained? The Bush administration has maintained that anyone it deems to be an "enemy combatant" should not have certain rights. It has also maintained that the courts should not second-guess its decisions on these matters. However, three cases challenging the Bush administration's stance made it to the Supreme Court.

First, *Hamdi v. Rumsfeld*. Yaser Hamdi was captured by the soldiers of the Northern Alliance and shipped off to Guantanamo. The U.S. military found out that Hamdi had been born in Louisiana and thus was legally a citizen of the United States. Once it was determined that he was a U.S. citizen, he was sent to a naval brig in Norfolk, Virginia, and classified as an "enemy combatant." The Bush administration argued that Hamdi was not entitled to habeas corpus because of his classification as an "enemy combatant." Hamdi, of course, needed the right of habeas corpus if he was to ever prove that he was not an enemy combatant. Thus he was caught in a vicious judicial circle that would be impossible to escape. However the Supreme Court intervened, agreeing that such a summary procedure violated the Constitution.

Second, *Rumsfeld v. Padilla*. Jose Padilla is an American citizen who was captured at O'Hare International Airport when he disembarked from a flight from Pakistan. John Ashcroft accused him of plotting to launch a "dirty bomb" in the United States. Thus Padilla was declared an "enemy combatant" and sent to a naval brig in Charleston, South Carolina. However, Padilla's habeas corpus petition suffered from a fatal defect on jurisdictional grounds. Essentially, the Supreme Court held that the head of the military brig in South Carolina, Commander Melanie Marr, not Defense Secretary Rumsfeld, was the person Padilla should have sued. So Padilla is still in jail awaiting trail because the Supreme Court threw his case out on a technicality.

Regarding American citizens such as Padilla, who are classified as "enemy combatants," the Cato Institute argues: "If America can no longer 'afford the luxury' of the Fourth Amendment, proponents of that view must try to persuade their fellow citizens to amend the Constitution."[16]

Third, *Rasul v. Bush*. The Supreme Court had to decide whether the federal judiciary has jurisdiction to consider the legality of detainees who are foreign nationals and captured on foreign soil. The Supreme Court ruled that the federal courts do have the right to consider the legality of such detentions. Rasul was interrogated over two hundred times by American and British security. He spent twenty-six months imprisoned in Afghanistan and Guantanamo. His situation is similar to two hundred people who have been detained, released, and never charged with a crime.[17]

According to the conservative Cato Institute, an ever-present argument justifying some of the Bush administration's behavior has been that "non citizens do not have the same rights as citizens." It points out that the claim that non-citizens do not have the same rights as citizens is both true and false. It depends on which passage is invoked. Sometimes the Constitution uses terms such as "citizens," but other provisions use words such as "persons" or "the people" or "the accused." For example, the Fourteenth Amendment states that "the right of citizens of the United States to vote shall not be denied or abridged . . ." while the Fifth Amendment states that "no person shall be held to answer for a capital, or otherwise infamous crime, unless on a presentment or indictment of a grand jury." Also, the Supreme Court has held that constitutional guarantees generally apply to aliens and citizens, as in the *Wong Wing v. United States* decision, which stated that an unlawful alien could not be imprisoned without a writ of habeas corpus.[18]

Regarding enemy combatants in general, the Cato Institute also points out that in addition to the Fourth Amendment prohibition against unreasonable search and seizures, the Fifth Amendment guarantees due process and the Sixth Amendment guarantees a speedy and a public trial. The Bush administration evaded these constitutional guarantees by declining to file any official criminal charges. Thus defense councils for prisoners have appealed to habeas corpus, often seen as a vital right that protects individual liberty. It is often referred to as the "Great Writ."

The president has always had less drastic options. One option, if there were not enough evidence to prosecute someone, would be for a suspect to be placed under surveillance. Another, perhaps less palatable option would be for the president to seek to persuade the Congress to suspend the writ of habeas corpus. The president does not have the right to bypass habeas corpus by merely designating "enemy combatants." The Non-Detention Act, 18 U.S.C. 4001(a) states, "no citizen shall be imprisoned or otherwise detained by the United States except as pursuant to an act of congress."[19] But even if some of the administration's policies did not violate civil liberty or international law, pragmatic concerns remain. It is not clear that these tactics increase American security. The Center for Constitutional Rights has challenged Bush on many of the administration's policies and has been in the forefront of the fight for detainee rights. Their attorney, Shane Kadidal, illustrates once more the need for habeas corpus:

> Yaser Hamdi spent two and a half years in detention not on suspicion of committing any crime but rather on suspicion that he might know something—anything—useful to the government. The government was wrong at every stage about the legality of his detention; it's not much of a reach to think they were probably wrong about whether he had useful intelligence as well.[20]

Unfortunately this case does not seem to be an anomaly. It is not clear that the United States is gathering detainees in the most efficient and effective way, or that it is going about its intelligence-gathering in the most useful way. Rumsfeld had hoped that Guantanamo detainees would provide a valuable source of intelligence. However, this does not seem to be the case. There has been a problem finding experienced analysts, interpreters, and interrogators. According to the *New York Times*, very few (if any) military intelligence officers had any significant expertise on Afghanistan or Al Qaeda. Also, the potential usefulness of detainees apprehended posed a problem. Lt. Col. Thomas S. Berg, a member of the original military legal team set up to work on the prosecutions, said, "it became obvious to us as we reviewed the evidence that, in many cases, we had simply got the slowest guys on the battlefield. We literally found guys who had been shot in the butt."[21]

There are also confirmed reports that the CIA is holding suspected terrorists in secret prisons. The sites are known as "black sites," and not too much is known about them. However, human rights groups are greatly concerned about these covert prisons due to abuses committed by the United States at Guantanamo Bay, Abu Ghraib, and Camp Nama. In May 2006, the United Nations released a report that urged the United States to close down Guantanamo Bay. The report stated that the detainees either need to be put on trial or released. It called for immediate measures to eliminate torture of detainees by U.S. military personnel. Also, the U.N. declared that the United States should refrain from interrogation techniques that use dogs or sexually humiliate the detainees. The United States claims that it is treating the prisoners humanely, though it still refuses to allow the U.N. to talk privately with detainees. The U.N. argues that private conversations with detainees is a necessary part of the investigation process. The Bush administration rejected the U.N.'s suggestions. Some officials say that the report is without merit and that those making the suggestions have never visited Guantanamo Bay.[22]

The downside of the administration's intelligence-gathering strategies may be more serious than alienating the United Nations or the monetary, manpower, and moral cost of rounding people up based on country of origin or hauling in whoever was shot in the butt. According to a *Washington Post* article dated October 6, 2004, Army Brig. Gen. Martin Lucenti said that most of the alleged Al Qaeda and Taliban inmates at the U.S. military prison at Guantanamo will be either released or sent to their home countries for further investigations. According to Lucenti, most of the detainees rounded up in this fashion are either not a big threat or are of very little intelligence-gathering value.[23] Thus the United States is perceived by many people to have contravened international law and civil liberties, without gaining any demonstrable increased security benefit.

Some individuals held at Guantanamo for years without being charged with anything may become more radicalized as time goes by, and it is unlikely that they can in fact be held indefinitely. The United States must be careful. If the detainees cannot be held indefinitely, the United States must seriously consider the gains by controversial interrogation techniques versus the costs of radicalizing detainees and losing international approval. By taking universal human rights seriously, the United States would be able to reconcile security and human rights more effectively than it has in the post-9/11 era. By respecting international law and human rights for detainees, security might actually be *increased*.

Humanitarian law has a rich and evolving history. *Jus in bello* (justice in war) is not a new concept. Throughout history, attempts have been made to put some restraints on actions in times of war and to codify these restraints. The

Code of Manu (Law of Ancient Hindus), Law 91, provides that a king who fights his foes in battle should not "strike one who has climbed on an eminence, or a eunuch, nor one who joins the palms of his hands [in supplication], nor one who [flees] with flying hair, nor one who sits down, nor one who says "'I am thine.'" In 634 A.D., Calif Abu Bakr charged the Muslim Arab army invading Christian Syria: "Do not commit treachery, nor depart from the right path. You must not mutilate, neither kill a child or aged man or woman."[24] These are just to title a few of the various theories of *jus in bello* throughout history.

By giving the impression that the United States may not take *jus in bello* as seriously as possible, the United States may lose credibility in much of the world. The United States has historically been seen as a leader in international law and human rights. If it wants to be able to intervene in states with brutal dictators, then it must be as impeccable as possible in its own record of human rights. Otherwise everything the United States says regarding human rights may be seen as mere rhetoric and political correctness. Words like "liberty" and "human rights" should fill people with feelings of respect, hope, and passion. They should not be viewed as empty words devoid of meaning, and only used as a political tool. Many people are already cynical. It would be tragic for the United States to squander its reputation as a humanitarian state for the sake of such ineffective policies.

As for the military tribunals, there are reports of inept translations, and there is a lack of independent review outside the chain of command. The international community is rightly concerned about whether the accused can get a fair trial. Unless the United States government presides over fair trials, their outcome will enjoy little respect in much of the international community. Recently, the United States Supreme Court ruled that the Bush administration went too far with its use of executive power. Justice John Paul Stevens wrote that the proposed military tribunals go against both U.S. law and the Geneva Conventions. The Bush administration will either have to follow the rules of military court martial that are already in place or ask Congress for permission to set up different military tribunals.[25] It is not clear what the Bush administration will do, though it may try to convince Congress to go along with some version of its current program.

As already noted, the perception that the United States disregards some of the international rules of war can put American troops in danger. If an enemy were only *prima facie* inclined to follow the rules of war, it could become disinclined rather quickly if it appeared that the United States were not following the rules of war.

Again, often all that is gained by aggressive interrogative techniques are false confessions. For example, Asif Iqbal gave interrogators a false confession. After extensive interrogation, he finally admitted that he was, indeed, in the videotape with Osama Bin Laden that the interrogators were trying to tie him to. Later, the British intelligence found proof that Asif Iqbal could not have been in that video. He had been in England at the time the video was made.[26]

It is known that excessive interrogation techniques often lead to false confessions. Thus any information gathered is of little use to military intelligence. United States officers have been trained to strictly follow the dictates of U.S. and international law. Deviation from such training could endanger United States troops. If the United States soldiers do not honor the Geneva Conventions and the Convention Against Torture and Other Cruel, Inhuman, or Degrading Treatment, then even if two wrongs do not make a right, our troops may in fact be less likely to be treated with the protection of POW status. The United States was founded on a respect for human dignity and human rights. This foundation is cherished by many Americans and respected by much of the rest of the world. It is a foundation that should not be chipped away at. Finally, the robustness of a country's constitution is not enhanced by *inter arma silent leges*. Indeed, a country grows stronger by showing a strong commitment to its constitution *during* times of war. The United States Constitution was written to provide checks and balances during times of war and peace. Security will not be obtained through false confessions, increasing worldwide animosity toward the United States, holding detainees incommunicado indefinitely, and so forth. Instead, it is by staying within the parameters of international law and the United States Constitution that America can best find an appropriate balance between both security, rights, and civil liberties.

## Notes

1. Martin Luther King, Jr., Letter from Birmingham Jail, The Nobel Prize Internet Archive, 1963, available at http://www.nobelprizes.com/.

2. J. Henry Dunant, *A Memory of Solferino* (Washington, D.C.: The American National Red Cross, 1939), http://www.icrc.org/WEB/ENG/siteeng0.nsf/htmlall/p0361?OpenDocument&style=Custo_Final.4&View=defaultBody2.

3. Burns H. Weston, Richard A. Falk, and Hilary Charlesworth, *Supplement of Basic Documents to International Law and World Order*, 3rd ed. (St. Paul: West Group, 1997), pp. 169–179. See specifically the Geneva Convention Relative to the Treatment of Prisoners of War, Article 4A(1–3), Article 5, Article 130.

4. Richard A. Serrano, "Response to Terror; U.S. Will Apply Geneva Rules to Taliban Fighters," *Los Angeles Times* on the Web, February 8, 2002, http://www.latimes.com.

5. Michael Ratner and Ellen Ray, *Guantánamo: What the World Should Know* (White River Junction, Vt.: Chelsea Green Publishing, 2004), pp. 127–128.

6. Ratner and Ray, *Guantánamo*, pp. 122–123.

7. Weston, Falk, and Charlesworth, *Supplement*, p. 513.

8. Shafiq Rasul and Asif Iqbal, The Center for Constitutional Rights, May 13, 2004, http://www.ccr-ny.org/v2/reports/docs/ltr%20to%20Sentate%2012may04v2.pdf.

9. Neil A. Lewis, "Broad Use of Harsh Tactics Is Described at Cuba Base," *New York Times* (Late Edition, East Coast), October 17, 2004, p. 1.1, http://www.nytimes.com/2004/10/17/politics/17gitmo.html?ei=5090&en=67208a988fb4 4907&ex=1255665600&partner=kmarx&pagewanted=print&position=.

10. Rupert Ticehurst, "The Martens Clause and the Laws of Armed Conflict," *International Review of the Red Cross*, 317 (April 30, 1997), pp. 125–134, http://www.icrc.org/Web/Eng/siteeng0.nsf/iwpList133/32AEA038821EA35EC1256 B66005A747C.

11. Theodore Meron, "The Martens Clause, Principles of Humanity, and Dictates of Public Conscience," *The American Journal of International Law*, 94:1 (January 2000), pp. 78–89.

12. Richard Cohen, "Lawless in Guantánamo," *Washington Post* on the Web, January 20, 2004, http://www.washingtonpost.com/ac2/wp-dyn?pagename=article&contentId=A30721-2004Jan20&notFound=true.

13. Alberto Gonzales, "Decision Re Application of the Geneva Convention on Prisoners of War to the Conflict with Al Qaeda the Taliban," January 25, 2002, http://www.visaportal.com/downloads/12502memo.pdf?.

14. Richard Cohen, "It's Not the American Way," *Washington Post* on the Web, June 3, 2004, http://www.washingtonpost.com/wp-dyn/articles/A11253-2004Jun2.html.

15. Tim Golden and Don Van Natta Jr., "Administration Officials Split Over Stalled Military Tribunals: Tough Justice—Second of Two Articles: A Policy Unravels," *New York Times* (Late Edition, East Coast), October 25, 2005, p. A1.

16. Timothy Lynch, "Power and Liberty in Wartime," *Cato Supreme Court Review*, September 17, 2004, p. 32, http://www.cato.org/pubs/scr/docs/2004/powerandliberty.pdf.

17. "Law of War: Defining the Detainees" (editorial), *Los Angeles Times*, November 21, 2004, p. M2.

18. Lynch, "Power and Liberty," p. 37.

19. Lynch, "Power and Liberty," p. 34.

20. "Hamdi Release Proves Need for Access to Counsel and Courts," The Center for Constitutional Rights, (n.d.), http://www.ccr-ny.org/v2/reports/report.asp?ObjID= QTArOLU0QU&Content=445.

21. Lewis, "Broad Use," p. A1.

22. "UN calls for Guantanamo Closure," BBC News on the Web (UK Version), February 16, 2006, http://news.bbc.co.uk/1/hi/world/americas/4718724.stm.

23. John Mintz, "Most at Guantanamo to Be Freed or Sent Home, Officer Says," *Washington Post* on the Web, October 6, 2004, http://www.washingtonpost.com/wp-dyn/articles/A9626-2004Oct5.html.

24. Covey T. Oliver, Edwin B. Firmage, Christopher L. Blakesley, Richard F. Scott, and Sharon A. Williams, *Cases and Materials on The International Legal System*, 4th ed. (Westbury, NY: The Foundation Press, 1995), pp. 1257–1258.

25. Associated Press, "Justices Say Bush Went Too Far at Guantanamo," MSNBC on the Web, June 29, 2006, http://www.msnbc.msn.com/id/13592908/.

26. Associated Press, "Britons Once Held by U.S. Claim Brutality," MSNBC, August 4, 2004, http://www.msnbc.msn.com/id/5602003/.

# Terrorism

## *A New Challenge for International Humanitarian Law?*

### ANISSEH VAN ENGELAND NOURAI

The attacks of September 11, 2001, and the War on Terror are a test for international law in general. They have substantially impacted the context in which humanitarian law and international human rights operate. These two branches of international law must now address issues that were not on their agendas previously and that present a series of challenges. It requested a lot of legal imagination from international humanitarian law lawyers and from the jurists of organizations such as the International Committee of the Red Cross to tackle the issues arising with the emergence of new types of war and transnational terrorist groups.[1] Indeed, in this new framework, international human rights and humanitarian law are disadvantaged rhetorically and politically.[2]

Immediately after the 2001 attacks, the question was raised as to whether international humanitarian law and the 1949 Geneva Conventions were capable of responding to the terrorist threat. Besides, the debate about the existence of Guantanamo, which has spread to life around the world and that is now very vivid in the United States, is linked to the issue of the enforcement of international humanitarian law to terrorism. The question is the following: Does humanitarian law cover all aspects of terrorism, even the most recent trends?

Firstly, I will examine the debate concerning the Geneva Conventions and whether they in fact apply to terrorism. Then I will consider the reasons why humanitarian law should cover terrorism where it does not yet seem to do so. Finally, in the third part, I will deal with the application of the Geneva Conventions to terrorists. The paper concludes by envisaging what the future developments of humanitarian law regarding terrorism might be.

## TERRORISM AND HUMANITARIAN LAW: WHY HUMANITARIAN LAW IS APPLICABLE TO TERRORISM

After 9/11, the United States authorities held that the Geneva Conventions did not apply to the new form of terrorism. This assertion was wrong. *Humanitarian law* is the enforcement of *international human rights* in times of war and armed conflict, while international human rights are intended to be enforced during times of peace. Thus, if we should decide that the "War on Terror" is a mere turn of phrase and that no war actually exists, humanitarian law does not apply and human rights do apply. No legal loophole exists. In this case, the international community decided that, after 2001, a state of war existed; so international humanitarian law and the Geneva Conventions do apply.

The United States and organizations representing the international community have very different rationales for their shared view that we are at war. Summarizing, the United States believes the country is under attack and therefore is at war. However, it does not recognize the application of international humanitarian law, based on diverse arguments, one being that Guantanamo is located outside its geographical jurisdiction. The U. S. government also holds that, though it is at war, this war is neither an international nor a non-international (civil) armed conflict, and so the Geneva Conventions do not apply. (This is similar to arguing that testing HIV positive falls under no established classification of diseases and therefore is not a disease.) The International Committee for the Red Cross (ICRC) replies that "terrorism, and by necessary implication, counterterrorism, are subject to humanitarian law when, and only when, those activities rise to the level of armed conflict. Otherwise, the standard bodies of domestic and international criminal and human rights laws will apply." The ICRC considers the post-9/11 situation, including terrorism and counterterrorism, to be an armed conflict.

The viewpoint of the United States Government can be found in President Bush's addresses. One example was his *Address to the Join Session of Congress and the American People*, September 20, 2001.[3] The ICRC viewpoint can be found in the ICRC Legal Advisor's declarations.[4]

Another argument advanced by the United States was that international human rights and humanitarian law were obstacles to the enforcement of security. This claim is erroneous. The aim of the human rights movement and humanitarian law is the same: both to ensure respect for human rights and to prevent the disruption of peace. The protection of human rights is in no way incompatible with the War on Terror. "The human rights regime adopts a legalist approach to limit the harm the powerful may inflict on the vulnerable."[5] The problem is to know how to balance the need for increased security with respect for human rights and humanitarian law.

How can a balance be established between, on the one hand, the civil right to life and the civil right to security and, on the other hand, civil liberty—all three guaranteed by Article 3 of the Universal Declaration on Human Rights ("Everyone has the right to life, liberty and security of person")? The United States Patriot Act is probably an example of what should not be done. Some civil rights activists describe the recent measures taken by the Bush administration and the United States Congress as still another war, one on civil liberties.[6] The 9/11 attacks and the War against Terror test the limits of the legalist approach.[7] New regulations surrounding visas have become so complex that many intellectuals can no longer enter the United States, as illustrated by the case of Tariq Ramadan, a French secular Muslim who was invited to teach at the University of Notre Dame but who was denied a visa on the grounds that he was a threat to national security.[8] If the Patriot Act violates human rights in the name of security, then what kind of regulation would ensure security and civil rights? The issue not only impacts students, journalists, professors and universities, but also concerns every citizen.

To what extent should a law be allowed to intrude on privacy? How far can a government go in violating civil rights or, in particular, prisoners' rights? Eventually the United States Supreme Court redressed the balance in the case *Rasul v. Bush* in 2004, saying that all the combatants seized in Afghanistan have a right to challenge their detentions.[9] The role of the courts is, however, to provide a solution to an existing problem. How can we prevent such a problem from arising? The problem exists not only in the United States; the United Kingdom and France also face the dilemma of finding a balance between rights and security. However, a country like France would not likely fingerprint its citizens or check the books they have borrowed from the library. Even though some criticize the French system, which allows the police to check personal identification in the streets, the system has found a balance. The criminal code and the jurisprudence guarantee detainees accused of terrorism rights such as the visit of a doctor, access to a lawyer, a seventy-two-hour interrogation limit, and protection against violence because police interrogations are taped and video-recorded. Furthermore, only criminals are listed in databases. The current French system might be presented as the sort of body of law that respects civil liberties, in a country that, of course, has a long history of dealing with terrorist actions.

International human rights and international humanitarian law also provide tools for such a balance in that all the texts, including the Universal Declaration of Human Rights and the Geneva Conventions are based, among others, on the principle of proportionality:[10] the right to life and security does not mean that anyone can violate the right of a detainee not to be tortured as laid down in Article 3(a) of the four Geneva Conventions (Article 3 is an article common to the four Geneva Conventions).[11] Having a right, such as the right to life and security, or protecting a person's rights does not entitle anyone to violate someone else's right, such as the right not to be tortured.

When confronted with terrorist attacks, we find ourselves debating whether an armed conflict exists.[12] Humanitarian law does not apply outside of an armed conflict, and according to the American authorities, terrorism is not an armed conflict. They argue that a difference exists between war and terrorism: terrorism involves sudden peaks of violence with specific targets, but war develops over the long term. Thus terrorist actions as such cannot be qualified as an armed conflict. The reply, however, is that terrorism can take place during a war, like an act of sabotage or sudden terrorist action against the enemy. Sometimes organized terrorist actions can initiate armed conflict. Morover, the very nature of terrorism, as just defined, changed in 2001, and it now involves a state of armed conflict, because the violence is not sporadic anymore but is a long-term threat of violence that can spring to new life at any time. The extension ad infinitum of the war zone and the random targeting of civilians also occur. Therefore, we are in a state of an armed conflict in which humanitarian law does apply and that falls within the scope of the Geneva Conventions.

Still, some could argue that terrorism does not meet the definition of international armed conflict because it is neither a war waged among states nor a non-international armed conflict because it takes place throughout the entire world. Therefore, the United States authorities refuse enforcement of the Geneva Conventions, since, according to them, no international or non-international armed conflict as defined in the Conventions exists. Yet challenges exist: the rules of the Geneva Conventions and the two protocols are not the same according to what type of conflict we are in.[13] For example, Article 3, which is common to the four conventions, grants important rights that apply only in a non-international armed conflict. Article 3 is considered by the International Committee for the Red Cross (ICRC) as a Convention in itself. It guarantees rights to detainees but also to civilians and to members of armed forces who have laid down their weapons, such as the right not to be tortured, killed, or taken hostage and the right to the respect of their dignity. Article 3 is enforced only during non-international armed conflicts. During international armed conflicts, parties can resort to Article 75 of Protocol I, which ensures the same rights. The major issue is that the United States has not ratified the protocol. So the way the War on Terror is characterized has weighty consequences for the prisoners in Guantanamo and other military bases. If the War on Terror is a non-international armed conflict, Article 3 is applicable. If it is an international armed conflict, Article 75 should apply; but as the United States is not a party to the protocol, we face a legal obstacle. Besides, according to the United States, neither type of armed conflict applies, so no humanitarian rights should be enforced, which is wrong: if there is no armed conflict, we are in peacetime, but then international human rights are enforced.

An extension or revision of the Geneva Conventions is thus needed, despite their *prima facie* application to terrorism. Some speak of terrorism as a *transnational* conflict instead of *international* violence. The law of armed conflict needs to be adapted to remain the main legal tool used in cases of terrorism. Such adaptation can easily take place because humanitarian law has never been a static body. Besides, this evolution is possible thanks to the flexibility of customary international law. Moreover, in their public documents, despite the above legal obstacle, humanitarian organizations reiterate that terrorism is covered by the Geneva Conventions and humanitarian law does apply to terrorism because there is a war.[14]

In order to solve the issue and close the debate, humanitarian agencies argue that there is no war without rules. Even though no *lex specialis* exists regarding the links between humanitarian law and terrorism, the Geneva Conventions and international humanitarian law are relevant. The scope of the Geneva Conventions has been enlarged in practice to answer the new terrorist challenges, just as the new forms of conflict are calling for an expansion of the concept of armed conflict. International humanitarian law is applicable to the fight against terrorism when such a fight amounts to or involves armed conflict.[15] Armed conflict requires, of course, some intensity of violence.[16] As the custodian of the Geneva Conventions, the ICRC is the main organization to present this argument

As a matter of fact, whether there is a situation of international or non-international armed conflict, humanitarian law has an answer for terrorism. According to humanitarian organizations, the 1949 Conventions do prohibit terrorism and provide tools for its repression.[17] The Conventions are not deficient, since they contain direct references to terrorism. Both Article 51 (2) of Protocol I (applying to international armed conflicts) and Article 13 (2) of Protocol II (applying to non-international armed conflicts) prohibit the "spread of terror" among the civilian population.[18] These are two of many articles in the Conventions that deal with terrorism.[19]

Many issues will still need to be answered by humanitarian law as terrorism evolves, some within the Geneva Conventions themselves. It might be suggested that humanitarian law should be applied on a case-by-case basis. In some situations violence might reach the level of war, but in other situations, this might not be so.[20] A case-by-case method would nevertheless undermine the credibility of international humanitarian law.

### WHY SHOULD INTERNATIONAL HUMANITARIAN LAW COVER TERRORISM WHEN IT DOES NOT YET APPEAR TO?

Some continue to question whether or not the Geneva Conventions and humanitarian law cover terrorism. If these documents did not cover them, there would be a risk of creating a "rights-free zone."[21] I have just shown that the Geneva Conventions do cover terrorism, but do they cover all aspects of it? For many reasons, humanitarian organizations hold that all forms of terrorism fall within the scope of the Geneva Conventions.

#### PROTECTION OF CIVILIANS

The aim of humanitarian law is to protect the security and well-being of populations affected by wars. Civilians are protected by the Fourth Geneva Convention as unlawful targets; international humanitarian law grants a limited "license to kill" on the battlefield only in the case of armed troops.

A problem raised by the 9/11 terrorist actions is that civilians are now randomly targeted everywhere by terrorism. Anyone in the world is a potential victim.[22] Thus the scope of application of the Conventions has never been so wide. The challenge humanitarian organizations face is to protect all civilians, everyone, everywhere, at any time.[23] The battlefield no longer has a geographical limit.

Civilians must also be protected in any war led against terrorism. Counterterrorist methods cannot violate international human rights or humanitarian law,[24] or else "the innocents would be exposed to double jeopardy and suffer twin violation of their human rights."[25] Counterterrorist actions must not violate the human rights of civilians while targeting terrorist networks. For example, the fight against terrorism does not justify fingerprinting or analyzing the library records of arbitrarily profiled individuals, since that would violate the right to privacy.[26]

### Protection of Terrorists

Humanitarian law is based on a key distinction between combatants and non-combatants. It guarantees that anyone, combatants or non-combatants, either engaged in or a victim of an armed conflict, will benefit from the protection of basic rights, including both suspected and actual terrorists. The United States authorities challenged the competence of humanitarian law on this issue: the U.S. government decided that combatants captured in Afghanistan are not protected by the Geneva Conventions. The Bush administration contends that, as terrorists are acting outside any acceptable warfare rules, they are outside the scope of the Conventions. The argument is that terrorist groups violate humanitarian laws, so why would an antiterrorist coalition have to respect the Conventions?[27] There is a culture of near-total impunity that is now developing and in which international humanitarian law is overlooked by some Western governments, not to speak of the terrorists themselves.[28]

### Protection of Humanitarian Workers

Humanitarian workers are the new targets and victims of terrorist blackmail. The fact that the United States and the allied coalition provides humanitarian relief and carries on military actions at the same time dangerously undermines the status of humanitarian workers and the working conditions in the field. Humanitarian workers are not trusted anymore, since they might be American soldiers or spies disguised as, or embedded among, humanitarian workers. Thus, humanitarian workers may no longer be perceived as impartial but may be seen as a part of the enemy's plan for invasion and occupation. The fragile link of trust between victims and humanitarian workers has been severely damaged by the wars in Afghanistan and Iraq. *Médecins Sans Frontières* was the first non-governmental organization to expose this problem.[29] In some parts of Afghanistan, white humanitarian workers are viewed with suspicion.[30] This raises tensions, and non-governmental organizations are in fact no longer able to communicate and dialogue anymore with all groups and people in the field.[31] This means that no humanitarian worker is safe anywhere and that humanitarian action has been emptied of its meaning. Therefore, terrorism and the War on Terror must be covered by the Geneva Conventions because they, along with other international texts, protect humanitarian workers by setting boundaries between warriors and humanitarian actors, eventually ensuring the credibility of humanitarians as independent, neutral, and impartial actors.

### The Interaction between the War on Terror and Humanitarian Intervention

The War on Terror seeks to subordinate humanitarian law actions and interventions to a political agenda. It gives a "human" aspect to the wars in Iraq and

Afghanistan, labeled "humanitarian wars." For a while, humanitarian law was removed from the political agenda while states opted for non-intervention in places such as Rwanda. Then humanitarian concerns were raised during the war in Kosovo. Since the 1990s, humanitarian actions have been put at the forefront of the public discourse. The war in the former Yugoslavia was from the beginning labeled a humanitarian war. However, with the wars in Iraq and Afghanistan, governments went a step further by performing humanitarian actions in the field, like throwing food from the air simultaneously with military actions. *Médecins Sans Frontières* denounced this subordination of humanitarian action to the anti-terrorist campaign.[32] Humanitarianism is used as a "smoke-screen" or to justify an intervention that is in fact motivated by other interests and, in the United States, is even branded as "compassionate conservatism."[33] The "military-humanitarian actions" or "military-humanitarian coalition," as the American and British administrations respectively refer to the War on Terror, is a threat to humanitarian law, firstly because the term "humanitarian" belongs to those professing humanity, but politicians have taken this concept and reshaped it for war. Secondly, if terrorism is a violation of humanitarian law, so are the so-called military-humanitarian actions.

## THE 1949 GENEVA CONVENTIONS AND TERRORISTS

It is crucial to determine the status of people taking part in terrorist actions. Are they protected under humanitarian law and the Geneva Conventions? If the Geneva Conventions apply to terrorism as an armed conflict, then they are protected. According to the ICRC, the wars in Afghanistan and Iraq amount to an armed conflict because of the intensity of the use of force, and they are, of course, international.[34] Thus the Geneva Conventions grant protection to terrorists, and humanitarian law protects, among others, combatants who have been seized on the battlefield during an international armed conflict. According to Article 5 of the Third Geneva Convention, a competent court should decide whether or not to grant the status of prisoner of war to the combatant seized. Until such a decision is made, the detainee is to be considered as a prisoner of war and entitled to the rights secured by the Conventions.

However, according to United States authorities, there are two types of combatants: lawful and unlawful. According to the criteria set forth in Article 4 of the Third Geneva Convention and Articles 43 and 44 of the Additional Protocol I, lawful combatants have the status of prisoners of war and have rights as stated in the Article 3 of the Third Geneva Convention.[35] As far as detention is concerned, Article 3 ensures that detained combatants (lawful or not) are treated humanely, without any discrimination based on sex, religion, race, or any other classification. The rights laid down in Article 3 of the Geneva

Conventions (which applies to non-international armed conflict) and Article 75 of Protocol I (applying to international armed conflicts) are considered the legal minimum.

The second category, unlawful combatants, does not appear in humanitarian law as such. However, the category is developed in the legal literature, in military manuals, and in case law. It is thought that there are combatants on the battlefield who act unlawfully, outside the laws of warfare, and who have no rights or protection under humanitarian law.[36] This is, however, a misunderstanding: humanitarian law does grant a protection to "unlawful" combatants. They are *unprivileged* combatants, but they are still granted minimal protection.

The notion of unprivileged combatants means that even if the prisoners cannot be granted the status of prisoners of war under the Third Convention, they still have protection and rights granted under the Fourth Convention, Article 4(1): "Persons protected by the Convention are those who at a given moment and in any manner whatsoever find themselves, in case of a conflict or occupation, in the hands of a Party to the conflict or Occupying Power of which they are not nationals."[37] This article certainly seems to apply to any person and could therefore be understood to include unlawful combatants. Thus, a person who has unlawfully taken part in a war is not excluded from protection. Also Articles 43 to 47 relax the standards regarding prisoner of war status, and Article 75 of the Additional Protocol I gives the minimal protection in case the detainees are denied any status or rights under the Fourth Convention. Unfortunately, the United States has signed but not ratified the 1977 Protocols. Article 3, common to the four Geneva Conventions, is, however, perceived as customary international law, so detainees accused of being terrorists are protected whether they are legal or illegal combatants. These issues notwithstanding, the debate about privileged and unprivileged combatants initiated by the Guantanamo case has had a negative impact for the image and credibility of humanitarian law.

## TERRORISM AND INTERNATIONAL HUMANITARIAN LAW: WHAT IS THE NEXT STEP?

After the 9/11 attacks, the question was raised as to whether a new convention in the field of humanitarian law might be needed. Non-governmental organizations, led by the ICRC, refused the option and presented proofs that the Geneva Conventions were able to meet the challenge of terrorism.[38] These organizations instead argue for changes through an extension of the Geneva Conventions and customary international law. Humanitarian law is not static but adapts to reality, to the new challenges posed by war, and to new types of wars. Humanitarian law has already evolved greatly since the First Convention, of 1864, and has become a complex network of laws that can be applied to any situation involving violence and war.

The defenders of a new convention remind us that in 1977, two additional protocols were written in response to new warfare methods, including guerilla combat and advances in weapons technology. These new weapons and techniques made it possible to extend the battlefield ad infinitum.[39] Terrorist actions like those in 2001 likewise reveal that far more potential victims exist and the battlefield has no limits. Considering this, it is perhaps time at least to further amend the letter of the Geneva Conventions in accordance with their spirit. For example, the interdiction of the spread of terror under Protocol I, Article 51 should perhaps be reinforced to ban more stringently terrorist activities and their extensions.

Another argument in favor of a new convention is the need to take into account the difficulties encountered by the states that lead the War on Terror so that a balance between their national security and human rights is maintained. However, the risk in amending the Conventions is that changes might be affected more by a political agenda than by a human rights agenda. Some states might take the opportunity of amendment to alter fundamental rights like the rules of detention, the right not to be tortured, or the right to a fair trial. Some countries might seek to demonstrate that the current rules under the Geneva Conventions are unsustainable. For example, it might offer an opportunity to suppress the protection for "unprivileged" combatants granted in Article 75 of the Additional Protocol I or to modify the rights and protection granted by Article 3.[40] Humanitarian organizations would have to fight off this threat and reaffirm their commitment to the already existing humanitarian laws.

What is needed is a better understanding of present humanitarian law, not a new law. The authority of law is better served by not tinkering with it. Consequently, better coordination and common understanding are needed between the humanitarian agencies. States should also fulfill their obligations under the Geneva Conventions.[41] This would be the most legitimate, the most respectful, acknowledgment of what the Conventions have meant. Humanitarian law is not perfect. However, if it is well understood, enforced, and respected, a new text is not needed.

Moreover, the War on Terror can proceed without violating basic rights by asset freezing, intelligence gathering, and judicial cooperation.[42] Nations leading the War on Terror should not invoke the ineffectiveness of humanitarian law to justify a challenge to human rights and humanitarian law just because of the terrorist challenge to them. Humanitarian law is the best tool with which to fight terrorism, since it speaks the exact opposite language of terrorism. It upholds universal fundamental values that are applicable at all times.

However, could it still be that by refusing any changes in the Conventions, humanitarian organizations are making a mistake? By sticking to the Conventions merely as they are, humanitarian organizations might overlook the challenges. They might have to surrender later to a convention created under international law that would not include humanitarian law or human rights references.

Other, more questionable changes are also possible. One might be preemptive assaults by military forces fighting terrorism undertaken to avoid the burden of legal redress: we have an example with the targeted assassination of Sheik Yassin.[43] Equally ominous would be a reconceptualization of counterterrorism as a new branch of international law, independent of human rights and humanitarian law. Counterterrorism could even become an exceptional branch within international law, a branch that would neglect international human rights or international humanitarian law. More than that, exceptions could also be fashioned within international humanitarian law itself: derogations could be established regarding the rules of detention, coercive interrogation, endlessness of an armed conflict, the right to a fair trial, and the principle of non-discrimination.

However, other, more positive developments could take place. Terrorism could be elevated to a war crime or crime against humanity. That would provide for stronger protection of civilians and victims. New theories exist to explain how and why terrorism could be considered as a war crime or qualified as a crime against humanity.[44] Terrorists could be judged by the International Criminal Court under Articles 7 (Crimes against Humanity) and 8 (War Crimes) of the Roma Statute. During the *travaux préparatoires* of the International Criminal Court, countries like Algeria or Israel tried to include terrorism in the competence of the future Court and failed to do so because of, paradoxically enough, the efforts of the United States. Redefining terrorist actions within humanitarian law would be contrary to U.S. policy and would expand the International Criminal Court's competence.

## CONCLUSION

International humanitarian law is not an obstacle to combating terrorism effectively. It is not because the Geneva Conventions did not specifically anticipate modern terrorism that they cannot not fully accommodate it.[45]

International humanitarian law gives boundaries and rules for fighting terrorism. However, non-governmental organizations cannot deny the challenges that have arisen after 9/11. The War on Terror should not be perceived as a threat to humanitarian law but rather as an opportunity to reveal the fuller scope of the Geneva Conventions. However, a new protocol may be needed to complete the rules already laid down in the Conventions and humanitarian law, providing a *lex specialis* within the humanitarian corpus dealing only with terrorism. The most important challenge would then be to convince all states to ratify such a *lex specialis*.

## Notes

1. Marco Sassoli, "La 'Guerre contre le Terrorisme', le Droit International Humanitaire et le Statut de Prisonnier de Guerre," *Canadian Yearbook of International Law* 39 (2001): 211–252.

2. Joan Fitzpatrick, "Speaking Law to Power: The War against Terrorism and Human Rights," *European Journal of International Law* 14, no. 2 (April 2003): 241–264.

3. George Bush, http://www.whitehouse.gov/news/releases/2001/09/20010920-8.html.

4. Gabor Roma, "When Is a War Not a War? The Proper Role of the Law of Armed Conflict in the 'Global War on Terror,'" presented at the International Action to Prevent and Combat Terrorism, ICRC Workshop on the Protection of Human Rights While Countering Terrorism, Copenhagen, March 15–16, 2004; available at http://www.icrc.org/Web/Eng/siteeng0.nsf/iwpList575/3C2914F52152E565C1256E60005C84C0#.

5. Fitzpatrick, "Speaking Law to Power," pp. 241–264.

6. Elaine Cassel, "Civil Liberties: Three Years Later: The Other War," *Civil Liberties Watch*, October 18, 2004, http://www.thirdworldtraveler.com/Civil_Liberties/Civil_Liberties_watch.html.

7. Fitzpatrick, "Speaking Law to Power," pp. 241–264.

8. Jane Lampman, "Muslim Scholar Barred from US Preaches Tolerance," *Christian Science Monitor*, September 21, 2004.

9. *Rasul et al. v. Bush, President of the United States, et al.*, United States Supreme Court, No. 03-334, June 28, 2004.

10. Sabine Von Schorlemer, "Human Rights: Substantive and Institutional Implications of the War against Terrorism," *European Journal of International Law* 14, no. 2 (April 2003): 265–282.

11. Article 3 is common to the four Conventions; it guarantees, among other rights, the right not to be tortured.

12. An armed conflict is a situation where parties resort to the use of force. The parties can be states waging an international war, which constitutes an international armed conflict. Then there might be use of force between two

parties, where one at least is a state: that is a non-international armed conflict.

13. See the Geneva Conventions or visit the ICRC website (www.icrc.org) for details.

14. ICRC, "What Does Humanitarian Law Say about Terrorism?" *International Humanitarian Law: Answers to Your Questions* (Geneva: ICRC, 2002).

15. ICRC, *International Humanitarian Law and the Challenges of Contemporary Armed Conflict*, Report for the 28th International Conference of the Red Cross and Red Crescent, and International Committee of the Red Cross (Geneva: ICRC, September 2003), www.icrc.org.

16. Rona, "When Is a War Not a War?"

17. ICRC, "Draft Convention on the Suppression of Acts of Nuclear Terrorism," United Nations General Assembly Resolution 51/210, statement of the ICRC, New York, October 6, 1998, http://www.icrc.org/Web/eng/siteeng0.nsf/htmlall/section_ihl_nuclear_weapons?OpenDocument).

18. ICRC, "What Does Humanitarian Law Say about Terrorism?"

19. There are also Protocol I, Article 53; Protocol II, Article 16; Article 3; Protocol II, Article 4 (2)a–b; and Protocol I, Article 75 common to the four Conventions.

20. Rona, "When Is a War Not a War?"

21. Fitzpatrick, "Speaking Law to Power," pp. 241–264.

22. Anton Camen, "International Humanitarian Law: Achievements, Current Status and the Outlook for New Developments," presentation given at the Organization of American States, Special Meeting of the Committee on Judicial and Political Affairs on Promotion of and Respect for International Humanitarian Law, ICRC, Washington DC, March 20, 2003.

23. ICRC, *International Humanitarian Law and the Challenges of Contemporary Armed Conflict*.

24. Rona, "When Is a War Not a War?"

25. Shri V. S. Verma, "Combating Terrorism under the Rule of Law," address at the Second Bodh Raj Sawhny Memorial Oration (December 4, 2001), transcript available at www.nhrc.nic.in.

26. Gerald L. Neuman, "Humanitarian Law and Counterterrorist Force," *European Journal of International Law* 14 (April 2003):283–298.

27. Ibid.

28. Magnus Rostrup, "War on Terror Ignores International Humanitarian Law," *New Perspective Quarterly* 20, no. 2 (Spring 2003).

29. Nicolas de Torrenté, "The War on Terror's Challenge to Humanitarian Action," *Humanitarian Exchange*, no. 22. London: Overseas Development Institute, 2002.

30. Ibid.

31. ICRC, *International Humanitarian Law and the Challenges of Contemporary Armed Conflict*.

32. Torrenté, "The War on Terror's Challenge."

33. Ibid.

34. Rona, "When Is a War Not a War?"

35. Geneva Convention III, Relative to the Treatment of Prisoners of War, August 12, 1949.

36. Robert K. Goldman and Brian T. Tittemore, "Unprivileged Combatants and the Hostilities in Afghanistan: Their Status and Rights under International Humanitarian and Human Rights Law," American Society of International Law, Task Force on Terrorism (December 2002).

37. Convention IV, Relative to the Protection of Civilian Persons in Time of War, Geneva, August 12, 1949.

38. ICRC, *International Humanitarian Law and the Challenges of Contemporary Armed Conflict*.

39. Jakob Kellenberger, *International Humanitarian Law at the Beginning of the 21st Century*, 26th Round Table in San Remo on Current Problems of International Humanitarian Law, the Two Additional Protocols to the Geneva Conventions: 25 Years Later—Challenges and Prospects (2002).

40. The United States is not a party to the 1977 Additional Protocol I. However Article 75 and Article 3 are considered as customary international law. If the protection granted by this article is expressly refused in a convention, the unlawful combatants might have no protection left.

41. ICRC, *International Humanitarian Law and the Challenges of Contemporary Armed Conflict*.

42. Camen, "International Humanitarian Law."

43. Fitzpatrick, "Speaking Law to Power," pp. 241–264. For an academic debate about preemption, see Abraham D. Sofaer, "Debate on the Necessity of Pre-emption," *European Journal of International Law* 14, no. 2 (April 2003): 209–226; and Michael Bother, "Terrorism and the Legality of Pre-emptive Force," *European Journal of International Law* 14, no. 2 (April 2003): 227–240.

44. Hans-Peter Gasser, "Acts of Terror, 'Terrorism' and International Humanitarian Law," *International Review of the Red Cross*, no. 847 (September 2002): 547–595.

45. Gabor Rona, "Interesting Times for International Humanitarian Law: Challenges from the War on Terror," *The Fletcher Forum of World Affairs*, 27, no. 2 (Summer/Fall 2003): 55–74.

# On the Judicial Treatment of Guantanamo Detainees in International Law
## ⁃ Saby Ghoshray ⁃

He begged not for human rights, but for rights equal to that of a dog. He had an erect proud gait. Now he walks with a stooping hunch, evidence of his shackles being too short. Routinely he was chained on the damp cement floor with hands and feet bound together. Recreation consisted of no more than his legs unshackled and walking up and down a gravel strip. His diet of rice and beans was piped through a tap into his cage. The water was yellow, which would be shut off most the time, especially before prayers. He was caged inside a small wire frame, which was open to the outside. He had no privacy and no protection from the elements or the rodents. His cage was next to a kennel housing a healthy and clean Alsatian dog that had air conditioning and green grass for exercise. The dog belonged to the United States military. Jamal al-Harith belonged to the United States military.

### INTRODUCTION

He is Jamal al-Harith,[1] formerly Ronald Fiddler, a British citizen from Manchester, England. After two years in detention without charges and without legal counsel, he was released, much to the chagrin of the military police who tortured him for two years. But more than five hundred of his fellow inmates are still chained, still drinking yellow water, and many facing indefinite detentions. Jamal bears the scars of Guantanamo. His life has changed forever.

As we approach that fifth anniversary of Guantanamo,[2] the world has discovered that the War on Terror included unaccountable and inaccessible military prisons filled with Jamals from all over the world. This has caused a loud hue and cry from the world community. As some of these detainees are entering their fourth year encapsulated in a legal black hole, many are descending rapidly into a psychological downward spiral.[3] Who should be held accountable?

The answer to the above questions can best be illuminated by the nature of the so-called global War on Terror. This is an unending and undefined war whose tentacles are so far-reaching and whose impact is so all-pervasive that it overwhelms the American psyche with a new landscape of fear. As a result, it is taking American jurisprudence through a metamorphosis. The Bush doctrine has created a buffer zone of ambiguity and uncertainty between United States domestic law and international law. This has resulted in President Bush's military order of November 13, which established military commissions.[4] This order states that any foreign national designated by the president as a suspected terrorist or as aiding terrorists could be detained, tried, convicted, and even executed without a public trial, without adequate access to counsel, without the presumption of innocence or even proof of guilt beyond reasonable doubt, and without the right to appeal.[5]

In this paper, I will examine the structural elements of the U.S. military commission in Guantanamo to establish its illegitimacy under both international law and the U.S. Constitution. I will further establish that indefinite detention defies international law, and the trial by an illegitimate military commission violates accepted legal norms in civilized countries. Finally, I will argue that only a standardized and universally accepted definition of terrorism can accommodate the due process rights of the defendants, a definition which must be accepted by the international community, including the United States.

## THE COMPLEXITIES OF UNITED STATES JURISDICTION OF GUANTANAMO BAY

The status of Guantanamo Bay implies a secretive spectacle played out in the name of security, off-limits to true global public scrutiny.[6] Prisoners, whether POWs or common criminals, cannot be shackled inside a zone closed to any legal scrutiny and beyond the territorial jurisdiction of the United States Constitution.[7] This is a tear in the legal fabric, a constitutional black hole covered by the shadow of imperial sovereignty. There have been more than five hundred prisoners of the War on Terror held in this zone of exception. They were taken captive on the new, ever-expanding global battlefields of the War on Terror.[8] They were captured in places such as Zambia, Sudan, Morocco, and Yemen.[9] In most cases, the detainees were initially housed in the temporary Camp X-Ray, then transferred to camps of preventive detention that are of a more permanently indefinite nature. Such camps include Camp Delta, Camp Iguana, and

Camp Echo.[10] To understand the significance of Guantanamo in this War on Terror this permanent and indefinite nature has to be understood.

Permanency is defined by the unilateral executive decision made to suspend the law governing detainees' status, their treatment, and the resolution of any guilt attached thereto. Indefiniteness means the postponement of the rule of law and of the determination of the detainees' status. As a result, time, indeed, is running out for these detainees. As the news trickles out of the prison camps of Guantanamo, the world has learned of the increase in detainees' attempted suicides,[11] depression, and psychological breakdowns.[12] Why could the United States administration have expected to be insulated from the consequences of such violations of international law?

The crux of the judicial issue hinges on the Guantanamo detainees' ability to invoke habeas corpus.[13] The government maintains that alien detainees outside the sovereign territory of the United States may not make a habeas corpus petition to try to secure their release.[14] But under whose sovereign right does Guantanamo exist? Guantanamo Bay has been under United States occupation for over a century. The United States Marines took control from Spain in 1898 at the start of the Spanish-American War. The United States government formalized its power over the territory via agreements signed with Cuba in 1903 and 1934, when Cuba was an obedient client state, well before Fidel Castro came to power.[15] There is but a single clause reserving ultimate sovereignty over this forty-five-square-mile tract of land to Cuba. According to the treaty,[16] the Republic of Cuba agrees that

> during the period of occupation of the areas covered by the terms of the agreement, the United States shall exercise complete jurisdiction and control over the said areas with the right to acquire (under conditions to be agreed upon by the two governments) for the public purposes of the United States any land or other property in those areas by purchase or by exercise of eminent domain with full compensation to the owners thereof.[17]

So the relationship is that of landlord and tenant with a rent-to-own option. Ultimate Cuban sovereignty in this case has little significance beyond creating a legal loophole that is convenient for the United States. Thus, the United States can argue that Guantanamo is foreign soil and therefore is beyond the reach of American courts.[18]

Focusing on the clause "the United States shall exercise complete jurisdiction and control" in the treaty, we can see that Cuban sovereignty exists only in the abstract. In the matter of sovereignty, we must consider the practical reality of control. This becomes clear if we ponder the question: Did the detainees fall into Guantanamo while committing acts against the United

States? The evidence suggests that they were brought captive to Guantanamo after being plucked from other parts of the world. We must clearly reject the argument of real Cuban sovereignty. We must conclude that the United States has the real control, and thus actions taken there should fall under the United States court system. The legal premise should be based not on "ultimate sovereignty" but on the practicality of the "real control." If the preponderance of evidence points to real American control, the treaty-based concept of ultimate sovereignty is not decisive. We must then take guidance from Article VI of the Constitution:

> This Constitution, and the Laws of the United States which shall be made in Pursuance thereof; and all Treaties made, or which shall be made, under the Authority of the United States, shall be the supreme Law of the Land; and the Judges in every State shall be bound thereby, any Thing in the Constitution or Laws of any state to the Contrary notwithstanding.[19]

Therefore, if the treaty with Cuba is to be followed, any part of the treaty that provides clear guidance as to the control of Guantanamo must be followed, which in turn should provide jurisdiction for the federal courts to decide on issues related to habeas corpus petition on behalf of the detainees. Why, then, does the government resist this point of argument? Both the language of the treaty and Article VI of the Constitution clearly mandate bringing into play the powers of all three branches of government. It becomes clear that the government's argument is on shaky ground. The government is an entity subject to the Constitution and bound by law not to act lawlessly, especially over an indefinite period of time. Therefore, Court decisions such as *Johnson v. Eisentrager*,[20] dismissing habeas petition, and the Alien Tort Claims Act, based on lack of jurisdiction over American-controlled military prisons in postwar Germany, appear constitutionally wrong.

## DEBATE OVER THE LEGALITY OF THE MILITARY TRIBUNALS

There are three features of the tribunals that strike at the very core of all established norms of criminal jurisprudence. First, the tribunals would allow for no confidentiality between lawyers and clients, a basic tenet of legal representation, which would make it virtually impossible to hold a fair trial. Second, hearsay and other types of evidence that are normally inadmissible would be allowed. Third, and most flagrant, there still does not appear to be any means of appeal beyond the tribunals to an independent judicial body. Several prominent legal scholars have presented strong comments on the military tribunals' lack of legality. Laurence H. Tribe of Harvard University writes:

> All the rules about proof beyond reasonable doubt and other similar

protections can look tremendous but not add up to anything in the end. There is no guarantee of an appeal outside the executive branch. The most important thing is that the appeal be to people who do not depend on the president's approval for their continuation in office.[21]

Similarly, Scott L. Silliman, a Duke University Law School specialist on the military, concurs: "If the administration really wants to go the final step to full, fair and impartial justice, they need to build in some kind of judicial appellate review,"[22] like in the Uniform Code of Military Justice."[23] The director of the United States program for Human Rights Watch, Jamie Fellner, said her group was pleased with the reports of guarantees of due process, but she added:

> [T]he matter of appeals goes to the heart of the process. You can't have justice without an independent and impartial proceeding, and they have not addressed that. You still have a system in which the President determines who should be tried, who the commissions will consist of, and the President will determine what punishment will be levied on the accused. He's the prosecutor and the ultimate judge.[24]

Therefore, the military tribunal consists of a system in which the prosecutor, at his sole and non-reviewable discretion, can decide to bring charges, convene a jury composed of people who work for him, select the defendant's attorney, and use hearsay evidence. The defendant has no right of appeal to any court, only to the prosecutor, who is the president of the United States. President George Bush defended this by saying, "whatever the procedures are for the military tribunals, our system will be fairer than the system of Bin Laden and the Taliban. That is for certain."[25] But is just being better than the Taliban what the United States is about? By following the perpetrators of terrorism in a scorched-earth policy of de-humanization and de-civilization, we are turning the hand of time back. The international society cannot be oblivious to the possible fallout from this medieval system of justice. If merely being better than the Taliban is the objective, then we can simply amputate the fingers of thieves, and not the entire hand. Clearly, the proposed military tribunal does not follow accepted procedural norms when it denies basic fundamental rights of people, even if they are accused of crimes against humanity.

*Appeal Procedure*

Under current regulations of United States military tribunals, the adjudication of guilt can be appealed only to the United States secretary of defense and the president, who in turn can convene a panel that would consist of military officers who report indirectly to the secretary of defense. There is no independent appeals court where the guilty verdict can be challenged, especially when convictions and sentencing required only a two-thirds vote of military judges. The procedures are substantially more restrictive than the United States Uniform Code of Military Justice (UCMJ),[26] which applies to the court-martial of United States military personnel, where the verdicts are not final until automatically reviewed by the Army Court of Military Review (ACMR).[27] If found guilty the defendant can go to the United States Court of Military Appeals (CMA),[28] which consists of five civilian judges, and can have further recourse to the United States Supreme Court to hear the case.[29] This lack of fundamental fairness in the appeals procedure calls into question the ultimate objective of these military trials. Is it the search for truth and justice? Or is it medieval vengeance wrapped under the facade of justice? The military review panel can only review the facts of probative value and any exculpatory evidence in accordance with the rules of the military tribunal, not according to United States Constitution or international law. The outcome can hardly be anything but a guilty verdict.

*Permissible Evidence*

Consider for a moment the translated words that were etched on leaflets that were dropped over the Afghanistan region. One leaflet reads:

> Get wealth and power beyond your dreams. Help the Anti-Taliban forces rid Afghanistan of murderers and terrorists.... You can receive millions of dollars for helping Anti-Taliban Force catch Al-Qaida and Taliban murderers. This is enough money to take care of your family, your village, your tribe for the rest of your life. Pay for livestock and doctors and school books and housing for all people.[30]

These leaflets or the propaganda generated from the leaflets gave rise to the detention of a large number of individuals on hearsay or secret evidence. A key structural flaw inherent in the military tribunals is the government's ability to use secret evidence to develop its case, argue before the tribunal, and secure convictions resulting in the death penalty. According to the tribunals' rules, hearsay evidence can be used, and witnesses providing such evidence need not testify under oath. The government argues that any evidence that has probative value to a reasonable person is fair game.[31] This severely restricts the defense counsel's search for justice for his or her client. It would appear this jeopardizes the minimum United Nations requirement of being fundamentally fair in these proceedings. It imposes no limitation on evidence gathering and witness conduct, so that the motivation for providing evidence could range from personal vendetta to a simple case of bounty collection,[32] which is especially true in some of the geographical regions from which the defendants of the military tribunals hail.

As the dust settled down, and the captured were questioned and examined, the evidence collected pointed toward an inordinate number of detainees being captured on extraordinarily weak evidence. An example of such weak evidence used by the U.S. government to categorize a detainee as an enemy combatant includes "guilt by association." Guilt by association requires a willingness on the part of the administration to ignore the gulf divide between actual evidence and mere allegations. Such examples of guilt by association include:

1. Association with unnamed and unidentified individuals and/or organizations;
2. Association even with organizations whose members would be allowed into the United States by the Department of Homeland Security;
3. Possession of rifles;
4. Use of a guest house;
5. Possession of Casio watches; and
6. Wearing of olive drab clothing.[33]

The above examples set the stage for capturing innocent people based on guilt by association. Numerous accounts have also detailed people captured because they worked as a car driver for a Taliban or even because they innocently traveled and shared a hotel room with an Afghani enemy combatant. Further, in a "Kalashnikov Culture" like Afghanistan, it is not unusual to see persons of all ages displaying a Kalashnikov rifle. It is also not unusual to witness these rifles in public, even in such places as a restaurant. There are estimates of around 10 million small arms in the region. In Afghanistan, it is impossible to distinguish good guys from the bad guys based on the mere possession of a rifle. Yet, "the evidence against 39% of the detainees rests in part upon the possession of a Kalashnikov rifle."[34]

These exceptionally loose standards of evidence are incorporated in the proceedings in an attempt to keep security secrets or hidden details, according to the United States government.[35] The results of this secrecy help guarantee conviction and prevent the defense from challenging any chain-of-custody. These proceedings also allow for no limitation on deliberately developing evidence or even planting evidence.

### Lack of Access to Effective Counsel

Under the new guidelines for the proposed rules of proceedings,[36] the divulging of any information that the government deems to be in conflict with the national security interest is prohibited and thus is subject to exclusion from custody challenges, cross-examination, and defense sharing with client. Therefore, if the government deems exculpatory information to be secret, the military defense counsel will have to keep that evidence hidden from his client and even the civilian co-counsel. These parameters leave no transparency between the defense counsel and the defendant, even though the defendant could be the best person to determine whether the evidence presented by the prosecution is to be challenged, either for its veracity or for determining deviations from chain-of-custody. This unfair advantage inherent within the rules of the tribunal is another example of the lack of fundamental fairness.

In this regard we must examine the issues of conflict of interest and the lack of experience of the defense counsel. Conflict of interest comes from the fact that the judge, the prosecutor, and the defense report indirectly to the president. In a defense already stifled by loose evidentiary standards, inadequate appellate procedures, and non-transparent attorney-client relations, how can a counsel jealously and vigorously defend the client as she is ethically bound? A defense counsel in such trials would be pitted against all of the government's resources and would have to prepare his or her case in a fraction of the time utilized by the prosecution to build its case. The defense counsel would be appointed by the government and would have to work within the restrictive covenant of the tribunals, where there is no recourse for repeated motions of continuance and challenges on evidentiary rulings. A defendant is permitted to hire a civilian defense attorney of his choice to assist in the case, but for detainees languishing without resources in Guantanamo or Afghanistan, the idea of affording private civilian legal representation borders on the ridiculous.

### Secrecy of Proceeding

In reviewing the rules and guidelines so far, one of the dominant themes appears to be the practicability issue. The proceedings are to be open to the public to the "maximum extent practicable," effectively closing it from the purview of the legal scholars, human rights watch groups, and the media.[37] Again, the national security interest has been invoked in making these tribunals virtually secret, even though public knowledge of the proceedings helps ensure a fair trial for any defendant. Given world suspicion towards the United States for fabricating false evidence[38] to justify the war in Iraq, the United States' reputation as the bastion of justice and liberty is already at risk. The international community eagerly awaits commencement of a first round of military tribunals, where the legality of the proceedings and their departure from international law will surely be tried in the court of public opinion. Only lifting the veil of secrecy from these tribunals will significantly reduce the gap between international law and such United States jurisprudence.

## THE SCOPE AND JURISDICTION OF THE MILITARY TRIBUNAL

Having analyzed the procedural issues of the United States military tribunals, we now turn to the scope and jurisdiction of the military tribunals. The hastily crafted guidelines of these tribunals have exposed their criminal jurisdiction over both the accused and the territory from which the accused can come to controversy. Confusion is also rampant as to how long these tribunals can continue, thereby discarding all legal precedents and frameworks of international law.[39] Therefore, three things have to be clearly defined. First and foremost, a clear definition of the enemy or the entity to be tried by these military tribunals is required. Second, the enemy territory has to be defined. And third, a time frame has to be plausibly established for the hostilities to end, beyond which the existence of the military tribunal has to be deemed illegal. Delving into the archives of American history, we find military tribunals have been utilized in many wars the United States has fought. The justification has always been that when a nation is at war, certain civil liberties must be derogated in the interest of national security. But those wars were formally declared against a finite number of clearly identifiable enemies. The public would also have an idea when the war was going to be over and when the military tribunals would no longer be needed. In the context of current military tribunals, the Bush doctrine has used the term "enemy combatants" to identify the defendants and, with far-reaching impact, has named the conflict the War on Terror, as we will now explore.

As the landscape of fear is making inroads into American jurisprudence, activists and observers from across the ideological spectrum agree that civil liberties have been constrained in the United States since the 9/11 attacks. In this context, David Cole, professor at Georgetown University Law Center, argued in his book *Terrorism and the Constitution*[40] that since 9/11 the emphasis on "preventive law enforcement" has already had dire consequences for American society. Perhaps none other than Benjamin Franklin summed it up best: "He who sacrifices freedom for security is neither free nor secure."

### ENEMY COMBATANTS

Most individuals detained by the United States military in its global initiative on terrorism and those who have the maximum likelihood of being tried under the rules of military tribunal are called enemy combatants. Any individuals that the United States government deems to be members of Al Qaeda or the Taliban, or to be participants in this armed conflict against the United States, are designated as unlawful or enemy combatants. According to the government, once the designation of enemy combatant is assigned to a person, he could be detained indefinitely and would have no right under the Laws and

Customs of War[41] or the Constitution to meet with counsel regarding detention or to understand the charges against the individual. This is in violation of the international humanitarian law under the guidelines provided in the four Geneva Conventions of 1949[42] and the Additional Protocols of 1977.[43] The detainees of the war in Afghanistan have the legitimate right to POW status accorded to them under the Third Geneva Convention. Article 4.1 of the Third Convention[44] states that "POWs are members of the armed forces of a party to the conflict who have fallen into the power of the enemy." Why, then, is the United States continuing to deny those rights to the Taliban members who were captured in the battlefield in Afghanistan?

The four Conventions and the Additional Protocols provide wide-ranging rights to POWs in armed conflicts, including the right not to be subjected to inhumane interrogation, as well as the end of their detention upon the cessation of hostilities. But by not according the combatants rights as POWs, the United States can detain the combatants for an indefinite period. Indefinite detention can be helpful when U.S. intelligence has no convincing evidence against the detainees, providing time to develop cases for military tribunals in which even hearsay and un-sworn evidence can put someone away for life or even impose the death penalty. Additionally, the War on Terror is a nebulous concept that can span the whole gamut of any territory the United States desires to invade in the future. It is a war on an idea under whose umbrella any person and territory can be placed according to the whims of the United States government and the military it commands. It is a conveniently marketed strategy that makes the United States government a sanctuary impervious to international law in which authorities can take the time to frame charges, manipulate judicial proceedings, and justify the harshest of punishments. In this context, the commentary "Even a 'Bad Man' Has Rights,"[45] written by Gary Solis in the *Washington Post*, is relevant. The commentary states:

> Until now, as used by the attorney general, the term "enemy combatant" appeared nowhere in US criminal law, international law or in the law of war. The term appears to have been appropriated from *ex parte Quirin*, the 1942 Nazi saboteurs case, in which the Supreme Court wrote that "an enemy combatant who without uniform comes secretly through the lines for the purpose of waging war by destruction of life or property [would exemplify] belligerents who are generally deemed not to be entitled to the status of prisoner of war, but to be offenders against the law of war subject to trial and punishment by military tribunals."

In the laws of war "combatant" commonly refers to members of an armed force. Members of a state's armed force are usually clearly distinguishable from civilians, including other government officials and employees.

Members of the force normally wear uniforms and carry distinctive identification cards or documents. In an organization such as a rebel group within an irregular armed force, the line between combatants and non-combatants is much less clear.[46] By deliberately ignoring the guidance of the Geneva Conventions, the United States government has used an antiquated case law, *ex parte Quirin*,[47] to justify its denial of POWs' rights to the detainees. In *Quirin*, a group of German soldiers smuggled themselves into the country, hid their uniforms, and planned sabotage in the United States before being caught. They were arrested, prosecuted for what were regarded as crimes of war, and convicted, and six were sentenced to death. The Court stated in *Quirin:*

> By universal agreement and practice, the law of war draws a distinction between the armed forces and the peaceful populations of belligerent nations and also between those who are lawful and unlawful combatants. Lawful combatants are subject to capture and detention as prisoners of war by opposing military forces. Unlawful combatants are likewise subject to capture and detention, but in addition they are subject to trial and punishment by military tribunals for acts, which render their belligerency unlawful.[48]

*Quirin* should not be applicable today, as it does not have sufficient precedent value, due to the disparity between the situation that led to *Quirin* and the armed conflict with the Taliban. The defendants in *Quirin* were uniformed members of the German military who entered the United States illegally and under the guise of plain-clothed civilians. The captured Taliban members were fighting an armed conflict resulting from U.S. aggression on Afghan territory controlled by the regime named as the Taliban. Secondly, *Quirin* does not provide a precedent for action in which detainees are captured and held in secret locations without access to counsel and due process. As noted, the defendants in *Quirin* were afforded the right to have counsel represent them. Additionally, the Fourth Geneva Convention of 1949[49] is closer in relevance to the case of detainees from the war in Afghanistan.

Protections under the Geneva Conventions

As noted, the Geneva Conventions of 1949, of which the United States is a party, provides the framework for analysis of the grounds and procedures for the detention and treatment of enemy combatants. The treatment of captured combatants during an armed conflict is addressed in the Third Geneva Convention Relative to the Treatment of Prisoners of War,[50] which defines POWs and gives guidelines for their protection. Even accepting non-POW status for the detainees, we can take guidance from the Fourth Convention, which addresses persons not entitled to POW status, including so-called unlawful combatants.

These persons are also entitled to protection in war. If the War on Terror is indeed a war within the meaning of armed conflict according to international law, then any detainee should enjoy the rights outlined in the Conventions.

International law governing the status of persons detained by the enemy forces in armed conflict has advanced since the World War II days of *Quirin*. We see clear guidance given to the government of the occupying power or the capturing entity in various situations dealing with combatants and enemies.[51] In a declared war, the opponents belonging to a specific organization or a state, and any prisoners belonging to them, are POWs and thus have rights insulating them from inhumane interrogation and unlawful and secret detentions. Is the Taliban or Al Qaeda a specific organization or a state for the purpose of assigning POW status to their captured members? It does not matter. Even if we do not consider the Taliban or Al Qaeda as a state, their members can be designated as having committed belligerent acts in or near the battlefield and were subsequently captured. This qualifies them as POWs according to the Fourth Convention. If we continue to espouse that it is still not clear if the combatants captured are POWs, we can turn to Article 5 of the Geneva POW Convention, which states:

> The present Convention shall apply to the persons referred to in article 4 from the time they fall into the power of the enemy and until their final release and repatriation. Should any doubt arise as to whether persons, having committed a belligerent act and having fallen into the hands of the enemy, belong to any of the categories enumerated in article 4, such persons shall enjoy the protection of the present Convention until such time as their status has been determined by a competent tribunal.[52]

Therefore, it is clear that whenever there is a doubt about the status of a captured individual, he or she must be accorded the full rights and protection of a POW until a legitimate and competent tribunal decides the status of the individual. In fact the United States has established Article 5 tribunals for thousands of individuals captured on the battlefield during the first Gulf War, and so possesses the technical expertise to conduct such determination and is cognizant of the international law governing such proceedings.[53]

We conclude by countering the United States government's argument that international humanitarian law may not cover every individual in enemy hands during armed conflict.[54] A review of the negotiating history behind the Fourth Convention states:

> Every person in enemy hands must have some status under international law: he is either a prisoner of war and, as such, covered by the Third Convention, a civilian covered by the Fourth Convention, or again, a member of the medical personnel of the armed forces who is covered by the First

Convention. . . . Nobody in enemy hands can be outside the law. We feel that that is a satisfactory solution—not only satisfying to the mind, but also, and above all, satisfactory from the humanitarian point of view.[55]

### INTERNATIONAL HUMAN RIGHTS LAWS AND TREATIES

Thus far we have debated the rights of the enemy combatants captured in armed conflict in the framework of *Quirin* and the various Geneva Conventions. We have also established that the Geneva Conventions are equipped to address current situations involving enemy combatants. Further, we established that the United States military commission's framework violates the norms of international law, international humanitarian law, the Code of Conduct of Civilized Nations, and, possibly, other recognized international agreements. But the question that is significant here is whether the existing modalities of international law can accommodate the legal status of detainees captured in Guantanamo.

#### THE UNIVERSAL DECLARATION OF HUMAN RIGHTS

Adopted in 1948, the Universal Declaration of Human Rights has been strongly supported by the United States. President Bush proclaimed December 9, 2001, as "Human Rights Day and Bill of Rights Week."[56] Relevant to what is at issue here are Articles 8 and 9 of the Declaration. Article 8 states that "everyone has the right to an effective remedy by the competent National tribunals for acts violating the fundamental rights guaranteed to him by the constitution or by law." Article 9 states that "no one shall be subjected to arbitrary arrest, detention or exile."

#### PROTECTION OF ALL PERSONS FROM DETENTION OR IMPRISONMENT

Principle 17(1)[57] of the Body of Principles for the Protection of All Persons under Any Form of Detention or Imprisonment was adopted by the United Nations General Assembly in 1988. It states, "Any detained person shall be entitled to have the assistance of a legal counsel. He shall be informed of his right by the competent authority promptly after arrest and shall be provided with reasonable facilities for exercising it." More importantly, Principle 18[58] provides the following:

> A detained or imprisoned person shall be entitled to communicate and consult with his legal counsel. A detained or imprisoned person shall be allowed adequate time and facilities for consultation with his legal counsel. The right of a detained or imprisoned person to be visited by and to consult and communicate, without delay or censorship and in full confidentiality, with his legal counsel may not be suspended or restricted save in exceptional circumstances, to be specified by law or lawful regulations,

when it is considered indispensable by a judicial or other authority in order to maintain security and good order.

*INTERNATIONAL COVENANT ON CIVIL AND POLITICAL RIGHTS*

The International Covenant on Civil and Political Rights (ICCPR) was adopted and opened for signature, ratification, and accession by United Nations General Assembly resolution 2200A (XXI) on December 16, 1966, and became effective in 1976, following ratification by the required number of states.[59] Article 14 of the ICCPR describes certain standards and procedures that should be used in all courts and tribunals.

Analysis of applicable statutes and case laws clearly shows that provisions of international humanitarian law are more than adequate to treat foreign nationals captured while fighting the United States forces. The United States proposal for a military tribunal, if consummated, would undermine all existing norms of customary international law, international humanitarian law, and human rights law as we know them today. True, there exists no bulletproof language addressing the treatment of foreign nationals captured fighting United States forces. But the lack of legitimacy and legality that the United States military tribunals encompass leaves us with no choice but to extend international humanitarian law, rather than the improvised law of military tribunals, to the enemy combatants captured in the battlefields of Afghanistan and beyond. But to understand the lack of legitimacy and the absence of legality of the United States military commissions, we must understand the legal premise the administration is using to justify its indefinite detention.

### THE GOVERNMENT'S LEGAL FRAMEWORK FOR DETENTION

The indefinite detention of an enemy combatant proceeds in three distinct phases. First, the detainee comes in contact with U.S. authorities, either directly or via enforcement officials of another country. Upon arrest, the individual immediately becomes the property of the U.S. military, which signals the beginning of the second phase.[60] During this second phase of detention, the individual is subjected to interrogation for intelligence gathering purposes. The next phase involves two possible scenarios: indefinite detention in U.S. controlled Guantanamo Bay, or extraordinary rendition.[61] Extraordinary rendition involves transferring the detainee to a third country that specializes in inhumane torture, when the particular detainee is not yielding to the interrogation technique at Guantanamo. This extraordinary rendition takes place in mostly CIA-operated detention centers where the detainees are subjected to mental and physical torture during the interrogation process.[62] During this extraordinary rendition phase, the detainee is subjected to inhumane and barbaric physical torture to extract a confession that could be used against him for prosecution in the War on Terror.[63] Then the detainee is either sent to Guantanamo for indefinite detention or brought to the U.S. to face federal criminal charges. The question we should be painfully posing is, Under what legal framework is this inhumane processing occurring?

When a detainee comes under the custody of the U.S. military, he is being processed under the criminal justice system for prosecution of a crime. If that is not the case, the detainee should be assigned the status of a POW, and the nature of interrogation should have a very narrow focus. That is, if he is considered a criminal suspect, then the interrogation should proceed under the advisement of the detainee's attorney. On the other hand, if he is not considered a criminal suspect, then he is to be accorded the status of POW, only to be detained until the end of hostilities and to be interrogated for limited information extraction purposes. The status given to Guantanamo detainees is neither that of criminal suspect nor that of POWs. This construct has both illegitimacy and illegality, as I shall explain below.

Under the existing norm of international legal standards, the legal rights of the detainees must be determined either within the criminal justice system or in accordance with the laws of war. Under the criminal justice model, the detainee is entitled to a set of rights. These rights include the right to prove his innocence within a specified time without unreasonable delay, the right to have legal representation, and the right to presumption of innocence. As the evidence of innocent bystanders from Afghanistan and elsewhere having been transported to Guantanamo keeps coming in, the rights of presumption of innocence become increasingly important. However, in reality we have seen none of these rights accorded to the Guantanamo detainees. The working legal framework under which they have been processed has been the laws of war model. Under this framework, the minimum threshold level of culpability for initial capture is much less stringent. The difference between a crime scene in the criminal justice model and a battlefield in the laws of war model is that the battlefield has a more expansive reach. Individuals can be captured for detention for merely being present in the theater of war and do not need to be given a presumption of innocence. It is therefore clear that the U.S. is applying the traditional laws of war model in capturing the detainees in its recent War on Terrorism post-9/11.

The second phase of these detention proceedings, as discussed above, contains structural ambiguities, I would submit. The status of detainees centers on a determination as to whether the 9/11 attack on the World Trade Center is an act of war or a criminal act, as each category needs to be prosecuted under a different framework. If the attacks are considered criminal acts, as has been made evident by the administration's initial response, the perpetrators are to be indicted, sought for capture, and, once captured, brought within federal criminal jurisprudence. If the attack is considered an act of war, a declaration of war has to be made, and individuals captured during the prosecution of this war must be processed in accordance with the laws of war. Judging on how hundreds of individual suspects have been swept away and detained, it is clear the U.S. administration is using the framework of laws of war, which I shall present below.

First, to detain individuals under the laws of war, a state is required to issue a declaration of war against a specified enemy. Second, the detainees are to be kept in confinement for the duration or until the end of hostilities. Third, the captured detainees are to be interrogated with a set of norms, comprehensively defined by both The Hague and Geneva streams of laws.[64] Fourth, the operating principle under this laws of war framework can never be divorced from the minimum threshold of rights and liberty accorded to every individual under international law. How does the U.S. government's adherence to these procedural norms of the laws of war stack up against existing modalities of the civilized world?

The detention of Al Qaeda suspects in Guantanamo indicates that the criminal justice model fails to explain the detention of such persons on several grounds. Declaring a detainee an enemy combatant requires a declaration of war identifying the enemy and naming the theater of operation, rationale, and duration of war. Implicitly through its actions, the Bush administration has identified the enemy in declaring War on Terror against Al Qaeda. This construct is weakened by the fact that the War on Terror is now becoming a nebulous concept, especially when five years after 9/11, we still do not see any end in sight. The laws of war dictate that the fate of an enemy captured in the battlefield must have an outcome, as there is supposed to be an end to the hostilities which brought about the detention in question. Therefore, under the laws of war, detention of enemy soldiers is inextricably linked with the hostilities attendant with a defined outcome available. Under the current operating norms unfolding in the War on Terror, there is no outcome or end-game in sight, which puts the detainees in an indeterminate state of rightlessness, undefined within the current modalities of laws of war. The Bush administration brings in the criminal law framework to plug in the gaps in legal framework not attributable to the laws of war model.

When the Guantanamo detainees were initially captured, the Bush administration branded them as unlawful combatants,[65] a separate status from POWs. This was done to deny the detainees well-established rights accorded to the POWs under international law. This was done because these individuals were not identified with any state engaged in active war with the U.S. Let me expand on this point. The traditional war model involves states and thus the laws of war involve interrelationships among states. As a result, the combatant involved in war can be given lawful combatant status, symmetrically applied to both sides of the warring factions. Because Al Qaeda is not connected with any state, as evidenced by the conglomeration of diverging nationalities detained in Guantanamo, any individual identified as an Al Qaeda fighter is declassified as a lawful combatant and reclassified as an enemy combatant.[66] This serves two purposes. First, by making the construct asymmetric, all actions by U.S. soldiers are given blanket immunity under the traditional laws of war. For example, the U.S. soldiers can blow up an entire building in trying to kill a few Al Qaeda fighters, even if such violence results in the death of excessive numbers of civilians. Second, by reclassifying Al Qaeda fighters as unlawful combatants they are taken out of any existing legal framework and stripped of all rights accorded to a free person in the twenty-first century.

Once the new classification of unlawful combatants takes effect, the length of detention goes away, or at least that is what the U.S. administration believes. They become static, inanimate objects, "property of the United States Marines."[67] Let us untangle the following quandary. If these detainees lie outside criminal jurisprudence and are considered to lie somewhat within the laws of war framework, how do we explain the indefinite detention? This has been the hue and cry of the international community, as well as the subject of some recent decisions by the U.S. Supreme Court.[68] In those decisions the Supreme Court clearly indicated that the detainee should have his day in court. This brings us back to the U.S. criminal law model of adjudicating guilt or innocence. Under the framework of criminal law, a detainee can thereby be kept in confinement until a hearing or trial takes place. The governing criterion is to indicate that the detainees are to be tried for certain designated crime against the U.S. government or U.S. nationals, which should put the issue within the federal criminal justice system, and the detainees within the control of the U.S. government until the trial takes place. So we are back to the criminal justice model, even though at the beginning of this process we were squarely within the authority under the laws of war model. This shifting of legal framework, depending how it suits the need of the government, has been the driving construct under which the U.S. authorities have been working since the first detainee was picked up and transported to the Guantanamo Bay Naval Base in Cuba.

The phenomenon of indefinite detention described above can be understood within the framework of three distinct steps. Even if we concede that the initial capture of detainees is done under the laws of war model and that the detention afterwards accords with the hybrid laws of war-criminal justice framework, how can we explain the aggressive, torturous interrogation of the detainees? Under the laws of war model, a designated POW "is bound to give, if he is questioned on the subject, his true name and rank, and if he infringes this rule, he is liable to have the advantages given to prisoners of his class curtailed."[69] Under the criminal justice model, a detainee is allowed interrogation within the framework involving *Miranda* rights.[70] Available evidence gathered so far suggests that neither was the case in the interrogation of Guantanamo detainees. These detainees are thus considered neither criminal suspects nor enemy combatants, but rather subjects of inhumane detention and interrogation techniques, insulated from all existing modalities of law in vogue in the civilized world.

We must then consider the question, Is the United States government working outside of any allowable legal framework? I submit that the initial inclination by the U.S. government has been to suspend all laws within its procedure for handling Guantanamo detainees. With the international pressure increasing, however, the government backtracked and provided a fuzzy explanation of its judicial treatment of detainees. Its reasoning thus far can at best be captured with a hybrid-model consisting of elements taken on an ad-hoc basis from both the criminal justice as well as the laws of war models.

The parallel application of both criminal law and the laws of war has never been applied on the global stage, as has now been attempted in the judicial treatment of Guantanamo detainees. This hybrid juxtaposition of models suffers from structural flaws. While the laws of war model is enshrined in the interrelationship among states, the criminal law is encapsulated within the interacting elements of a state model. Clearly, there exists inherent tension between the two legal systems, which makes the application of such a hybrid model in defining the framework of detention in Guantanamo extremely difficult, if not downright illegitimate. Therefore, I will argue, this illegitimacy, coupled with other procedural difficulties within the Guantanamo Military Commission discussed earlier, breeds illegality within the legal framework. The lack of legitimacy and legality that the United States military tribunals encompass leaves us with no choice but to extend international humanitarian law, rather than the improvised law of military tribunals, to the enemy combatants captured in the battlefields of Afghanistan and beyond.

## JUDICIAL ANALYSIS OF RECENT SUPREME COURT DECISIONS

The fear of unknown enemies and the mystique surrounding classified security secrets influenced the legislative process and confused the Judiciary. The Executive sought absolute power. Congress gave a blank check, and the Judiciary cashed it. The Supreme Court finally intervened in July 2004, when it stated that Congress failed to oversee executive excesses, which culminated in two landmark decisions: *Rasul v. Bush* and *Hamdi v. Rumsfeld*.[71] These cases are significant in charting a future course for the fate of Guantanamo detainees, as these new rulings imply that the detainees held at Guantanamo must have access to the United States courts. While the legal world is hailing the rulings as a victory for liberty and the rule of law, the positive implications of the Court's rulings are yet to be fully understood. Furthermore, we must not lose sight of the fact that over five hundred detainees are still languishing in the Soviet-Gulag-like[72] prison camps of Guantanamo. The window of opportunity has opened slightly for many detainees, but it is still uncertain whether the rulings have done enough to restore the credibility of both the Judiciary and the United States government in the eyes of the world. Let us better understand the significance of the rulings by analyzing the individual opinions of some of the justices involved in the decision-making process.

The fundamental question in the Supreme Court decision in *Rasul v. Bush* was whether the federal court has jurisdiction over persons detained in Guantanamo. Even though the Court, in essence, ruled in favor of granting habeas relief to the detainees,[73] the majority opinion and the dissenting opinion clearly exhibit narrow and cautious decisions. The Supreme Court did not want to collide with the Executive branch. Thus, the decision essentially is no triumph for liberty. The Court rightfully corrected the narrow interpretation on which the court of appeals based its earlier ruling against the detainees' judicial rights of habeas corpus. One significant consequence of the Court's ruling in *Rasul* was that the Court no longer saw *Eisentrager* as a stumbling block that precludes a detainee from resorting to the judicial system of the United States, regardless of the place of capture and the nationality of the person. This is a sharp departure from the earlier lower court's decision in which the judiciary sided with the executive excesses of the U.S. government. Additionally, the Court called attention to the still-outstanding issue of indefinite detention under military custody by ruling that the type of custody is immaterial to the jurisdiction issue under review by the district court.

The Supreme Court ruling in *Rasul* can be seen as only the tip of the iceberg of a much broader issue surrounding the indefinite and arbitrary detention of Guantanamo aliens. The Court did not rule on the executive detention of the detainees; rather it rendered a cautious verdict in determining that the district court can hear cases of detention. The Court wanted to avoid a collision course with the Executive branch. Its ruling could not be hailed as a victory for liberty because the decision in *Rasul* will not end the languishing detention for the over five hundred people captured by the United States authorities under varying circumstances. These cases of detention involve even being captured on the battlefield while on a medical mission, being kidnapped for ransom by the Taliban or others, and simply being at the wrong place at the wrong time.

An interesting aspect of *Rasul* ia the way two distinct lines of argument were applied in arriving at the majority decision of granting habeas corpus relief to the detainees. (1) Four out of nine judges concurred with the Judiciary's long-standing reliance on *Eisentrager*, which now no longer poses a constitutional impediment against granting habeas corpus relief to the Guantanamo detainees. (2) Interestingly, however, Justice Kennedy concurred with the majority conclusion by following a different line of argument preserving the principle in *Eisentrager*. He explored the scope of *Eisentrager* to show how the facts in *Rasul* differ significantly from those of the alleged precedent. His retention of *Eisentrager* was important, because it has been somewhat of a constitutional bedrock, heavily relied upon in dealing with habeas corpus rights of wartime detainees in all pre-*Rasul* cases. While preserving reverence for the ideology of *Eisentrager*, Justice Kennedy went on to show that the "implied protection" by the United States as petitioned in *Eisentrager* actually holds in Guantanamo because of the special status of Guantanamo, in which, contrary to military prisons in Germany, the United States retains practical sovereignty. Additionally, Justice Kennedy's line of inquiry shows a clear distinction between the *Eisentrager* petitioners' trial with subsequent conviction and the indefinite detention without trial in the case of the Guantanamo petitioners.

Having stated the implications of the majority decision of the justices in *Rasul*, we owe some analysis of the dissenting opinion of Justice Scalia.[74] In implying the limited jurisdiction of the federal courts on the issue of habeas corpus relief for the detainees, Justice Scalia invoked the doctrine of constitutional avoidance to justify the narrow scope of *Eisentrager* in refuting the majority ruling. The doctrine of constitutional avoidance comes into play when "a statute is susceptible of two constructions, by one of which grave and doubtful constitutional questions arise and by the other of which such questions are avoided." It is expected as the duty of the Court to adopt the latter. The immediate and short answer to application of the doctrine to the case of *Rasul v. Bush* is that the granting of habeas relief to Guantanamo detainees is simply not "susceptible of two constructions." A careful analysis of *Eisentrager* lies at the very core of the resolution in *Rasul*. If practical sovereignty of Guantanamo is assumed, then neither the issue of constitutional avoidance nor the precedent of *Eisentrager* becomes a stumbling block in arriving at the majority opinion. In response to Justice Scalia's remark about the Court's springing a trap on the Executive branch, we conclude that as long as executive excesses are kept within the confines of legislative due diligence and the constitutional framework, the majority decision in *Rasul* did not jeopardize the Executive's wartime conduct and did not compromise military preparation of the United States in wartime.

In his dissenting opinion, Justice Scalia further laments: "In abandoning the venerable statutory line drawn in *Eisentrager*, the court boldly extends the scope of the habeas statute to the four corners of the earth." In response, we would emphasize that for the first time in this protracted War on Terror since 9/11, a small window of opportunity has opened. It is our belief that through this small opening the protection of all future and present detainees from executive excesses of the U.S. government in all four corners of the earth will come—assuming that the line between practical and ultimate sovereignty applies to the United States. The decision in *Rasul*, therefore, could be hailed as a harbinger to protect innocent people from the gallows of illegal detentions by the United States, whether in Guantanamo or in Falluja. This much-needed opening must be made transparent and apparent wherever the unending War on Terror creates an ambience of practical United States control that passes beyond the threshold created in *Rasul*.

Let us now turn our focus from the judicial treatment of the detainees to the military tribunals. We have already aired procedural flaws in the organization of these tribunals, but we must also explore issues affecting the future of customary international law as we know it today. The legality of the jurisdiction of the United States military tribunals can be dissected as follows. First, procedures of the tribunals conflict with international humanitarian law. Secondly, the denial of POW status to the detainees is simply not in conformity with the established legal norms of global jurisprudence. The rules of the tribunals are fundamentally unfair in the light of United Nations requirements, and the designation of detainees does not follow customary rules of engagement in international armed conflict.

International law dictates that a person detained outside the United States' geographic boundaries falls under the criminal jurisdiction of the United States if the crime committed is so grave that it seriously risks affecting relations between the nations. This is a universal principle dependent on the notion of *hostis humani generis*.[75] The person in question may be tried and punished by any state that establishes control over him or her, regardless of nationality, of whether the person's country of origin is at war, and of the location of the crime. This calls for assigning the label "crimes against humanity," as in the Nuremberg Trial, which is broader than the concept of regular war crime.[76] Yet this still leaves the question of linking enemy combatants to high crimes like crime against humanity.[77]

It is now certain that we need a comprehensive, universally accepted definition of terrorism because the current definition is based on a sliding scale driven by the hegemonic need to wield powers global in breadth rather than on jurisdictional and judicial consistency. Only within the fabric of a standardized and universally accepted definition of terrorism can we incorporate the due process rights of the defendants, which must be accepted by the international community, including the United States. Despite the imperfections of international law, it is still the only legal framework for today's focus on combating global terrorism.

The terrorist attacks in New York and Washington D.C. on 9/11 have further underscored the weakening influence of international law and the isolation of United States domestic law. We have analyzed President Bush's controversial military order of November 13, 2001, establishing a legal framework to prosecute terrorists via military tribunals, both in the context of the United States' current stance against the International Criminal Court and within the parameters of legal precedents.

Analyzing the broad applicability of Geneva Conventions and reviewing the case laws regarding past tribunals, we have established that these military tribunals, with their extraordinary scope, are in violation of international law. Where the application of international law guarantees military justice for every segment of the population in the combat zone, the military tribunal extends its tentacles to ordinary citizens thousands of miles away from the actual combat. There is nothing in such tribunals to grant enemy combatants humanitarian protection from unlawful detention and torture, rights so fundamental that no deviation from their implementation can be accepted. The spirit of international law makes it incumbent upon us to redefine POWs and their rights as the United States expands its global reach in combating terrorism.

## CONCLUSION

The United States Supreme Court may have placed some restraint on the unbridled executive excess of its government, but the Court has left numerous lacunae in our understanding of what rights detainees can claim, the standards and procedures that will apply to such petitions, and whether habeas jurisdiction also covers American detainees at other foreign locations. This makes it both interesting and puzzling to predict how the future courts will deal with the issue of applying habeas at other United States-controlled sites while still assuring combat effectiveness in the War on Terror. On the other hand, the debate over the rights of the defendants and the types of defenses that could be allowed within the framework of a military tribunal will not end without establishing a definition of terrorism under international law. The unprecedented and alarming new penchant for United States government secrecy and the abandonment of legal precedents has given rise to a slew of unanswered questions, such as, What should be the international law on terrorism? What should be the due process accorded to the accused? Does merely the declaration of a war on terror justify detaining people without recourse to due process? Humanitarian law can still prevent civilized nations from falling into decadence, chaos, and violence by extending the rhetorical battlefield. International law can address the issues that, in a more perilous way, the military tribunals propose to address. We must renew our faith in the concepts of civil rights, judicial protection, and human rights. We must prevent international law from becoming a vanishing point in global jurisprudence.

## NOTES

1. Jamal al-Harith is the first detainee to shed light on the barbaric and torturous acts of military personnel in Guantanamo Bay's Camp X-Ray and Camp Delta prison camps. The accounts first surfaced in a series of interviews in the *Daily Mirror:* Rosa Prince and Gary Jones, "My Hell in Camp X-Ray," *Daily Mirror,* March 12, 2004, http://www.cageprisoners.com/articles.php?aid=890. See also the statement of Jamal al-Harith in *The Lawfulness of Detentions by the United States in Guantánamo Bay,* Committee on Legal Affairs and Human Rights of the Council of Europe Parliamentary Assembly, Paris, December 17, 2004, available at http://www.blink.org.uk/print.asp?key=5438. Jamal al-Harith was a school administrator in the United Kingdom before being captured and sent to Guantanamo. He was ultimately released with no charges brought against him, and he joined a lawsuit with other detainees that were held illegally in Guantanamo.

2. Kate Allen, "Guantánamo Bay: Two Years Too Many," *Observer* (UK), January 11, 2004, available at http://www.commondreams.org/cgi-bin/print.cgi?file=/views04/0111-06.htm. As director of Amnesty Internationally she writes about the phenomenon of Guantanamo Bay as it unfolded. Almost two years have since passed, and the fates of over 500 detainees remain in uncertain, inhumane conditions. As noted by Jennifer Shook, "Over 9,500 troops are stationed at Camp America, the main section of the base at 'Gitmo.' Since the first president of Cuba, an American citizen, signed the lease in 1903, the U.S. has had 'complete jurisdiction and control' over the territory, but Cuba retains sovereignty. In Rumsfeld's words, it seemed the 'least worst place' to detain suspected terrorists"; see Jennifer Shook, "Guantánamo: Honor Bound to Defend Freedom," Timeline Theatre Company, February 2006, available at timelinetheater.com.

3. Since the latter part of 2003, increasingly numerous news articles have published corroborative reports of escalating psychological problems among Guantanamo detainees. In an October 2003 report, the International Committee of the Red Cross (ICRC) issued scathing criticism of the United States government for its treatment of detainees. The ICRC observes: "We have observed what we consider to be a worrying deterioration in the psychological health of a large number of the internees"; "US Prisoner Treatment Causes Mental Health Problems," Mental Health Blog, October 11, 2003, available at http://mentalhealth.about.com/b/a/033814.htm; See also Don Van Natta, Jr., "Questioning Terror Suspects in a Dark and Surreal World," *New York Times*, March, 9 2003, available at http://www.nytimes.com/2003/03/09/international/09DETA.html?ei=5070&en=504). Also worth noting are the proposals by authorities to open a special ward for detainees with mental problems, as documented in the articles "US Plans Mental Ward for Detainees," Associated Press, March 7, 2003; and "Suicide Attempts at Guantánamo Reach 32," Talkleft, August 26, 2003, available at http://www.eightlinks.com/archives/000900.html.

4. For a better understanding of the president's military order on detainees, review "President Issues Military Order," White House Publication, 13 November 2001, available at http://www.whitehouse.gov/news/releases/2001/11/20011113-27.html.

5. For a general understanding of the ordeal detainees endured, see generally Megan Lane, "Letters from Guantánamo Bay," *BBC News Online*, July 17, 2003, available at http://news.bbc.co.uk/2/hi/uk_news/magazine/3072529.stm.

6. Guantanamo Bay, Cuba is a strategic location to hold Al Qaeda and Taliban detainees captured in the war in Afghanistan. Initially built as a 612-occupancy detention facility, Camp Delta is located in Guantanamo Bay and currently has the capacity to hold over 2,000 in detention. As GlobalSecurity.org outlines, "To be eligible for transfer and detention at Camp Delta, Guantánamo, prisoners taken in Afghanistan must meet any one of the following criteria: (i) be a foreign national; (ii) have received training from Al Qaeda; or (iii) be in command of 300 or more personnel. Located on Cuban territory, it is the 'legal equivalent of outer space,' according to one United States government official, unlike military bases on United States territories. These other locations were ruled out as prison sites because they fall under the jurisdiction of the Ninth United States Circuit Court of Appeals." See Guantánamo Bay—Camp Delta, GlobalSecurity.org, April 26, 2005, available at http://www.globalsecurity.org/military/ facility/Guantánamo-bay_delta.htm.

7. Legal scholars and human rights organizations have voiced their

opinion regarding the perceived attempt by the United States government to put the status of Guantanamo Bay, Cuba into a legal limbo. See Lord Johan Steyn, "Guantánamo Bay: The Legal Black Hole," Twenty-Seventh FA Mann Lecture, British Institute of International and Comparative Law and Herbert Smith, Lincoln's Inn Old Hall, November 25, 2003. See also the article in the *Guardian* newspaper in which attorney Louise Christian, who represents the four UK detainees, presents a scathing attack on the Blair government, describing Guantanamo Bay as a legal black hole; Richard Phillips, "'Friend of Court' Applications Denounce Guantanamo Bay Detentions as Illegal," World Socialist Web Site, January 19, 2004, available at http://www.wsws.org/articles/2004/jan2004/guan-j19.shtml.

8. Several detainees in Guantanamo were captured away from the battlefield in Afghanistan. Some were kidnapped and, in some cases, captured in other parts of the world and later handed over to United States authorities. For example, three of the British detainees were captured by local authorities in Africa, interrogated, transferred to the custody of United States military, and found their way to Guantanamo. Similarly, six Algerians were captured in Bosnia by local authorities but were transferred to United States custody in Guantanamo, overruling the release order by the Bosnian high court. The case of a detained Sudanese cameraman with Al-Jazeera television network is also a well-known fact; more details available from Alicia Upano, "Al-Jazeera Cameraman Detained by U.S. Military," The Reporters Committe for Freedom of the Press, October 1, 2002, available at http://www.rcfp.org/news/2002/1001aljaze.html.

9. Detainees have come from all parts of the world. The Pentagon has produced a list which is to contain the names and citizenship of 558 people that were detained in Guantanamo for the year 2004–2005. To view this list, visit the website available at http://www.timesonline.co.uk/article/0,,11069-2143034,00.html.

10. Detention facilities at Camp X-Ray were initially single-occupancy only. As the War on Terror became both unending in scope and unlimited in its geographical reach, the demand for occupancy space grew. The United States government has detained an estimated 2,000 prisoners or more at Guantanamo Bay. As a result, the construction of a larger, more permanent detention facility, Camp Delta, began on February 27, 2002. Camp Echo is the detention facility for the detainees whom the president of the United States has selected for the military tribunals, who are kept separate from the general population in Camp Delta. Camp Iguana is the detention facility dedicated for juvenile prisoners aged between 13 and 15 years. See GlobalSecurity.org, available at http://www.globalsecurity.org/military/facil-

ity/Guantánamo-bay_delta.htm. See also "The Threat of a Bad Example: Undermining International Standards as 'War on Terror' Detentions Continue," Amnesty International, August 19, 2003, available at http://web.amnesty.org/library/Index/ENGAMR511142003.

11. According to a July 10, 2006 report, "... recent deaths by suicide of three detainees at Guantánamo have raised questions about both the conditions under which such individuals are held and their dangerousness. The recent 'success' of the suicide attempts by the three detainees has led the Government to characterize these three suicides, and previous actions of detainees, as acts of 'Asymmetrical Warfare.'" See Mark Denbeaux and Joshua Denbeaux et al., "Report: The Guantánamo Detainees During Detention, Data from Department of Defense Records," Seton Hall University School of Law (July 10, 2006). The report documents statistical breakdown of various incidents, including the higher rate of self-injurious behaviors than acts of disciplinary violations. This concept of asymmetrical warfare, hunger strike or suicide, interestingly is not documented in any of the incident report by the guards.

12. See note 3 above.

13. The Supreme Court and any justice may grant writs of habeas corpus. They may also decline to entertain an application for a writ of habeas corpus and may transfer the application and determination to the district court having jurisdiction to entertain it. See 28 USC 2241, Power to Grant Writs.

14. There are two Supreme Court cases that test the limit of the presidential power to detain people in the United States government's War on Terror. The *Hamdi v. Rumsfeld* case involves Yaser Hamdi, who was captured by the Northern Alliance in Afghanistan, turned over to the United States military, and transferred to Guantanamo Bay. Upon discovery of his United States citizenship, he was transferred to a United States naval brig and held there as an enemy combatant. His lawsuit claimed relief on the basis of his being a relief worker in Afghanistan. On the other hand, the government claimed he was a Taliban fighter and, therefore, had to be held without charges indefinitely. In *Rasul et al. v. Bush,* two Australians and twelve Kuwaitis who were captured during the United States invasion of Afghanistan in 2001 filed suit under federal law challenging the legality of their detention. The United States District Court recognized the suits as habeas petitions and dismissed them for lack of jurisdiction, invoking *Johnson v. Eisentrager,* according to which territories beyond U.S. sovereignty may not invoke habeas relief. Upon affirmation by the Court of Appeals, this case went to the Supreme Court. See Supreme Court decision 339 US 763 (1950).

15. See Lease of Lands for Naval and Coaling Stations, 23 February 1903, US-Cuba, Art. III, T.S. No. 418. A supplemental lease agreement, ex-

ecuted in July 1903, obligates the United States to pay an annual rent in the amount of "two thousand dollars, in gold coin of the United States" and to maintain "permanent fences" around the base. See also Lease of Certain Areas for Naval or Coaling Stations, July 2, 1903, US-Cuba, Arts. I-II, T.S. No. 426, http://washingtonpost.findlaw.com/supreme_court /briefs/03-334/ 03-34.resp.html.

16. Ibid., and Treaty Defining Relations with Cuba, 1934, US-Cuba, Art. III, 48 Stat. 1683, T.S. No. 866.

17. See Art. III, T.S. No. 418: "While on the one hand the United States recognizes the continuance of the Ultimate sovereignty of the Republic of Cuba over the above described areas of land and water, on the other hand the Republic of Cuba consents that during the period of the occupation by the United States of said areas under the terms of this agreement the United States shall exercise complete jurisdiction and control over and within said areas with the right to acquire (under conditions to be hereafter agreed upon by the two Governments) for the public purposes of the United States any land or other property therein by purchase or by exercise of eminent domain with full compensation to the owners thereof."

18. The decision to create Guantanamo Bay, Cuba, as an indefinite detention center for prisoners in the United States government's unending War on Terror is a deliberate but illegal maneuver. By its sole reliance on *Johnson v. Eisentrager* (339 US 763), the United States government sets procedural roadblocks to restrict the detainees from accessing the United States legal system. On the other hand, using the perceived complexity of Guantanamo sovereignty, the government wants to create a legal gray zone, where the laws of military tribunals collide with the due process of civilian court system. See David Cole, *Enemy Aliens: Double Standards and Constitutional Freedoms in the War on Terrorism* (New York: New Press, 2003).

19. For more detailed explanation about the United States Constitution, Article VI, refer to http://www.yale.edu/lawweb/avalon/art.6.htm.

20. The Supreme Court (339 US 763) denied a group of convicted German war criminals the right to seek federal court review of their sentences. Court emphasized that occupied Germany, where the prisoners were held, was foreign territory.

21. Laurence Tribe, "Trial by Fury: Why Congress Must Curb Bush's Military Courts," *The New Republic*, December 10, 2001. Professor Tribe writes, in essence, that President Bush's executive order on military tribunals is severely flawed and calls for using civilian tribunals. See also Neal Kumar Katyal and Laurence Tribe, "Waging War, Deciding Guilt: Trying the Military Tribunals," *Yale Law Journal* 111 (2002).

22. Scott L. Silliman, "Freedom and Security in 21st Century America: Are Our Individual Liberties at Risk?" North Carolina Bar Center, February 15, 2002. Professor Silliman discusses the prosecutorial options for the prisoners at Guantanamo Bay. According to Professor Silliman, one option might be a trial in federal district court—as with the first World Trade Center bombing and as with embassy bombings—although this could not be implemented due to security concerns. The second option, the international tribunal, requires relinquishing a certain amount of control, something the United States opposes. According to Professor Silliman, the option of the military commission is a creature of international law predicated on the right of military commanders to try war crimes on foreign soil as recognized by the United States Supreme Court in World War II. The problem, Professor Silliman notes, is that the executive order extends too far, depending on the level of legal procedure the prisoners will be afforded. The tribunals will have only the level of procedure the creators of the tribunal build into it. There is, however, a floor, or base level, of procedure beneath which the commission cannot go in accordance with international law.

23. See the Uniform Code of Military Justice, available at http://www.au.af.mil/au/awc/awcgate/ucmj.htm.

24. Jim Lobe, "Military Tribunals Fall Short of Standards, Say US Rights Group," OneWorld.net, March 22, 2002, available at http://www.commondreams.org/ headlines02/0322-04.htm.

25. "Military Tribunal Don't Make the Grade," *The Daily Diatribe*, January 2, 2002, available at http://www.therationalradical.com/dsep02/01/tribunal-regulations.htm.

26. See Uniform Code of Military Justice (UCMJ) is the congressional code of military criminal law applicable to all military members worldwide. Enacted in May 1950 by replacing the articles of war, the UCMJ governs the trial, prosecution and punishment of all military personnel, including warrant and commissioned officers. It is the federal law that is the basis for the system of justice in the military. It discloses what conduct is a crime, establishes the types of court and sets forth procedures to be followed in administering military justice.

27. Ibid. The Army Court of Military Review (ACMR) is located in Washington D.C., and is the first leg of the appellate body in a military trial. If military personnel under the UCMJ receive a punitive discharge or confinement for more than one year, this appellate body automatically reviews the case.

28. Ibid. If, in a court martial case, the ACMR rejects the military personnel's case, the appellant can further appeal the conviction to this higher court,

the United States Court of Military Appeals, also located in Washington D.C.

29. Ibid. Even in a military trial, the last recourse is the United States Supreme Court. It is to be noted that even within the court martial system of law there is an adequate appeals procedure, and a civilian court is held as the ultimate appellate body; none of these elements are remotely available in the case of proposed military tribunals.

30. The lure of wealth has increased false allegations and the ultimate capture of many innocent people. Here I offer the obvious examples of bounty hunters gone awry. Find a target, perhaps a class of people who are different, voiceless or on the outer fringes of society and capture them. Collect your money, save your family. It is that simple. This style of bounty hunters or reward-seekers run amok is reflected in the capture of the Chinese-Muslim class of Uighers. With porous borders between Afghanistan and Pakistan, it was easy for the bounty hunters to capture the Uighers in neighboring Pakistan. "The Uighers were sold for $5,000 a head—at least my clients, and probably more, to US forces. And by the time people figured out who they were, they were on a sort of one-way escalator to Guantanamo and were never able to get off." See Mark Simkin, "Chinese Muslims Stuck in Guantanamo Limbo," Australian Broadcasting Corporation, TV program transcript, 1/17/06, available at http://www.abc.net.au/7.30/content/2006/s1549632.htm.

31. In the proposed military tribunal, the defendant is proven guilty if prosecutors produce evidence that has "probative value to a reasonable person." That standard of proof is as minimal and ambiguous as to be meaningless. The government will encounter few obstacles in meeting this standard. The accused will be hard-pressed to prepare a defense because, unlike a normal criminal proceeding, the government will have no obligation to advise him beforehand of the nature of the evidence against him.

32. See Mark Denbeaux and Joshua Denbeaux et al., "Report: The Guantánamo Detainees During Detention, Data from Department of Defense Records," Seton Hall University School of Law (July 10, 2006), 17.

33. Ibid., 19. See also National Education Association, Report: NEA's Statements on Afghanistan and the Taliban, Arms and Child Soldiers, available at http://neahin.org/programs/schoolsafety/september11/materials/nmneapos.htm.

34. Ibid.

35. The need for secrecy is driven by national security concerns, which has brought an interesting twist to the rules of the military tribunals. The concern is, therefore, to determine when the hearsay or unsworn evidence ceases to have probative value to a reasonable person. This evidence establishes such a loose standard, according to international law, that it is inadmissible.

36. These military tribunals are not bound by procedures followed in civilian courts, which derive from the rights guaranteed in the Constitution. According to Defense Department guidelines, military tribunals for foreigners suspected of terrorism will use juries of three to seven panelists, all of them military officers rather than the twelve-member public panels used in federal criminal courts; will require a two-thirds vote for conviction and sentencing, except in cases where the death penalty is involved, in which case seven panelists must reach a unanimous decision; will admit evidence including secondhand evidence and hearsay, which are banned from traditional courts, so long as they have "probative value to a reasonable person"; will not require prosecutors to establish the "chain of custody" of evidence—that is, to account for how the evidence was transported from where it was found to the courtroom; will provide defendants with military lawyers and allow them to hire civilian attorneys, albeit at their own expense; and will not allow defendants to appeal decisions in federal courts, but instead will allow them to petition a panel of review, which may include civilians as well as military officers. The president, as commander in chief, will have final review. See "Terrorism Q&A: Military Tribunals," Council on Foreign Relations, 2004, available at http://cfrterrorism.org/responses/tribunals_print.html.

37. Duties of the Commission During Trial, Military Commission Order No. 1, March 21, 2002, Sec. 6B. The commission shall: "(3) Hold open proceedings except where otherwise decided by the appointing authority or the presiding officer in accordance with the President's Military Order and this Order. Grounds for closure include the protection of information classified or classifiable under reference (d); . . . The Presiding Officer may decide to close all or part of the proceeding on the Presiding Officers' own initiative or based upon a presentation, including an *ex parte, in camera* presentation." See also Jess Bravin, "War on Terror, List of War Crimes Qualifying for Military Tribunals Set," *Wall Street Journal,* February 28, 2003; Jess Bravin, "US Readies Tribunal System to Prosecute Terror Suspects," *Wall Street Journal,* December 10, 2002; and Neil A. Lewis, "Administration's Position Shifts on Plans for Tribunals," *New York Times,* November 2, 2000.

38. Andrew Buncombe and Marie Woolf, "Cheney under Pressure to Quit over False War Evidence: Anger Grows on Both Sides of Atlantic at Misleading Claims on Eve of Iraq Conflict," *Independent Digital* (UK), July 17, 2003, available at http://www.rense.com/general39/CHENY.htm. An increasing body of evidence suggests that the United States fabricated evidence, exposing itself to increasing global resentment.

39. The terms "international law," "international humanitarian law," "law of armed conflict," "*jus in bello*" and "laws of war" are here interchange-

able. While there is sometimes disagreement on the relative scope of the terms, they all point to the body of law that governs the *jus in bello* conduct of hostilities and the protection of victims within the framework of the Hague and Geneva streams of law. See Karma Nabulsi, "Jus ad Bellum / Jus in Bello," *Crimes of War: The Book, 1999–2003,* available at http://www.crimesofwar.org/thebook/jus-ad-bellum.html.

40. See David Cole, James X. Dempsey, and Nancy Talanian, *Terrorism and the Constitution: Sacrificing Civil Liberties in the Name of National Security,* 3rd ed. (New York: New Press), 2006.

41. On September 18, 2001, Congress's joint resolution (Public Law 107-40, 115 Stat. 224) authorized the president "to use all necessary force against those nations, organizations, or persons he determines planned authorized, committed, or aided the terrorist attacks on September 11, 2001, or harbored such organizations or persons, in order to prevent any future acts of international terrorism against the United States by such nations, organizations or persons." War may exist when a state of war has been declared or when activities involving the use of force rise to such a level that a state of war exists. Absent a declaration of war, there may be some uncertainty whether a state of war exists, depending on the level and nature of hostile activities. Based on the above the United States inferred from combat operations in Afghanistan that it was at war with Al Qaeda, the organization deemed responsible for the 9/11 attacks; see http://www.stcl.edu/faculty-dir/bergin/AUMF%20-20115%20STAT%20224.pdf.

42. Convention for the Amelioration of the Condition of the Wounded and Sick in the Armed Forces in the Field, 75 UNTS 31; Convention for the Amelioration of the Condition of the Wounded, Sick and Shipwrecked Members of Armed Forces at Sea, 75 UNTS 85; Convention relative to the Treatment of Prisoners of War, 75 UNTS 135; Convention relative to the Protection of Civilian Persons in Time of War, 75 UNTS 287.

43. Protocol Additional to the Geneva Conventions of August 12, 1949, and relating to the Protection of Victims of International Armed Conflicts, June 8, 1977, 1125 UNTS 3; and Protocol Additional to the Geneva Conventions of August 12, 1949, and relating to the Protection of Victims of Non-International Armed Conflicts, June 8, 1977, 1125 UNTS 609, available at http://www.unhchr.ch/html/menu3/b/93.htm.

44. Article 118 of the Convention (III) relative to the Treatment of Prisoners of War, August 12, 1949, provides that "prisoners of war shall be released and repatriated without delay after the cessation of active hostilities." The Third Geneva Convention is available at http://www.icrc.org/ihl.nsf/7c4d08d9b287a42141256739003e636b/6fef854a3517b75ac125641e004a9e68.

45. Gary Solis, "Even a 'Bad Man' Has Rights," *Washington Post*, June 25, 2002. The author points out the danger to the Constitution and to the military in holding American citizens.

46. The Bush administration has used the term "unlawful combatant" and "enemy combatant" interchangeably and with effective use to stress that the detainees are not considered POWs. However, the administration, in its zeal to combat terrorism, has failed to comply with its obligation under customary International law to make a clear distinction between combatants and non-combatants. As a result, many civilian non-combatants were captured and detained as enemy combatants.

47. The constitutionality of military tribunals was questioned before the Supreme Court during World War II in the case of *ex parte Quirin* (317 US 1 [1942]). Defense lawyers argued that the accused spies were entitled to a speedy and public trial by an impartial jury, as well as the other constitutional protections contained in the Bill of Rights. The attorney for the spies, relying on Milligan, argued that the Constitution applied even during war. By the time the case was appealed to the Supreme Court, there was a great deal of political pressure to uphold the convictions. The *Quirin* decision upheld the use of a military tribunal as used under the specific circumstances of that case because the accused spies were "unlawful belligerents." Nevertheless, many experts argue that it does not provide blanket authorization for the use of military tribunals. Justice Douglas also regretted the ruling. "It is extremely undesirable to announce a decision on the merits without an opinion accompanying it," he said, referring to the fact that the Court entered a brief order upholding the tribunals shortly after the arguments, but did not issue a full opinion until many months later. Justice Stone, in writing the opinion, admitted that "a majority of the full Court are not agreed on the appropriate grounds for the decision." The Court also recognized that a military tribunal could not try some offenses because our courts do not recognize them as violations of the law of war or because they are in the class of offenses that can only be constitutionally tried by a jury. Although the *Quirin* decision appears to authorize military tribunals for "unlawful belligerents," the court failed to articulate specific criteria that must be present in order for a military tribunal to be valid. The Court stated, "We have no occasion now to define with meticulous care the ultimate boundaries of the jurisdiction of military tribunals to try persons according to the law of war. It is enough that petitioners here . . . were plainly within those boundaries." The Court narrowed its decision to avoid any sweeping statement regarding military jurisdiction and provided little guidance for application to future cases.

48. 317 US 1 (1942), 30–31.

49. The international humanitarian law of armed conflict for the protection of war victims, which includes the customary law on the subject as well as conventional or treaty law, is human rights law in the most fundamental sense. It provides a basic or minimum standard of human rights protections for individuals that are to be applied in the situation of war or international armed conflict, including belligerent occupation. The governments that have created this law have acted on the assumption that even urgent military necessity cannot be allowed to deprive human beings of certain elementary protections. The overriding purpose of the Geneva Conventions of 1949, as reflected in the negotiating history, was to avoid a repetition of the atrocities and massive deprivations of human rights that were inflicted upon civilian populations during the Second World War by the Nazis in Europe and Russia and by the Japanese militarists in Asia.

50. See supra note 40.

51. The genesis of the stream of law contained in the Geneva Conventions and the Hague Declarations clearly is much broader in applicability to combatants captured in "armed conflict" anywhere in the world. See Convention (III) Relative to the Treatment of Prisoners of War, August 12, 1949, 75 UNTS 135, entered into force October 21, 1950.

52. Operational Law Handbook, International and Operational Law Department, Judge Advocate General's School, Charlottesville (VA), 1977, 18-8.

53. Hans-Peter Gasser, "Acts of Terror, Terrorism and International Humanitarian Law," *International Review of the Red Cross* 84 (September 2002), pp. 547, 553–554.

54. J. S. Pictet, *Commentary of the Fourth Geneva Convention* (Geneva: International Committee of the Red Cross, 1952), p. 5. See also Convention IV, Article 4. Even though the nationals of the detaining authority and of neutral and co-belligerent states are not "protected persons," even they must have some legal status. See International Covenant on Political and Civil Rights, Articles 16 and 42, available at http://www.unhchr.ch/html/menu3/b/a_ccpr.htm.

55. The Universal Declaration of Human Rights strives to provide the inherent dignity and equal and inalienable rights to all members of the human family. By proclaiming Human Rights Day, Bill of Rights Day, and Human Rights Week, the United States president assures the universal principles of democracy, justice and individual liberty embodied in the U.S. Constitution's Bill of Rights and the support and encouragement of civilized people worldwide in the mutual fight against terrorism. By proclaiming the Universal Declaration of Human Rights, the United States is supposed to promote and protect human rights through joint efforts with its allies worldwide, as well as

with non-governmental and other international organizations, recognizing that the respect for human rights contributes to security, stability, and prosperity, available at http://www.un.org/Overview/rights.html.

56. See generally the Body of Principles for the Protection of All Persons under Any Form of Detention or Imprisonment, United Nations General Assembly Resolution 43/173, December 9, 1988, available at http://www.unhchr.ch/html/menu3/b/h_comp36.htm.

57. See supra note 51.

58. International Covenant on Civil and Political Rights, United Nations General Assembly Resolution 2200A (XXI), March 23, 1976.

59. Id.

60. See Joseph Margulies, "You Are Now the Property of the U.S. Marines," chapter 4 of *Guantanamo and the Abuse of Presidential Power* (New York: Simon and Schuster, 2006), 68.

61. Extraordinary rendition is excellently summed up in the words of columnist David Ignatius. He writes, "Rendition is the CIA's antiseptic term for its practice of sending captured terrorist suspects to other countries for interrogation. Because some of those countries torture prisoners—and because some of the suspected terrorists 'rendered' by the CIA say they were in fact tortured—the debate has tended to lump rendition and torture together. The implication is that the CIA is sending people to Egypt, Jordan or other Middle Eastern countries because they can be tortured there and coerced into providing information they wouldn't give up otherwise." See David Ignatius, 'Rendition' Realities, Wednesday, March 9, 2005; page A21, available at http://www.washingtonpost.com/wp-dyn/articles/A18709-2005Mar8.html.

62. The concept of outsourcing torture under the guise of extraordinary rendition is a painful reality to many detainees. One such documented case is that of Canadian citizen Maher Arar, who was a victim of the U.S. policy of extraordinary rendition. He was detained by U.S. officials in 2002, accused of terrorist links, and handed over to Syrian authorities, who tortured him. Arar spoke publicly about his torture by the Syrians, he recalled:

> . . . without no warning the interrogator came in with a cable. He asked me to open my right hand. I did open it. And he hit me strongly on my palm. It was so painful to the point that I forgot every moment I enjoyed in my life. This moment is still vivid in my mind because it was the first I was ever beaten in my life. Then he asked me to open my left hand. He hit me again. And that one missed and hit my wrist. The pain from that hit lasted approximately six months. And then he would ask me questions. And I

> would have to answer very quickly. And then he would repeat the beating this time anywhere on my, on my body. Sometimes he would take me to a room where I could, where I was alone, I could hear other prisoners being tortured, severely tortured. I remember that I used to hear their screams. I just couldn't believe it, that human beings would do this to other human beings.

See Maher Arar, "The Horrors of Extraordinary Rendition," Letelier-Moffitt International Human Rights Award, Institute for Policy Studies, October 18, 2006, in Washington, D.C. available at http://www.counterpunch.org/arar10272006.html.

63. Ibid.

64. See note 39 above.

65. The Bush administration has used the terms "unlawful combatant" and "enemy combatant" interchangeably to stress that the detainees are not considered POWs. However, the administration, in its zeal to combat terrorism, has failed to comply with its obligation under customary international law to make a clear distinction between combatants and noncombatants. As a result, many civilian noncombatants were captured and detained as enemy combatants. In the law of war a "combatant" commonly refers to members of an armed force. Members of a state's armed force are usually clearly distinguishable from civilians, including other government officials and employees. Members of the force normally wear uniforms and carry a distinctive identification card or document. In an organization such as a rebel group with an irregular armed force, the line between combatants and non-combatants is much less clear. By deliberately ignoring the guidance of the Geneva Conventions, the U.S. government has used an antiquated case law, *ex parte Quirin*, to justify its denial of POWs rights to the detainees. In the case of *Quirin*, a group of Nazi saboteurs attempted to sneak into the United States for the purpose of destroying United States infrastructure. They were captured almost immediately and tried by military tribunal. Defense lawyers argued that the accused spies were entitled to a speedy and public trial by an impartial jury, as well as the other constitutional protections contained in the Bill of Rights.

66. See ibid.

67. See Margulies, *Guantanamo and the Abuse of Presidential Power*, 68.

68. See *Rasul v. Bush*, 124 U.S. 2686 (2004); *Hamdi v. Rumsfeld*, 124 U.S. 2633 (2004); *Hamdan v. Rumsfeld*, 548 U.S. (2006).

69. See Laws of War, Laws and Customs of War on Land (Hague IV); October 18, 1907, available at http://www.yale.edu/lawweb/avalon/lawofwar/hague04.htm.

70. *Miranda v. Arizona*, 384 US 436 (1966).

71. See note 68 above.

72. There is significant structural difference between the Soviet-Gulag and the American version of the Gulag of the twenty-first century. The former was created to detain mainly the dissidents of the regime at home, whereas the latter is aimed at indefinite detention of prisoners of the War on Terror abroad but similar in the torturous tactics of its predecessor. The invoking of the term "gulag" is more symbolic of an escalating super-imperialism, in which the United States seems to have lost sight of all legal, moral, and political perspective against its scorched earth policy of incarcerating foreigners for life without trial. For a better understanding of the Soviet-Gulag prisons, visit the website available at http://www.paulmitchinson.com/gulag.html.

73. See note 68 above. See also, in the Supreme Court decision of *Rasul v. Bush*, while rendering the majority opinion, Justice Stevens argues: "Eisentrager itself erects no bar to the exercise of Federal Court jurisdiction over the petitioners' habeas corpus claims. It therefore certainly does not bar the exercise of Federal-Court jurisdiction over claims that merely implicate the 'same category of laws listed in the habeas corpus statute.' But in any event, nothing in *Eisentrager* or in any of other cases categorically excludes aliens detained in military custody outside the United States from the 'privilege of litigation' in US Courts" (321 F. 3d, at 1139).

74. In his dissenting opinion, Justice Scalia directly opposes the majority opinion as he asserts while arguing against granting habeas rights to the detainees that nothing in the Constitution extends such a right, "nor does anything in our statutes." He further added: "These prisoners at no relevant time were within any territory over which the United States is sovereign, and the scenes of their offenses, the capture, their trail and their punishment were all beyond the territorial jurisdiction of any court of the United States."

75. Sir Edward Coke used the term *hostis humani generis*; see http://web.amnesty.org/library/pdf/IOR530042001ENGLISH/$File/IOR5300401.pdf. See also Sir William Blackstone, *Commentaries on the Laws of England*, "Of Offences Against the Law of Nations," book 4, chap. 5 (1769), available at www.lonang.com/exlibris/blackstone/bla-405.htm. As detailed, *hostis humani generis* is used to describe such persons who committed the crime of piracy, or robbery and depredation upon the high seas, "an offence against the universal law of society." Because such an enemy of mankind has "renounced all the benefits of society and government, and has reduced himself afresh to the savage state of nature, by declaring war against all mankind, all mankind must declare war against him; so that every community has a right, by the rule of self-defense, to inflict that punishment upon him, which every individual

would in a state of nature have been otherwise entitled to do, [for] any invasion of his person or personal property."

76. See "Nuremberg Trial Proceedings," *The Avalon Project*, volume 1, 1996–2005, available at http://www.yale.edu/lawweb/avalon/imt/proc/v1menu.htm.

77. In this context, the applicability of *hostis humani generis* is severely flawed, as society has evolved since the Middle Ages, especially with the evolution of the Hague and Geneva Conventions' streams of law. See Geneva Conventions of 1949 and 1977, available at http://www.genevaconventions.org.

PART 2

# THE JUDICIAL-MORAL TREATMENT OF THE OTHER

# Gandhi's Alternative to the Alien Other
## *Nonviolent Social Action*
### ☞ RICHARD JOHNSON ☜

Growing up during the British Raj, Mohandas K. Gandhi saw himself from the British perspective in many ways as an Alien Other in his own land, an Indian colonial whose culture and polity were inferior to those of the British rulers. He chaffed at times under the yoke of the supposed British moral superiority to him and his compatriots, but he believed that the British Empire was, overall, a force for good until his final break with the Raj in 1920, when he was 51 years old. From his first encounter with racist violence in South Africa in 1893, he had developed an increasing awareness of the racism, materialism, and violence of the British Empire. As he examined his own experience and the experience of Indians with whom he worked in South Africa and in India, he came to understand that Indians themselves had to create a strong sense of their own identity to overcome the British image of them as Alien Others. Over time, Gandhi developed nonviolent social action, a practical and successful alternative to British rule and to Indians' internalization of the Alien Other image. In India, he developed programs which helped Indians themselves join together and overcome treating each other as Alien Others across ethnic and religious divides.

In the process of understanding the racism of South African whites, who viewed themselves as superior to dark-skinned Indians—Alien Others as racially inferior as black Africans—Gandhi came to realize that he himself had initially been treating others as inferior to him. As a middle-class man, the poor and women were, in many ways, Alien Others to him. In South Africa and India, he learned to overcome to a large extent his classism and sexism and to work side by side with the poor, women, Untouchables, and others to uplift all who were oppressed. From ancient Hindu and modern Western sources, Gandhi forged nonviolent action, an approach to social change which included two basic elements: *satyagraha* (literally clinging to truth), nonviolent resistance to British rule, and the Constructive Programme, a wide range of initiatives to create social harmony and justice.

His nonviolent action was a movement of sociopolitical transformation which won fundamental rights for over 400 million Indians without resorting to violence. A relatively small number of *satyagrahis*, nonviolent social activists, lived Gandhi's belief that only by devotion to *dharma* (duty) could these rights be assured. Activists since Gandhi have shown that his theory and practice of nonviolent social action can provide viable alternatives to the Alien Other, a widespread and pernicious social construct used by ruling elites to maintain their power.

Born in 1869, Gandhi lived at a time when the British Raj had gain supremacy throughout all of India. The British used two forms of power to control the Indian people: military force and imperial ideology. In 1857, just 12 years before Gandhi was born, the British responded with overwhelming military force to put down the greatest single threat to their power, the Sepoy Mutiny. Sepoys were Indians who made up 96 percent of the British army. The British made public display of the sepoys that they killed: "Captured sepoys were bayoneted or sewn into the hides of pigs or cows and fired from cannons.... The road from Kanpur to Allahabad was lined with the corpses of Indian soldiers who had been hanged."[1]

Although Gandhi was aware of the mutiny, he and his generation were controlled primarily by imperial ideology, not military force. The British, who maintained a limited number of civil servants and soldiers in India, needed loyal middle-class Indians to carry out the administration of the Raj. Imperial ideology was disseminated through the various institutions the British created to indoctrinate Indians: the media, the educational system, the courts, and so forth.

However, Gandhi found school difficult, in part because the higher the grade, the more the instruction was in English. He and his friends dreamed of ending the Raj, but simultaneously they imbibed ideas and values that served to buttress British control. Gandhi's best friend convinced him, for a time, to eat meat because it would make them as physically strong as the British. Although he broke off meat-eating after a while because he could not continue to deceive his parents, who thought he was following their vegetarian diet, he believed that he would have been stronger had he continued. He and his friend did not understand that they intended to defeat the British by adopting British practices and assumptions. If they had turned to Indian traditions instead, they would have had a greater chance to overcome the internalized image of themselves as inferior to the British.

Moreover, no matter how much young Indians may have yearned to end Indian rule, it was clear that the only way for them to advance economically and socially was to work in British institutions, which furthered British rule. A few years after the death of his father, Gandhi asked his mother and older brother to send him to London to study law. His caste elders opposed the plan because they believed that leaving India for three years would take the young Gandhi away from Indian traditions. When he refused to follow their demand to remain, they declared him an outcaste, a serious sanction at the time.

In his early months in London, he sought to become as British as possible. He took dance lessons, studied French, yearned to eat meat, and found himself drawn to a relationship with an English girl, even though he had been married in India at the age of 13. After a while he realized that his desire to become a proper British gentleman made no sense. No amount of training in the social graces could actually make him British. Moreover, he could not afford such a lavish lifestyle on his modest budget. And as a dutiful Indian son, he was sworn to follow the vow he had made to his mother not to be involved with women, drinking, and meat-eating. Even though he recognized that he could not become British, his stay in London deepened his belief in the moral mission of the British Empire to civilize the world, including, of course, India. He was proud to be a member of the empire and confident that Indians would profit from their association with the British.

He loved the British constitution and celebrated the anniversary of Queen Victoria's Royal Proclamation of 1858, promulgated after the Sepoy Mutiny, which promised Indians freedom from racial or religious discrimination. It seemed to him, at the time, that the true purpose of the British Empire was to bring about the rule of law to the benefit all colonials. Gandhi recognized that imperial practices often fell short of the high imperial ideal, but overall he believed that the British had the well-being of Indians at heart and that the empire would correct injustices in pursuit of an ever-expanding moral order. In 1895, after he had begun his public service to rectify wrongs against Indians in South Africa, he wrote that Indians "are proud to be under the British Crown, because they think that England will prove India's deliverer." In 1906 he wrote, "we have no hesitation in saying that one of the greatest secrets of the success of the Empire is its ability to deal out even-handed justice."[2]

In fact the British were themselves of two minds. There were those who used their claims of moral superiority to exploit colonials, and there were those who genuinely wished to contribute to the growth and development of colonials as free and independent human beings. The more cynical, hypocritical, and often deeply racist British were involved in the imperial enterprise for profit and power. The more sincere British, those who believed in dealing out "even-handed justice," recognized that colonials had to have the same rights and prerogatives that British citizens enjoyed. It took Gandhi many years to understand that his dear friends who belonged to the even-handed group were not, in fact, those in power. His belief in the rule of law was not shared by those British who made much of their constitution while denying constitutional rights to colonials.

Gandhi understood that there was a conflict between the real and the ideal of the empire, but he did not understand early on that empire and democracy are opposing systems of thought and practice. Jonathan Schell's critique of U.S. imperialism applies as well to British imperialism: "empire is incompatible with democracy, whether at home or abroad. Democracy is founded on the rule of law, empire on the rule of force. Democracy is a system of self-determination, empire a system of military conquest."[3] True democracy—later in his life Gandhi asserted that Western democracies were not true democracies—is inclusive of all who are gathered within its community; empire sets up a fundamental dichotomy between those who control and those who are controlled, the colonizers and the colonized. True democracy deconstructs inequities between citizens so that all are equal before the law; empire reifies difference and requires the maintenance of the Alien Other. Imperial ideology assumes that those who enjoy democratically established legal rights are, by their nature, different from and better than those who do not have these rights.

Gandhi's long process of freeing himself from imperial ideology began in London. He was accepted as an equal by many British friends and associates. Gandhi learned from British theosophists that Hindu and Christian scriptures revealed essentially the same truths. Two theosophist brothers asked Gandhi to help them read the *Bhagavad Gita* in the original. Influenced by a general British contempt for Hinduism, he had himself inclined "somewhat toward atheism."[4] He had not experienced the depth of faith and understanding that he gained later in reading the *Gita*. Gandhi's internalization of British imperial ideology is apparent here in that British admirers of Hinduism influenced him when other Indians had not. These theosophists and others, as well as many devout Christians, set Gandhi on a religious quest that led him to a life-long love of the *Gita* and other Hindu, Jain, and Buddhist traditions as well as Western sacred texts, particularly the New Testament and the Qur'an.

Central to Gandhi's religious quest was his growing awareness of the unity of being, a central tenet of all the Indian traditions. According to Gandhi, "the chief value of Hinduism lies in holding the active belief that *all* life (not only human beings, but all sentient beings) is one, i.e., all life comes from the One universal source, call it Allah, God, or Parameshwara."[5] Unlike most Indians, however, Gandhi sought to bring this religiously based sense of unity into the sphere of politics. In South Africa, as he faced racism and economic exploitation of the Indian minority, he increasingly understood and asserted that Indians were the equals of the whites who treated them as Alien Others. After he was thrown off the train toward the end of his first week in South Africa, he thought about his options and realized that he had to fight for Indians' rights.

> I began to think of my duty. Should I fight for my rights or go back to India, or should I go on to Pretoria without minding the insults, and return to India after finishing the case? It would be cowardice to run back to India without fulfilling my obligation. The hardship to which I was subjected was superficial—only a symptom of the deep disease of colour prejudice. I should try, if possible, to root out the disease and suffer hardships in the process.[6]

This was an extraordinary decision at the time for a young man of 23. Gandhi could see that there was no essential difference between Indians and the whites in South Africa. Behind the disease of racism was his deeply held belief in healthy human relations based on the fundamental unity of all people, whatever their color, nationality, or creed. And as important, he believed that he and others could root out this disease.

Over time, from this decision in 1893 to the launching of the first *satyagraha* campaign in 1906, Gandhi continued bringing together his religious quest for unity and his political commitment to the Indian minority in South Africa. He began with petitioning the British and litigation, but he learned that they and the Afrikaners were not inclined to end their racism and economic exploitation as a result of these methods. Beginning spontaneously in 1906 and reaching a fully conceived rationale in 1909 in his *Hind Swaraj (Indian Home Rule)*, Gandhi developed a new way to resist oppression. To be sure, others had already practiced "passive resistance," tactical civil disobedience campaigns. But Gandhi's *satyagraha* was different. He took the tactics from the passive resisters and sought to "spiritualize the political,"[7] to initiate a moral/spiritual approach to politics that relied on principles of unity, truth, and love. It was a process of transforming the struggle from one side against the other side to a relationship of equals. He sought to win over the opponent, not to win the battle. He chose self-suffering rather than inflicting suffering on the opponent.

In his political work in South Africa, Gandhi was engaged in transforming his sense of self. He was less and less the Alien Other within the imperial ideology of British superiority and more and more an activist seeking spiritual liberation in the political arena. In his concept of *swaraj*, which to Gandhi was both individual liberation and national liberation, he melded the personal and the political. *Swaraj* meant to engage in the life-long (lives-long) process of *moksha* (spiritual liberation from the wheel of birth and death) and, simultaneously, the liberation of India from British rule. As he wrote in *Hind Swaraj*, "if we become free, India is free. And in this thought you have a definition of swaraj."[8]

Based on his close reading of the *Bhagavad Gita*, Gandhi strove his whole life to become a spiritually liberated person and to help others come closer to this ideal. The *sthitha-prajna* (the person of steady wisdom) in the *Gita* was the model for the *satyagrahi*. By working resolutely to live the disciplines of knowledge, devotion and action (*jnaniyoga*, *bhaktiyoga* and *karmayoga*), a *satyagrahis* would be able to transform themselves and India.[9] Gandhi believed that Jesus, Buddha, Muhammed, and Socrates were highly realized *satyagrahis,* and that the greater the spiritual freedom of a *satyagrahi*, the greater his or her impact on society as a whole. He often wrote that a perfect *satyagrahi* could transform a nation completely.

From the *Gita* he learned that the person of steady wisdom seeks always to discover and perform his or her *dharma*, generally translated into English as "duty" but in fact a deeper spiritual essence for Gandhi: "*Dharma* does not mean any particular creed or dogma. . . . *Dharma* is a quality of the soul and is present, visibly or invisibly, in every human being. Through it we know our duty in human life and our relations with other souls. It is evident that we cannot do so till we have known the self in us. Hence *dharma* is the means by which we can know ourselves."[10] This "natural *dharma*," as Anthony Parel calls it, was foundational for Gandhi. He sought to live as a soul. He believed that humans have an animal and a spiritual self and that the true self is spiritual in nature. It is on this spiritual level that we know ourselves and we know ourselves as one. The animal self remains separate, alone, and capable of committing violence out of ignorance of *dharma*.

Gandhi took the vows of the individual *yogi* of Patanjali's *Yogasutra*[11]—nonviolence, truthfulness, nonstealing, chastity, and greedlessness—and added six more that would serve in social change—*swadeshi* (caring about one's own country), removal of Untouchability, bodily labor, control of the palate, fearlessness, and respect for all religions. He developed for himself and other *satyagrahis* a commitment to inner growth and to social transformation, a major blending of Indian and Western thought. As Parel states, "There is no question that Gandhi is drawing out the civic potential inherent in spiritual freedom."[12]

He also created the politically focused ashram to provide a place for *satyagrahis* to develop spiritual and civic freedom. The ashram had been used for spiritual growth in India for centuries, but it was a major innovation of G.K. Gokhale, Gandhi's political mentor, to seek to apply the spiritual model to political action. From his years in South Africa and continuing in India, *satyagrahis* could learn together and refuel themselves in the ashrams so that they could become the leaven in the transformation of society. Humans acting as souls were, to Gandhi, naturally social beings. As he wrote, "Man is not born to live in isolation but is essentially a social animal independent and interdependent."[13]

Gandhi intended that *satyagraha* be a way to bring this essential social nature into the political arena to transform politics and society. He did not seek to destroy or overwhelm opponents but rather to include them in spiritually and socially transformed human relations. He wrote in 1946, "A nonviolent rebellion is not a programme of seizure of power. It is a programme of transformation of relationship ending in a peaceful transfer of power. It will never use coercion. Even those who hold contrary views will receive full protection under it."[14] In these transformed relationships, the Alien Other would no longer exist.

From Gandhi's perspective, in the Indian independence movement, Indians were not the Alien Others of the British, nor were the British the Alien Others of the Indians. Gandhi believed that violence on either side perpetuated the belief that human beings were separate from each other across national, religious, or ethnic lines. As soon as we realize fully the unity of being, it becomes impossible to practice violence. Violence against another human being is violence against oneself, since we are one. According to Gandhi, the Alien Other is a construct of minds that divides human beings into false categories. He rejected the notion that others were fundamentally different from him, and he therefore rejected the politics of difference.

As he confronted and overcame the South African construct of him and of other Indians as the racial Alien Other, Gandhi slowly began to examine and change his own internalized classism and sexism. He was a middle-class man and therefore had certain privileges over women and lower-class individuals. But he worked extensively with poor, indentured Indian workers in South Africa, and he began to observe his oppression of his wife, Kasturbhai. Out of classist and sexist assumptions, he had created a movement to aid Indians in South Africa that was largely limited to middle-class Indian men. As he began to see women and the poor as equals, as he began to recognize his class and gender privileges, he was able to welcome women and the poor into his *satyagraha* campaign. His ability to see not only whites' oppression of Indians, but also his own oppression of women and lower classes, was a crucial element in the final success of *satyagraha* in South Africa.

In 1913, he asked women to join the campaign because white judges had ruled that non-Christian unions of a woman and a man were not legally binding marriages. This meant that Indian men's wives were concubines and that their children had no rights of inheritance. Gandhi realized that this ruling affected women and men alike and decided for the first time that women could be as effective as men in the campaign for equal rights. Indian women, including Kasturbhai, became active and initiated a campaign with indentured Indian miners and their families. At this point, *satyagraha* extended beyond middle-class Indian men. With thousands of fresh recruits, the "Great March" of 1913 led to the most significant success of *satyagraha* in South Africa.[15]

Upon his return to India in 1915, Gandhi spent time exploring the Indian political and cultural landscape before initiating *satyagraha* there. After a few successful local campaigns, he felt ready to launch a nationwide campaign against the Rowlatt legislation in 1919. Gandhi and many Indians were opposed to Rowlatt bills, intended to curb terrorism in India, because the British refused to include Indians in discussions about this legislation. As more and more Indians joined the campaign, called the Rowlatt *Satyagraha*, British violence against Indians reached its highest point since the Sepoy Mutiny in 1857. There were several incidents in which the British acted, in Gandhi's terms, "in the spirit of terrorism."[16] The most extreme British terrorism took place in Amritsar, in an enclosed space where hundreds of Indians were engaged in nonviolent protest. Without warning, General Reginald Dyer ordered his troops to fire on the protesters, who had no means of escape. Nearly 400 were killed and more than 1,500 were wounded.

As a result of British violence in Amritsar and other injustices during the Rowlatt *satyagraha* and during Gandhi's non-cooperation campaign a year later, Gandhi made his final break with the British Empire in 1920. He believed that the empire took Indians and the British away from their essential divine nature. Submitting to and committing oppression subverted moral integrity. He observed Indians becoming passive and compliant as colonials, not free persons engaged in opposition to injustice; and he observed Indian extremists practice terrorism, which to him played into the hands of the British authorities. Indian terror served to justify the counterterror of the British. Gandhi asserted that the terrorism of the Indians and the British was essentially the same, since both resorted to violence in power politics and both denied the common humanity of the Enemy Other.[17]

After Gandhi broke off his non-cooperation campaign in 1922 as a result of Indian violence against the British, he began to reevaluate *satyagraha*. He believed that *satyagrahis* needed to develop their sense of unity, quest for truth, and love of their opponents and that with sufficient inner harmony and group cohesion, they could persuade the British to leave India. But he did not believe that *satyagraha* alone could transform Indian society. The extreme differences between rich and poor, the divisions between Hindus and Muslims, and the oppression of women and Untouchables were worsened by British rule, but in fact, Indians were oppressing other Indians. Indians treated Indians as Alien Others. Unless Indians began to work with each other to heal the divisions in their own society, Indian independence would only replace British oppressors with Indian oppressors. For Gandhi, independence meant a transformation of consciousness down to the village level: "Mere withdrawal of the English is not independence. It means the consciousness in the average villager that he is the maker of his destiny, [that] he is his own legislator through his chosen representatives."[18]

Gandhi developed the Constructive Programme, a set of initiatives to end these social divisions among Indians and to bring the needed transformation of consciousness to all.[19] The educated would work directly with the uneducated to create *purna swaraj* (complete independence) to bring about a transformation of the Constructive Workers, those they worked with, and Indian society and polity as a whole. Until his death in 1948, he spent more time in the Constructive Programme than he did in *satyagraha* campaigns. *Satyagraha* was intended to be carried out by a small cadre of *satyagrahis,* but Gandhi hoped to train many more Constructive Workers, since he wanted them in all of India's 700,000 villages and wherever Indians were divided from Indians. If Indians could find unity among themselves through interfaith cooperation, spinning, sharing wealth, removing Untouchability, and the uplift of women, true *swaraj* would take place naturally, like a ripe fruit falling from a tree. Relationships would be transformed by overcoming artificial separations of clothing, religion, caste, class, and gender. Gandhi believed that all humans are, as souls, one.

By the time he wrote his pamphlet, *Constructive Programme: Its Meaning and Place*, in 1941, Gandhi had come to believe that civil disobedience without a series of constructive initiatives would not work. He wrote that civil disobedience "without the co-operation of the millions by way of constructive effort is mere bravado and worse than useless."[20] He concluded his pamphlet with a haunting image: "my handling of civil disobedience without the constructive programme will be like a paralysed hand attempting to lift a spoon."²¹ Indeed, civil disobedience in the war years was in a state of paralysis, with no real impact on either the British or Indians. Gandhi's first item in his *Constructive Programme*, indispensable to true *swaraj*, was "communal unity," an "unbreakable heart unity"²² among all faiths in India. He wrote in 1940, "Abolish all caste and religious or race distinction from your heart."²³

The Constructive Programme was his effort to lift up the Indian people, a way of saying yes to "heart unity" among Indians whether or not the British were in power in India. *Satyagraha* was his effort to resist British injustices, a way of saying no to oppression.²⁴ Gandhi's nonviolent social action—his affirmation of Indian unity through the Constructive Programme and his resistance to the British Raj through *satyagraha*—did win wide-ranging human rights for Indians. They gained political independence with very little violence perpetrated against the British, and they were able to achieve an unusually high degree of cooperation with the British in the process.

However, even though he and his fellow *satyagrahis* were instrumental in bringing about marked improvements in human rights among Indians, Judith Brown is correct in asserting that Gandhi's "thinking was not embedded in the human rights discourse of Western liberal thought."²⁵ As an Indian, Gandhi's primary focus was not winning of rights but rather the performance of *dharma*. Parel explains:

> Beneficial and necessary though rights were to . . . [the peaceful political well-being of humans], they needed to be complemented by duty (*dharma*). Given the basic unity of human nature, Gandhi saw no reasonable basis for positing a fundamental opposition between rights and duties. In his view, the opposition that modern Western theory of rights posits between rights and duties is owed to the particular anthropology and epistemology it chose to adopt rather than to any self-evident truths about human beings.²⁶

Gandhi believed that *satyagraha* was the result of his efforts to do his duty to serve the Indian minority in South Africa, but he was not seeking separate rights for them. His intent was that all people have basic rights: "Fundamental rights can only be those rights the exercise of which is not only in the interest of the citizens but that of the whole world. . . . Rights cannot be divorced from duties. This is how *satyagraha* was born, for I was always striving to decide what my duty was."²⁷ For Gandhi rights were a natural result of duties performed in the service of the common good.

*Satyagrahis* and Constructive Workers made significant progress in Gandhi's lifetime in creating a more equal relationship with the British and in building Indians' belief that they could in fact practice self-rule. However, Gandhi and many others were devastated by the savage civil war between Muslims, Hindus and Sikhs in northern India and Pakistan. At least one million died in this war, and millions more were displaced from their homes. Indians treated each other as Alien Others with deadly earnest. The communal efforts came to an end at Gandhi's death, as it had in his fasts in Calcutta and Delhi in the final months of his life. Gandhi struggled his whole life to create Hindu-Muslim unity, but in his final years, the civil war and the partition of India demonstrated how far India was from what he so fervently wanted. His assassination at the hands of a Hindu fanatic who feared Gandhi was giving too much to Muslims was yet another sign of violent disunity in India. Many leaders in India since Gandhi's death are closer in worldview to Gandhi's assassin than they are to Gandhi himself.

In the last half-century, enormous gains have been won by nonviolent activists in the American civil rights movement, in Eastern Europe and the former Soviet Union, in the Philippines, in South Africa, in Serbia, and in many other countries. Moreover, if we understand that local, national, and international non-governmental organizations can be seen as modern-day equivalents to Gandhi's Constructive Programme, then the impact of nonviolent social action is even wider than most would see. Hundreds of thousands of activists are working with millions of disadvantaged people all over the world.

These activists are contributing to a growing and powerful people's movement to abolish the Alien Other and to establish brother/sisterhood in the world. It would be false optimism to assume that this movement will prevail over entrenched elites who use national, ethnic, gender, and class divisions to oppress minorities. The Alien Other exists in every theory, and practice of oppression is present in the world now, as it always has. However, it would be an equally false pessimism to ignore the strides that have been made and the possibility of further social transformations. Gandhi's first *satyagraha* campaign was launched on September 11, 1906, a century ago. Violence and other forms of social injustice have been practiced far longer. Gandhi wrote in 1937, "Out of my ashes a thousand Gandhis will arise."[28] It remains to be seen to what extent we answer Gandhi's call to co-create a just and moral world order.

## Notes

1. Chalmers Johnson, *The Sorrows of Empire: Militarism, Secrecy, and the End of the Republic* (New York: Metropolitan Books, 2004), 139.

2. *Collected Works of Mahatma Gandhi* (*CWMG*), 100 vols. (New Delhi: Publication Division, Ministry of Information and Broadcasting, 1958–1994),

1:285, the first quote; and 5:250, the second quote. Cited in Judith Brown, *Gandhi: Prisoner of Hope* (New Haven: Yale University Press, 1989), 64.

3. "Pre-emptive Defeat, or How Not to Fight Proliferation," in *The Iraq War Reader: History, Documents*, ed. Micah L. Sifry and Christopher Cerf (New York: Touchstone, 2003), 516.

4. *An Autobiography: The Story of My Experiments with Truth* (Boston: Beacon Press, 1957), 34.

5. *Harijan*, 12-26-36, cited in Raghavan Iyer, ed., *The Moral and Political Writings of Mahatma Gandhi* (Oxford: Clarendon Press: 1986–1987), vol. 1, 515.

6. *Autobiography*, 112.

7. Gandhi believed that it was the intent of his political mentor, G. K. Gokhale, "to spiritualise the political." See Gandhi, in *Gandhi's Experiments with Truth: Essential Writings by and about Mahatma Gandhi* (Lanham, Md.: Lexington Books, 2005), 134. See also Richard L. Johnson and Eric Ledbetter, "'Spiritualizing the Political': Christ and Christianity in Gandhi's *Satyagraha*," *Peace & Change*, 22:1 (Jan. 1997), 32–48.

8. Gandhi, in *Gandhi's Experiments with Truth*, 85.

9. Cf. Anthony J. Parel, "Gandhian Freedoms and Self-Rule," in *Gandhi, Freedom, and Self-Rule*, ed. Parel (Lanham, Md.: Lexington Books, 2000), 16.

10. Gandhi quote cited in Parel as well as Parel's expression "natural *dharma*," 9.

11. Patanjali, who lived in India around 2,000 years ago, wrote the *Yogasutra* as a guide to right living through deep meditative practices.

12. "Gandhian Freedoms and Self-Rule," 16.

13. *Hind Swaraj*, 155.

14. *Harijan*, 2-10-46.

15. See Richard L. Johnson, "Gandhi's Soul Politics in South Africa," *Gandhi Marg*, 19:3 (Oct.–Dec., 1997), 2270–71.

16. *CWMG*, 15:164, 172, 174–175.

17. See Richard L. Johnson, "*Satyqraha*: The Only Way to Stop Terrorism," in *Gandhi's Experiments with Truth*, 228–236.

18. *CWMG*, 42:469.

19. See Michael Nagler, "The Constructive Programme," in *Gandhi's Experiments with Truth*, 253–259.

20. *CWMG*, 75:165.

21. *CWMG*, 75:166.

22. *CWMG*, 75:147.

23. *Harijan*, 3-16-40, cited in Iyer, vol. 1, 63.

24. Nagler, in *Gandhi's Experiments with Truth*, pp. 253–254.

25. "Gandhi and Human Rights: In Search of True Humanity," in *Gandhi, Freedom, and Self-Rule*, 87.

26. "Gandhian Freedoms and Self-Rule," 9.

27. *CWMG*, 88:230.

28. *Harijan*, 1-16-37.

# The Closed Society versus the Rights to Emigrate and Immigrate

## ⌐ W. L. McBride ⌐

This paper proved more difficult to prepare than I anticipated when I accepted the challenge of creating it. For what I am calling for, in effect, is a radical rethinking of such fundamental notions as nationality and citizenship at the very time when there has been a serious retreat and hardening of attitudes concerning these notions in many places, most notably in the United States. One example of the forces of discouragement, as they might be called, that are currently at play is a background story connected with the recent intelligence service reorganization legislation. The details of the act itself or whether its impact will ultimately lessen, exacerbate, or prove neutral with regard to the ongoing closing of our society will not be the focus of this paper. What strikes many scholars very forcefully about the news reports, in a way that added to my discouragement, was the fact that the two powerful congressional chairs who managed to block the bill until the last moment were both eager to add provisions that would further restrict immigration and the rights of immigrants. This is precisely the opposite of what this article advocates.

The notion of a "closed society" has many different meanings. Even in the predominantly spatial sense of closed borders, to which, for the moment, I shall limit this paper's focus, it can have several quite different, though interrelated, functions: it can be a working model, it can be a description, and it can be a norm—today, usually a negative norm.

As a working model, the "closed society" has dominated much—far *too* much—of Western political and economic theory. Plato and Aristotle, as we know, took the *polis* to be the basic structure within which the good life was to be pursued. This did not entail disregarding the larger world—both of them traveled, both of them, especially Aristotle, lived in different *poleis* at different times, and in their political models, both of them acknowledged the great significance of travel and commerce. But Plato forbade travel to the rulers in his Republic, and Aristotle emphasized the achievement of self-sufficiency, to the greatest extent possible, as a supreme political goal. Both also looked down on the barbarians, meaning all non-Greeks, for, among other things, the nomadism of some, such as the Scythians, and the excessively vast territories of others, such as the Babylonians and the Persians. Paradoxically, it was Aristotle's erstwhile pupil, Alexander, who followed his father Philip's lead in unifying first the Greek city-states and then much of the vast territories to the east and south of Greece, including Persia itself. In a fit of pique, Alexander, a fitting predecessor of self-righteous invaders and conquerors right up to the present time (although the latter, of course, possess far more potent firepower than he), burned the great palace of Persepolis to the ground. Thus was the ancient world first unified and the *polis* model rendered defunct.

During the period of the Roman Empire, which soon succeeded, the model of the cosmopolis took hold, at least among philosophers.[1] In medieval times, even while smaller and larger kingdoms and principalities were the dominant units of sociopolitical life (except, perhaps, for the theoretically long but practically very brief period of hegemony of Charlemagne's Holy Roman Empire), the model that had greatest importance in both intellectual and popular minds was that of the spiritual City of God, which of course knows no physical borders. But in early modern times, the period of the rise of modern nation-states, what I am calling the closed society as model again came to prevail. It was the model that was assumed by the social contract theorists from Hobbes onward, it was Hegel's apparent model in Prussia when he spoke of the state as the way of God in the world. It was obviously Fichte's model in his work *The Closed Commercial State*, which is at the same time, for Fichte, a positive norm; and it was even the explicit working model of that great internationalist, Karl Marx, in this respect aping Adam Smith and other political economist predecessors, in his analysis of capitalism as a global system.[2] For while Marx clearly acknowledged that trade, colonial exploitation, and related external phenomena are of significance in making the system what it is, the focal point of his detailed calculations was a single national unit, with England being, of course, his most important historical referent.

In his significant if now already dated work of the last century, John Rawls self-consciously employed the same closed society model until his brief and rather unsuccessful late work, *The Law of Peoples*. By way of illustration, here is a citation from Rawls's middle-period book, *Political Liberalism*:

> I assume that the basic structure is that of a closed society: that is, we are to regard it as self-contained and as having no relations with other societies. Its members enter it only by birth and leave it only by death. This allows us to speak of them as born into a society where they will lead a complete life.[3]

Rawls goes on to admit that this conception is abstract, but he justifies it on the grounds of its usefulness, and he repeats this language, using very much the same words, in a number of other passages throughout the book.

So much, then, for the closed society as a model. Next there is the closed society as an empirical description. As with many such descriptions, the classifications soon become messy, and closedness versus openness is in some ways a matter of degree. A maximally closed society would be one that allowed no one to enter from outside and no one to leave. There is no such society of which I am aware today—not even North Korea or Myanmar, which are closer contemporary approximations than most to this extreme. But I think it is fair to say that certain developments in the twentieth century, beginning with the two world wars and continuing with the Cold War, have led to greater efforts in the direction of legally restricting movements of individuals between nation-states, even while, paradoxically, actual migrations of populations have been taking place on an unprecedentedly vast scale. Passport and visa requirements were by no means as universal in earlier modern times as they have become today: Gavrilo Prinzip, for example, was apparently able legally to travel to the Austro-Hungarian territory of Bosnia and Herzegovina, where he then carried out the assassination of Archduke Ferdinand, which ignited World War I, even though he was a member of a Serbian terror organization.

For those of us who lived through all or part of the Cold War period, the most obvious empirical instantiations of a closed society that are likely to come to mind are the countries of the Soviet Bloc, and especially the USSR itself. Although there was some cross-border travel, primarily by organized tour groups, available within most of the countries of Eastern Europe for their own citizens, during most of the Cold War period travel to those countries from the West was encouraged only up to a point and on a limited basis, and exodus *to* the West was strongly discouraged, with severe sanctions being threatened for those who attempted it and imposed on those who failed, as well as, often enough, on successful escapees' family members who remained behind. Most notorious in this respect, in part as a result of its geographical location and particularly the peculiarity of the divided city of Berlin, and in part because of the especially repressive nature of the regime itself, was East Germany, the self-styled German Democratic Republic. Fittingly enough, then, one mechanism that greatly contributed to bringing down this regime and ensuring the total collapse of the Eastern Bloc was the opening of its borders to East German citizens by the new government in Czechoslovakia following the so-called "Velvet Revolution."

But the comparative closedness of the Soviet Bloc was not confined merely to restrictions on the movements of human bodies across frontiers: of considerable significance, as well, were its policies of restricting and manipulating information. The jamming of radio and television broadcasts from the West was a routine practice, and to listen to them surreptitiously could be a very serious offense, with the degree of seriousness depending on the particular country and year in question. Meanwhile, during the 1980s, the new electronic era was dawning, and a sophisticated nascent electronics industry was beginning to develop, particularly in Bulgaria. But the very idea of the sort of instant and massive cross-border communication that we now know as the World Wide Web appeared to the authorities of the Bloc as a threat, as indeed it was. As a result, investment in electronics development was curtailed, and this in turn, at least according to some analysts, helped contribute to the overall industrial stagnation that began to set in during what turned out to be the last days of those regimes—some of which, such as East Germany and Czechoslovakia, had during an earlier period maintained robust levels of productivity, competitive with the West. We may reasonably conclude from this that closed societies may well pay a terrible price for their closedness even in economic terms, to say nothing of their cost to the human spirit.

With this thought, we have begun to touch on the third sense of "closed society" that I listed at the outset: the closed society as a norm, today usually a negative one. When Rawls, in the passage cited earlier, unequivocally declared that the basis of his analyses was the closed society as what I have called a "model," he showed no apparent awareness of the sense in which that term has come to acquire negative normative connotations. That is because the context in which he was using it was seemingly so different from the evaluative context to which I am now pointing. Nevertheless, for reasons that would take too long fully to explicate here, I am convinced that the two contexts are not entirely unrelated, and that to be thoroughly at home with the idea of a closed society as a *model* importantly influences a person's way of thinking about sociopolitical ideals, particularly about the choice between nationalist and cosmopolitan values. I shall return to this issue, but for the moment, however, let me explicitly point out what is, in any case, thoroughly obvious about the normative implications of the idea of a "closed society," to wit, that its contrast term is the apparently very popular "open society." It was Sir Karl Popper who, in his book *The Open Society and Its Enemies*, popularized this term among philosophers with his slashing critique of Plato's *Republic* and of similar ways of thinking that he detected in later writers. Plato favored censorship and, as I have already mentioned, forbade his Guardians to travel abroad, for reasons that were clearly connected with his absolutist metaphysics and epistemology; Popper presented himself as the opponent of absolutisms and totalitarianisms in all domains. In more recent years, an individual who sat in on Popper's courses for a time and was greatly influenced by them, namely, George Soros, has lavished considerable resources on a foundation designed to encourage the growth of anti-totalitarian ways of thinking and practices, particularly in Eastern Europe, and has named it the Open Society Foundation. On the surface, then, the attractiveness of the idea of an open society, to which lip service is so widely paid, would seem to imply that the closed society norm or ideal is in full retreat.

But is it? Hardly. At the present time, thanks in large measure to terrorist threats but thanks also to a resurgence of xenophobia, a regression in policies and attitudes is taking place throughout the world, particularly in the United States. This country's government has instituted new border control measures which are supposed to promote domestic security, but the clear effects of which are to treat as suspect, often to humiliate, and generally to make much less welcome than before all potential visitors to the United States, both short-term and long-term. This is especially ironic with respect to potential tourists, who are by definition short-term visitors, because the dramatic decline in value of the dollar has made the United States a comparatively cheap vacation spot, and the arrival of tourists in larger numbers would do a good deal to ease the country's huge trade deficit. As for longer-term visitors to the United States, notably graduate students and older scholars, there is unmistakable statistical as well as anecdotal evidence that the new policies of exclusion, together with popular perceptions of the new border procedures, which are sometimes even more extreme than the procedures themselves, have brought about a serious decline in their numbers, with a potentially devastating effect on American higher education. It is somewhat surprising that these new United States government border policies have thus far not generated more severe reciprocal retaliatory policies on the parts of most other governments, although the beginnings of such a development can be observed—for example, in Brazil's visa and immigration regulations for Americans. But the general global trend is obvious, whether it be an anti-immigrant referendum in Arizona or anti-Muslim acts of violence in, of all places, the Netherlands. The widespread nostalgia for a return to a more closed society, at the very time at which the evolution of travel, commerce, and communication has made such a return more difficult than ever and technically attainable only by very harsh measures, is quite evident.

In this paper so far, no reference has been made to the central theme of this volume, the judicio-moral treatment of aliens. That is about to change. First, let me strike a serious note of caution. All too often individuals who hold comfortable academic positions succumb to the illusion that talking about the twin ideals of fair judicial treatment of aliens and of human rights automatically makes them *bien vus* in the eyes of the powerful, or even of many ordinary citizens, in this country today. On the contrary: academics would be well regarded by them only to the extent to which the latter might try to show that they actually respect and promote these ideals. But that would be nonsensical. With a national administration, buoyed by a relatively small but still significant electoral majority, that chose as its attorney general an individual who is known to have dismissed international codes governing the humane treatment of prisoners as quaint and outmoded, scholars cannot pretend that to uphold the ideals in the name of their positions as researchers gives them any positive aura within the contemporary American *Zeitgeist;* on the contrary, to do so renders them abject in the eyes of many. In the current climate, to speak colloquially, international law is for sissies.

I shall proceed then, pusillanimously, to highlight one of the most abject fragments of international law, if it can even be regarded as a genuine part of it, the Universal Declaration of Human Rights. A clause in Article 13, part 2 reads: "Everyone has the right to leave any country, including his own, and to return to his country." I have always contended that it makes sense to treat this as a right in the real world if and only if there is at least one other country that is willing to receive the emigrant.[4] In short, with all due consideration being given to the need for regulations dealing with questions of physical security, job security, the avoidance of dangerous overpopulation in one particular city or region, and so forth—which could and should be addressed much more seriously than they are being addressed at present (thanks to the free market ideology that maintains that outsourcing is "cool")—the right to move from one country to another has been established, through this clause of the Universal Declaration, as a human right that is guaranteed by international law—has it not? No, not really, according to philosophers such as John Rawls, for example. In a footnote in *The Law of Peoples*, he acknowledges the possibility that an argument along the lines that I have just indicated—that a right to emigrate implies a right to immigrate—could be made, but then immediately dismisses it by saying that "many rights are without point in this sense: to give a few examples, the right to marry, to invite people into one's house, or even to make a promise. It takes two to make good on these rights."[5]

I am not opposed in principle to arguments from analogy, and indeed, I believe that true masters of analogy, such as Aristotle, often contribute greatly to thought by making brilliant and illuminating connections. Rawls's analogies here, however, certainly do not fall under that description. His three examples of supposed "rights," which are rather odd choices and, in fact, not even very similar to one another, have little in common with the precise rights to emigration and, at least by implication, immigration that are specified in Article 13 of the Universal Declaration. Why does this quintessential liberal democratic philosopher take such an intellectually sloppy and dismissive stance on such an important issue? A significant and still insufficiently recognized book by a British philosopher, Phillip Cole, entitled *Philosophies of Exclusion*, helps us better to understand this, though not to excuse it. In his book Cole does not, in fact, take account of the text that I have cited from *The Law of Peoples*, although he does express doubt about the consistency of Rawls's liberalism with regard to this issue on the basis of Rawls's earlier writings. Cole's sweeping and forceful conclusion, after two hundred pages of careful review of older and recent literature on the topic, is that immigration policy is the reef on which liberal democratic theory as a whole founders. As he says:

> Any solution that has been offered to justify exclusive membership—and therefore immigration and naturalisation regulations—has given rise to an incoherence between the liberal polity's internal and external principles: those within its boundaries are subjected to liberal principles and practices, while those at the border are subjected to illiberal principles and practices.[6]

Liberalism, in its classic historical sense as distinguished from the contemporary idiom that has reduced it to the status of just one more epithet, is centrally committed to the freedom and equality of all human beings; and yet, liberal thinkers have constantly attempted to defend the nation-state's alleged right to maintain its own exclusivity, that is, to restrict its own membership like a private club. "Liberal nationalism," a notion that has been defended by the Israeli theorist Yael Tamir and others, is thus little better than a contradiction in terms. Restrictive immigration and naturalization regulations are simply incompatible with liberal ideals.

In the strictest, most literal sense of the term "human rights," the rights to emigrate and immigrate, on which I am focusing here, are not human rights, although in a broader sense, they are. By way of explaining, we must recall one of the most famous claims of one of the founders of liberal thought, John

Locke, that "a child is born a subject of no country or government. He is under his father's tuition and authority till he comes to age of discretion, and then he is a freeman, at liberty what government he will put himself under, what body politic he will unite himself to."[7] Locke attempts to justify this claim as one that is upheld by the practices of governments themselves—he refers to the case of a child born to an English couple in France—"as well as by the law of right and reason." For Locke, both civil societies, which are the basis of what are more loosely called "countries" in the text quoted, and governments, which can even be dissolved by revolution without this necessarily entailing the dissolution of the civil societies that undergird them, are ultimately constructs, the outcomes of conventions. Emigration and immigration are meaningless notions apart from the realities of geographical national borders, which are created on the basis of such conventions. Hence, if the notion of "human rights" is understood in the very strict sense of those claims that we have on one another by virtue of our simply being human beings, there is no human right to emigrate or immigrate because, at the conceptual level of humanity as such, there are no national borders: "a child is born a subject of no country or government." At the same time, the rights that we have by virtue of our common humanity seem to entail rejection of restrictive immigration practices as constituting negations of that humanity.

Although Locke was not universally consistent throughout his writings, and his personal behaviors were not, on the whole, consistent with this broad humanitarian outlook, his humanitarian outlook itself, however unrealistic it may seem in light of contemporary practice, strikes me as both attractive and theoretically coherent. What is incoherent, by contrast, is the set of practices, notably the practices of exclusion, which are the product of ideological nationalism.

There are those who have no difficulty finding fault with, for example, Serbian nationalism or Ivoirean nationalism (the views put forward by certain intellectuals in the southern Ivory Coast, according to which most of those who live in the north are not true Ivoireans, that have helped fuel the divisions leading to the recent conflict there), who may even find such ideas ridiculous, but who at the same time fail to realize that the most virulent nationalism of all today—the most virulent because so closely connected with such overwhelming, hegemonic power—is *American* nationalism. Expressed as it is these days in so many well-rehearsed ways,[8] this attitude, it is worth observing, exhibits characteristics traditionally associated with the notion of radical evil, even though some of those who display it claim to be religious people. This country, which contains slightly less than 5 percent of the world's population but consumes several times that percentage of its fuel supplies and houses some 25 percent of its prisoners, used to pretend to exercise a kind of global moral leadership, and this claim was, in fact, widely accepted. As poll after poll reminds us—and, after a while, such overwhelming evidence must merit some credence even among those who, like me, are highly skeptical of polls—this is no longer the case: the United States is seen by most non-Americans who have any view about it as more of a world menace than a world hope. And yet the response of a great many Americans, so reminiscent of Serbian nationalists I have known in the past, is one of rancor and of defiance toward those "Others" who "hate us because of our freedom."

Meanwhile, many of the same individuals (who still believe that "Operation Enduring Freedom" was an appropriate name for the military operation that led to thousands of prisoners and suspects and just ordinary civilians' being forced to endure the often obscene liberties that American soldiers were encouraged to feel free to take with them) also applaud the introduction of increasingly repressive measures with respect to immigration as well as to other areas of national life. Under terms of the USA Patriot Act (I mean, of course, the Uniting and Strengthening America by Providing Appropriate Tools Required to Intercept and Obstruct Terrorism Act of 2001, for which "USA Patriot" just *happens* to be the acronym), for example, government agencies were empowered to seek information about individuals from universities, libraries, and so on while compelling the authorities of these institutions to keep silent about their inquiries. Powerful interests, generally aligned with the government, exert heavy-handed control over large portions of the media. The Internet itself, which has so greatly facilitated communication, just as the Soviet authorities once feared, is becoming increasingly subject to a universal surveillance that many of the custodians of the newly, rather chillingly christened United States "Homeland" are ever more eager to exert as the technical means to do so become increasingly refined. These were the kinds of practices that, a couple of decades ago, were routinely identified with Soviet totalitarianism—in other words, with closed societies. This is what Americans are now becoming, or perhaps have already begun to become—although, like the Soviets on several notorious occasions, this country has not become so completely closed as to impede its government from sending its armed forces beyond its borders in the tens of thousands to engage in conquest and occupation when of a mind to do so.

In a certain sense, I am tempted to stop at this point, much like Rousseau near the end of his pessimistic *Discourse on the Origin of Inequality,* where he says, concerning the situation of absolute despotism, which he thinks human history has attained: "Here is the ultimate stage of inequality, and the extreme point which closes the circle and touches the point from which we started."[9] Here, indeed, we at least stand on the threshhold of the closed society, the point from which we started. For several years now, I have been suggesting, with some obvious sarcasm but at the same time in earnest, that political philosophy, if it is to live up to what I regard as its obligation to respond to actual lived experience, needs to come to terms with new real-world circumstances by devoting less attention to democracy, rights, freedom, justice, peace studies, and so forth and revisiting issues of despotism, totalitarianism, global injustice, and war.[10] To some extent that is actually happening, and not just in what I myself say and write.

To note just one straw in the wind, in his recent writings and talks Jürgen Habermas has begun to call attention to the extreme discrepancy between the cosmopolitan constitutionalism advocated by Kant and others, Habermas included, in that tradition and the flouting of this ideal by the current hegemony.[11] I am by no means simply indulging in ironic rhetoric when I say that the era of Rawls, which can perhaps best be epitomized in the expression that he frequently used when implicitly alluding to the United States in *A Theory of Justice*, the "nearly just society," is mostly past and dead (although one can, of course, still detect, in writers such as Rawls's erstwhile colleague Michael Walzer, some traces of that time of intellectual self-congratulation and of asserting how much better "we" are than all other societies, even those that are relatively "decent," to say nothing of "outlaw states," to employ two notorious Rawlsisms that pervade *The Law of Peoples*).

Today, the very thought of worrying about promoting some sort of distributive justice even in a single society—which was, after all, Rawls's central concern in *A Theory of Justice*—much less all over the globe—which turned out not to concern him in *The Law of Peoples*—seems, in the context of the dominant *Zeitgeist*, rather "quaint" (to use the U.S. attorney general's apt expression). The dear old Homeland really is, I believe, in a period of extended crisis, the likely eventual outcome of which seems to be a diminution of its own standing. (One early herald of this is the diminution of the standing of the dollar.) Such an outcome, when taken by itself might well be a good thing, but perhaps the rest of the world will have to pay a considerable price for it. All of this amply warrants considerable pessimism and cautions against self-indulgence in pointless utopian thinking—thinking that may in some ways resemble what is reported about the current methamphetamine craze: the drug user experiences an extreme, erotically tinged "high" the first time, but after a while the relevant part of the brain is burned out, and, to paraphrase Scripture, the last state is worse than the first.

Nevertheless, there is, no doubt, another side to all this: we cannot give up, we must carry on—after the example of Rousseau himself, who drafted his quite utopian *Social Contract* some years after having published the *Discourse on the Origins of Inequality*. Social and political philosophers, while in my view they are indeed bound to respect the lived experiences of their own epoch, however wretched and disheartening, are at the same time entitled to offer some glimpses—utopian, if you will—of a better possible future world. They should exhibit a model, to recall the words that Plato puts in Socrates' mouth in the *Republic*, that is "laid up in heaven," but one that can also serve as an ideal referent for us here below. One possible route toward reversing the closing of society that is currently taking place is to introduce, as Carol Gould does in her recent book, *Globalizing Democracy and Human Rights*, a notion that has become very popular of late, especially in business ethics, namely, stakeholder theory, while drawing more sweeping conclusions from it than she does. When reconsidering the question of workplace democracy, which has long interested her, she quotes from a work by Christopher McMahon in which he argues against extending the net of those to be considered stakeholders in corporations widely enough to include all those affected by them:

> A little reflection shows that this is not a principle we accept in the political sphere. Virtually everyone in the world is affected by the foreign policy decisions of the United States government, but we do not suppose that they therefore have a right to participate in making these decisions or in choosing those who make them.[12]

Well, contrary to McMahon, a little more reflection might lead to the thought, "Why not?" Granted, it would be a challenge to try to work out formulas for weighting votes relative to the extent to which particular individuals and groups are affected, and the recent failures in accurately counting even American citizens' votes show how technically difficult and liable to fraud any attempt to give some voice to those affected by American foreign policy around the world would be; but it seems to me that the idea itself is an excellent one. I fearlessly predict, however, that it will not be implemented in even the most modified form in the foreseeable future.

Nevertheless, the perspectives of non-Americans affected by U.S. policy do have a chance of "counting" indirectly precisely to the extent to which United States government officials participate in international organizations such as, in particular, the United Nations and make any effort whatsoever to accommodate their actions to the concerns of representatives of the affected individuals in other countries. They have done so in the past, and that they will do so again in the future is by no means inconceivable—in fact, it is certain. Meanwhile, although the outright elimination of visa and immigration requirements—which would not, I wish to repeat, entail eliminating security procedures or regulations concerning housing and employment designed to prevent overpopulation of already saturated areas and job losses by prior residents—is clearly not in the cards for the foreseeable future, it is nevertheless true that there are some in power who resist the trend toward a closed society that I have been identifying. They may still have some success, and it is not entirely unthinkable that the trend could be partially reversed before too long.[13] We can recall that in an executive memorandum dated 19 April 2000, President Clinton directed heads of executive agencies, working with the private sector, to "review the effect of United States government actions on the international flow of students and scholars as well as on citizen and professional exchanges, and take steps to address unnecessary obstacles, including those involving visa and tax regulations, procedures, and policies."[14] It is not unthinkable that the pendulum might swing in this direction once again some day.

Finally, to take the broadest view, what needs to be remembered is that such notions as "citizen" and "nation" are not truly universals, in the sense of retaining the same meaning, or perhaps any meaning at all, across the whole of time. As my initial survey of the idea of a closed society as a model over time also implied, such notions are the products of history—just think of the complex connotations that *civis Romanus*, which became anything but a mere ethnic or national designation, took on over the long course of ancient Roman history—and, as such, are subject to the inevitability of change. My utopian hope is that sooner or later, at some future time, we will supplement the Renaissance saying, "Nihil humani [or humanum] a me alienum puto,"—I think of nothing human as alien to me—with "Nullum hominem a me alienum puto"—I think of no human being as an alien to me.

## Notes

1. I am thinking especially, of course, of the Stoics, who coined the term.

2. "The difference in the rates of surplus-value in different countries, and consequently the national differences in the degree of exploitation of labour, are immaterial for our present analysis. What we want to show in this part is precisely the way in which a general rate of profit takes shape in any given country." Marx, *Capital* (Moscow: Foreign Languages Publishing House, 1962), vol. 3, part 2, ch. 8, p. 141.

3. John Rawls, *Political Liberalism* (New York: Columbia University Press, 1996), p. 12.

4. See my "The Rights of Aliens and of Other Others," in *Challenges to Law at the End of the 20th Century: Proceedings of the 17th World Congress of the International Association for Philosophy of Law and Social Philosophy (IVR), Bologna, June 16–21, 1995*, ed. Rex Martin and Gerhard Sprenge (Stuttgart: F. Steiner Verlag, 1997), vol. 1, pp. 192–99.

5. John Rawls, *The Law of Peoples* (Cambridge: Harvard University Press, 1999), p. 74.

6. Phillip Cole, *Philosophies of Exclusion: Liberal Political Theory and Immigration* (Edinburgh: Edinburgh University Press, 2000), p. 202.

7. John Locke, *The Second Treatise of Civil Government*, in *Two Treatises of Government* (New York: Hafner, 1947), ch. 8, para. 118, p. 181.

8. Such examples include the rejection of international treaty initiatives; a willingness to scrap or redefine existing treaties as the government pleases; an assertion of the right unilaterally to decide which countries to attack militarily and when; and of course the unbridled contempt for the lives and dignity of non-Americans, especially those who have been designated *les ennemis du jour*, which has so clearly manifested itself in Guantanamo, Abu Ghraib, and Felluja.

9. Jean-Jacques Rousseau, *Discourse on the Origins and Foundations of Inequality among Men*, in *The First and Second Discourse*, ed. R. D. Masters, trans. R. D. and J. D. Masters (New York: St. Martin's Press, 1964), p. 177.

10. See, for example, "Sartre et l'avenir de la démocratie libérale," *sens-public*, 3 (2005), http://www.sens-public.org/article_paru3, and printed in *Jean-Paul Sartre, violence et éthique*, ed. Gérard Wormser (Lyons: Editions Sens-public): 151–59; "Globalization and Intercultural Dialogue," *sens-public*, 3 (2005), http://www.sens-public.org/article_paru3; and "Sartre and the Twilight of Liberal Democracy as We Have Known It," in *Sartre Today: A Centenary Collection*, ed. Adrian van den Hoven and Andrew Leak (New York: Berghahn Books, 2005) [special issue of *Sartre Studies International* 11 (1/2) (2005)], 311–18.

11. See (and hear), for example, Habermas's lecture of October 15, 2004 at Purdue University, West Lafayette, Indiana, "The Kantian Project of Cosmopolitan Law," http://www.cla.purdue.edu/academic/idis/phil–li.

12. Carol Gould, *Globalizing Democracy and Human Rights* (Cambridge, UK: Cambridge University Press, 2004), pp. 226–27. The citation is from Christopher McMahon, *Authority and Democracy: A General Theory of Government and Management* (Princeton: Princeton University Press, 1994), p. 11.

13. Senator Richard Lugar of Indiana deserves some recognition here, I think, as a person who has been seriously concerned in maintaining exchange

relationships with "Others." His support of initiatives involving exchanges with young people from the Middle East, in which Donald Mitchell of the Department of Philosophy at Purdue University has played a leading role as coordinator, is one laudable example of this.

14. McBride, "Cultural Differences and Cosmopolitan Ideals: A Philosophical Analysis," *Fulbright Newsletter* (Bulgarian-American Commission for Educational Exchange) 21 (Spring 2000), p. 8.

# Human Rights and Living Wages
## ⁓ Milton Fisk ⁓

Researchers must dig deeply into current United Nations declarations and reports on human rights before coming across any mention of wages. To be sure, the right to a living wage features prominently along with other labor rights in earlier United Nations declarations.[1] However, the United Nations' Millennium Development Goals of 2000 calls for cutting in half by 2015 the number of those eking out an existence on less than a dollar a day, without mention of the issue of wages.[2] The focus instead is on economic aid and growth. Yet in reality, wages are a major issue as corporations scour the world for labor that will work for poverty wages. Even the United Nations' International Labor Organization in its 1998 declaration on rights at work focuses on issues other than wages.[3]

This downplaying of wages is but another sign of our neoliberal times. Still, the wage issue has not completely disappeared from consideration within United Nations human rights bodies. For example, in a 2004 report on five countries, the Committee on Economic, Social, and Cultural Rights notes its concern that Azerbaijan and Chile have minimum wages that are insufficient to ensure a decent living for workers and their families.[4] This committee monitors implementation of the 1974 covenant that, among many other things, sets a standard for minimum wages in countries ratifying it.

In a world beset with terrorism, violence against women and minorities, state torture, and inter-state belligerence, it is crucial to enforce human rights against such violence. This may tempt us to treat economic human rights as secondary and to suspend their enforcement at least until the agents of violence are under control. President Lula of Brazil inadvertently responded to the failure to give poverty wages a crucial place among human rights abuses by claiming that poverty is the world's most powerful weapon of mass destruction. He was saying that poverty destroys lives by shortening them, by creating vulnerabilities to disease, by closing off opportunities, and by breeding aggression.

Multiplying these effects of poverty by the best estimate of the number of the world's poor will give some idea of the magnitude of the violence done by poverty. Roughly, 1,400,000,000 people, or one half of the world's wage earners, earn, in terms of purchasing power parity, less than two dollars a day. In many poor families, someone has employment. Usually their jobs do not retain them for more than a short time or pay wages that provide an escape from poverty. Therefore, we cannot justify downgrading the importance of poverty wages as a human rights violation on the grounds that, regrettable as it may be, a poverty wage is not an act of overt violence against human beings. There is no firewall between rights against violence and rights against poverty wages and other economic abuses.

## AGREEMENT AND DISSENT OVER HUMAN RIGHTS

Nor can we set aside the problem of low wages by saying low wages occur only outside the mainstream of capitalism. Far from being a symptom of backwardness, the problem is at the heart of the most advanced corporations of our global economy.

The largest corporation in the world, Wal-Mart, employs millions of workers in merchandising, in the United States and elsewhere, who fail to make anything we might reasonably call a "living wage"—one that covers basic requirements for a working family of shelter, food, clothing, child care, education, health care, and transportation. Moreover, Wal-Mart's relations with the corporations that make the products it sells maintain millions of production workers at below the living wage levels appropriate in their countries. Given Wal-Mart's economic prowess, its suppliers have little choice but to accept the low prices Wal-Mart dictates for the products they sell. These low prices encourage the rock-bottom wages those suppliers pay.

General Electric (GE) is far from a backwater of capitalism. It is a transnational production and financial corporation. In the United States, it pays wages for a good living thanks to the efforts of its organized workforce, efforts spearheaded for many years by the United Electrical Workers with the support of other unions. GE has been moving production from jobs that pay for a good living in the United States to jobs elsewhere that fail to pay a living wage. In 2000, 1,400 jobs went from GE in Bloomington, Indiana, to jobs paying eight dollars a day at GE subsidiary Mabe in the state of Guanajuato, Mexico. Although far from being the lowest wage in Mexico, this is still not a living wage. The transnationals are setting global standards for wages that are below what workers and their families need to live on.

In setting the global standards for wages so low, these corporations are in violation of some of the human rights listed in the Universal Declaration of Human Rights (Universal Declaration) of 1948: "Everyone who works has the right to just and favorable remuneration ensuring for himself and his family an existence worthy of human dignity and if necessary supplemented by other means of social protection."[5] To make clear that earning a living does not mean taking on multiple jobs and long hours, the Universal Declaration says, "Everyone has the right to rest and leisure, including reasonable limitation of working hours and periodic holidays with pay."[6] The same points were expressed in the 1974 International Covenant on Economic, Social, and Cultural Rights,[7] which was signed by President Carter in 1978 but has not been ratified by the United States Congress.

The United States and other wealthy countries show, by their failure to ratify this covenant, their unease at recognizing certain economic requirements as genuine human rights. What in fact does it mean to say that something is a human right? Formally, it means that the right in question is one every human being has. Its scope is then universal. This though leaves open the question as to where a human right gets its authority. The authority behind such a right is never just an institution—a legislative body, a religious body, the market economy, or a covenant among nations. Ultimately, this authority comes from human beings recognizing that the right is a needed protection for the way they want to live together. Thus, in addition to having universal scope, a human right has authority coming from a common recognition of the basic requirements for a form of social existence.

A third aspect of human rights, as of other rights, is struggle. Many groups fight back against arbitrary and burdensome exclusions from benefits by others who enjoy a dominant position. Think here of the general strikes in the United States against employers' privileges in the early 1930s, of India's struggle against colonialism in the 1940s, and of the struggles of women against domination in the 1970s. The language of such struggles becomes the language of rights. Victories in those struggles tend to embed those rights in a people's spirit as a common recognition that a requirement of their living together is to avoid those exclusions. The tendency to struggle against exclusions perceived as arbitrary and burdensome becomes an attitudinal and behavioral feature of those who adopt rights.

However, a cautionary note must be included alongside my discussion about common recognition. There are always dissenters from human rights, and hence there is never a truly common recognition of the basic requirements of living together. The dissent is even broader as regards economic human rights, as shown partly by the refusal of some nations to ratify covenants of both the United Nations and the International Labor Organization, founded as an adjunct to the League of Nations in 1919 but now a specialized agency of the United Nations.[8] What this means is that human rights are inevitably political rather than articles of dogma. Those who wish to enjoy the benefits of excluding others do not change their minds just because of a victorious struggle against them. Yet what is striking is that since the United Nations Universal Declaration, the struggles against exclusion have spread the culture of human rights so widely. We need then to settle for this majoritarian culture as a basis for the authority of human rights. We cannot go beyond it by appealing, as some philosophers do, to the dubious prospect of universal agreement at some indefinite point in the future.[9] What we have is a widespread, but contested, recognition of these rights. Hence, some people will contest the kind of life together we want these rights to protect.

It is instructive to note the source of the criticism of economic human rights and, in particular, of the right to a living wage. When those rights appeared in the Universal Declaration, most of the major countries were advancing strongly social democratic policies. The 1944 Bretton Woods Accords on international finance protected strong welfare states from the vagaries of capital flows between nations.[10] Such capital flows could lead, as they did in the 1980s and 1990s, to the underfunding of welfare measures. In the 1944–1948 context, social protection for the unemployed, joining trade unions, equal pay for equal work, a living wage, and leisure from work seemed like the appropriate thing to demand.

However, from the perspective of the neoliberal elite of today's world, rights like these are seen as corrupting the market, which leads this elite to attack these rights, whether by stealth or frontal assault. In its view, the market takes precedence over any such alleged rights. In its view, the market delivers any legitimate benefits these rights guarantee workers more efficiently. From this neoliberal perspective, the Universal Declaration betrays its out-of-date nature by appealing in Article 1 to human beings to act in a spirit of concern for one another.[11]

In reality though, respect for rights can only exist in a context of concern for others. At the end of World War II people understood where the lack of economic regulation had led. They were asking how their leaders could have allowed the Great Depression with its global misery and then the brutishness in Stalingrad, the Holocaust, and Hiroshima-Nagasaki. They were open to the call to rebuild their world within a context of a concern for others strong enough to defend a wide range of rights for them.

### RECIPROCITY REQUIRES THE LIVING WAGE

In the Universal Declaration, the right to a living wage is described as "a just and favorable remuneration insuring for himself and his family an existence worthy of human dignity." Considering this assertion, my purpose is to show that it is as strong a right as other human rights. In fact, the structure of reasoning someone would use to defend other human rights applies perfectly well in the case of the right to a living wage.

In a pure market system, the focus would be on labor power, which is what an employer buys by paying a wage and what an employee sells in taking a job for a given wage. In such a system, labor power is a mere "commodity" in the sense that its price is determined by the supply of it and the demand for it. If labor power is considered to be a commodity, there will be nothing objectionable about a wage that cannot support the life of an employee. This would simply reflect the fact that the labor supply is so ample that employers can recruit labor at an extremely low wage. This pure market perspective, it turns out, has become the main basis for denying that employed people have a right to a wage on which they can live. However, such a denial is a consequence of our treating human beings as no more than board pieces in a game of supply and demand.

To proceed critically in examining this denial of the right to a living wage, we must ask whether we are prepared to treat labor power as a commodity and the employee as a mere seller of it.[12] To treat labor power in this way is to treat it as no more than something potentially useful to a buyer. In the case of any commodity, there is a seller who hopes to get at least the market price for it. The difference in the case of labor power is only that the employee who sells it also embodies it. Still, the employee gets no consideration of his or her needs, and it is only by chance that the marketplace meets the needs vital to the employee. Without such consideration for the employee, other significant human relations are absent as well. There is no respect for labor power or its bearer as something with legitimate needs. Finally, there is no recognition of equality, since the employer can degrade the employee as much as the market will allow without a corresponding sacrifice. Undoubtedly, even the market system accords some rights to sellers of commodities. For example, there is the right to sell labor power on a competitive market rather than to an employer who has monopolized it. However, these are not human rights, but rather the institutional rights deriving from the rules of the market.

In sum, to treat the wages for which human beings sell their labor power as no different from the prices for which other human beings sell vegetables and computers is to treat labor power as a commodity. From the perspective of an employer in a pure market, labor power and the human beings embodying it appear simply as means to running a business. It becomes irrelevant to the employer what the ends of those human beings are. What the ends of those human beings are whom the employer is using becomes irrelevant to the employer. Specifically, it becomes irrelevant that job seekers have one interest in common, which is to make a living through taking a job.

The employer then needs—in order to avoid treating employees as mere means—to drop the abstraction of the pure market by considering the ends of employees.[13] What is in question is not an intellectual consideration of employees' ends but a consideration that amounts to a commitment to do something about them. Similarly, it is not respect in the sense of admiration that is in question, but respect that will not allow the object of respect—the employee—to fall into misery by frustrating his or her basic ends. Certainly, there will be ends that are tangential to the employer's focus on employment. Though employees may want to be taken more seriously in the political system, the employer cannot be held directly responsible for improving the voice of employees in politics. Only in the area of work and its conditions, including wages, does the employer's consideration of employees' goals and needs take effect. Employers will try to address the work-related interests of employees, and there will be many such concerns. Settling even some of the issues that arise will free the employer from the charge of using the employee solely as a means. What, then, is the reason that a living wage in particular is a concern that an employer has an obligation to address?

To answer this question, it is crucial to consider the idea of reciprocity. It takes us beyond the indefinite point to which we have come so far. So far we know only two things. We know first that we need to show some concern for other people to avoid treating them simply as means for our benefit. We know second that people whose position puts them in a special relation to others must show concern for those others in a way that addresses some of the interests those others have due to standing in that relation. In particular, anyone who is in the position of an employer needs to show concern for his or her employees in a way that addresses some of their work-related interests. This is still quite indefinite, since employees will have many such interests, and perhaps only some in particular have to engage the concern of the employer. The idea of reciprocity comes in to help determine which interests must be of concern.

In looking for specific interests that employers must try to satisfy, we need to consider the economic system in which wage work plays a key part. Are there employee interests that arise from the existence of this system, a system that features employers who want to hire labor? There are many such employee interests, but one in particular is more important here. As this economic system spread, it displaced many other sources of making a living. It then forced a majority of people to look to it in order to make a living. For them this system created an interest in making a living wage. There are jobs that people do not rely on to make a living, such as a job a wealthy person takes for prestige or a second job that a person of moderate means takes to afford the purchase of a luxury. The basic situation, though, is that employers want to hire people, but the system of employment itself creates a dependency in those they hire, for people who come into the system for a job typically cannot make a living outside it. They depend on it for making a living. Surely, they may exit the system at any time they think they can make a success of self-employment or retire on savings.

This gives us the elements needed for requiring reciprocity. Employers have refined and spread the system of wage labor as something that benefits them. A person who enters this system as an employee will typically not have another avenue of making a living and will then depend on wages in the system to make a living. Reciprocity requires that employers make the benefit they derive from turning people into employees correspond to the benefit of a living wages for employees. For their advantage, employers have put employees in the situation of having to take wage work to make a living. Employers need to reciprocate for this advantage given them by employees through paying employees the living wage they seek in entering the wage system.

Behind this reciprocity lies concern. Reciprocity functions here only to indicate which among a variety of work-related interests an employer should satisfy. The assumption is, though, that the employer has concern for the fulfillment of at least some among these employee interests. Reciprocity as an abstract principle of balancing benefits cannot have moral force without the backing of concern for others. The element of concern came in above as an alternative to the instrumental view of persons. Without it, anyone could simply ignore the dependency of employees on their job for making a living.

### THE REJECTION OF RECIPROCITY

There are sure to be objections to reciprocity as a basis for a living wage. It is time to consider a few of them before going on to uncover a basis for reciprocity itself.

The first objection is that there need be no such reciprocity, since employees enter voluntarily into the wage contract, thereby accepting a given wage rate and absolving the employer of any responsibility to pay more. This objection ignores the fact that, given its spread, the system of employment itself makes many people dependent on it for making a living. The responsibility of the employer to reciprocate with a living wage comes from the fact that he or she is perpetuating a system that many people cannot avoid entering if they hope to make enough to live by. Since the employer is getting a benefit out of this system, he or she needs to reciprocate with a living wage. A voluntary agreement on a poverty wage cannot void the requirement of reciprocity; instead, reciprocity is the background within which any voluntary agreement should fit.

Second, another objection, a favorite of libertarians, claims that only those who are unwilling to take several jobs can fail to make a living from low wages. In commenting on it, we need to appeal to the interrelatedness of human rights. The Vienna Declaration from the 1993 World Congress on Human Rights and Program of Action states, "All human rights are universal, indivisible and interdependent and interrelated. The international community must treat human rights globally in a fair and equal manner, on the same footing, and with the same emphasis."[14] This is relevant because, as already noted, the Universal Declaration says in Article 24, "Everyone has the right to rest and leisure, including reasonable limitation of working hours and periodic holidays with pay." As a means to a living wage, multiple jobs that together last longer than a normal working day conflict with the requirement of rest and leisure needed for human dignity.

Here, the right to rest and leisure and the right to a living wage support one another. The right to rest and leisure would be unenforceable without a right to a living wage for a reasonable workday, and the right to a living wage for a reasonable workday will be unenforceable when employers deny employees the right to rest and leisure through mandatory long workdays.

Moreover, the two rights have parallel structures of justification. The right to rest and leisure from wage-paid activity depends on a context of concern for interests others have when employed. Since employees have many interests, a person needs a specific reason why concern centers on rest and leisure. Reciprocity becomes the key here, as it did with the living wage itself. Once drawn into the system of employment, employees must depend on it for allowing freedom in the form of rest and leisure. If the system does not deliver this freedom, then employers, who nonetheless benefit from their employees, have broken reciprocity with those employees.

Third, we hear some employers protesting that they would have to close down if they paid a living wage. The assumption is that making a living from their businesses is a higher obligation than paying a living wage to their employees. It is difficult to justify this assumption, since it is incompatible with the reciprocity between the two sets of actors. In effect, the assumption refuses to acknowledge any reciprocity.

The response is usually that the working poor are better off than those who are rotting in pools of unemployment. There is, though, a broader picture to consider. Employers who cannot pay a living wage put downward pressure on the wages of employers who can. Thus, what appeared to be a hand helping a few workers move out of unemployment becomes a market force creating the misery of working poverty for many.

## SOCIAL GOALS AS THE BASIS FOR RECIPROCITY

After this discussion of objections, I now return to the notion of reciprocity. As the basis for his principles of justice, John Rawls pointed to an interesting link between reciprocity and his idea that a society is a cooperative venture.[15] Cooperation, he agreed, is necessary for everyone's well-being. However, the failure of reciprocity would be a deterrent to cooperation. To illustrate his point, imagine that Pat and Jerry are poor members of a remote community who cooperate in getting a medical clinic set up in their community, but once it is set up, Jerry manages to get control of the clinic. As a result, Jerry is able to determine fees for users that will make profits for him. The fees are high enough to exclude the poor, including even Pat, who helped establish the clinic. Pat will feel that Jerry took advantage of her cooperation, since, in the end, he denied her any benefits from it. If this kind of thing happens regularly, many in the community will withhold their cooperation from projects that could ostensibly benefit the community.

This, I think, deepens our understanding of the principle of reciprocity. People need not view it as a stand-alone principle, but they can view it as a requirement of social goals, which are a vital ingredient in any society. The kind of society that people make for themselves depends, in part at least, on their social goals. They will perhaps want to make it an educated society, a healthy one, one in which the courts are fair, one at peace within the global community, one that is democratic, and one with a high degree of equality. In making for themselves a certain kind of society, people organize cooperative efforts to pursue social goals. After all, in pursuing the same goals, they have every reason to work together.

Reaching goals for the society as a whole leads to benefits that accrue to individual members of the society. The struggle to realize a social goal is a struggle to change the society, and this is not the same as the struggle of an individual to get the benefits for him- or herself of living in the changed society. We can make our society, but not an individual in it, into one with a court system that is fair. Ultimately, we want to realize social goals only because a society that has realized such goals can benefit its individual members in corresponding ways. With a fair court system, individuals can benefit by having their grievances heard and handled with fairness. There is no way to guarantee these benefits for individuals directly without structuring the society with the potential for doing so.

Goals such as these have then two distinctive features. One is that they are literally the same, and not just similar, for all who pursue them; the other is that people pursue them, not on their own through competition with others, but through cooperation.[16]

A failure of reciprocity would undermine both of these features. It would mean that, despite the cooperative effort to realize a social goal, some of the cooperators would benefit considerably from this cooperative effort, whereas others would gain little or nothing. It denies some people the benefits that they hoped to get from cooperating with others in an effort to realize a social goal. They lose their benefits so others can reap larger benefits.

The effect of this lack of reciprocity is that, instead of realizing the social goal of the cooperative undertaking, the process realizes the goal of gain only for some. This goal fails the first requirement of a social goal, for the goal of gain only for some ceases to be the same goal for all. Moreover, lack of reciprocity leads to a lack of cooperation, and thus fails to satisfy the second requirement of a social goal. Those who end up pursuing their own interest rather than the social goal cease to cooperate with those genuinely interested in the social goal and end up manipulating them for their private interest. If the lack of reciprocity becomes a pattern, people will hesitate to accept proposals to cooperate in realizing social goals, suspecting that intentions to manipulate them lie behind such proposals. Such suspicion undermines the identity of a society by leaving it without institutions benefiting all.

The point to which this leads is that reciprocity, on which the human right to a living wage as well as other human rights depend, makes the foundation of human rights into the social goals that define the kind of society in which we hope to live. Reciprocity is not a stand-alone principle but one we accept because violations of it undermine the cooperative efforts needed in the pursuit of our social ideals.

How, specifically, does this apply to the case of the right to a living wage? The relevant social goal that is widely accepted in the United States and in much of the rest of the world is that of a prosperous society within which there is a widespread market that includes a labor market. Broad acceptance of this goal depends on the understanding that a prosperous society is one in which all enjoy prosperity, even if in different degrees. There is, then, room for inequality, provided it is not so great as to destroy cooperation in seeking to realize this goal. However, prosperity is universal, leaving no room for poverty that flows from requirements of the economy. Since the labor market is the means through which employees are to gain their prosperity, their cooperation in realizing and maintaining this ideal will depend on employment that earns them at least a living wage.[17]

Even when we consider a noneconomic right, such as the right to freedom of thought, conscience, and religion, which is called for in Article 18 of the Universal Declaration, a similar pattern connects this right to one or more social goals. Here the goal is a society that does not hide diversity but rather treats it as an asset. In the cooperative effort to reach this goal, reciprocity is essential. Otherwise, some will take advantage of the willingness of the rest to cooperate in order to make their thought or belief hegemonic. This leaves the rest without recognition for their views; cooperation will evaporate, and then only dissenters will champion the social goal of a tolerant society.

Thus enough similarity is found between the basis for economic and noneconomic human rights to make implausible the view that the economic ones are weaker, less binding, or secondary. For example, no one can appeal to the differences between the two kinds of rights to give priority to democratic reforms while leaving labor reforms to the end. There are different stages in the process of making a society more democratic; democracy does not show up all at once.[18] Without implementing labor rights along the way, the advance of democracy is blocked. Then employees are subject to vital decisions about the labor market and the economy generally that they have had no part in making. The basis for this interdependence of rights lies in the equal value given to the social goals those rights protect.

## CONFLICT AND CONSENSUS OVER SOCIAL GOALS

In times past, an active role for social agreement and historical trends played no part in the common good. People found the common good, as opposed to the goods of individuals and groups, in human nature by the light of reason. It did not matter if half of humanity, through a supposed distortion of temperament, failed to find the common good or misidentified an individual good as a common good. The contemporary replacement for this metaphysical notion of the common good is a consensual notion of the common good, which, in the terms I have been using, is a set of social goals. Under this replacement, people agree upon what their social goals are, and this agreement becomes the basis for a cooperative effort to try to realize them. People enter into the cooperative effort freely because of having agreed, and human rights protect their unobstructed access to the benefits resulting from their cooperative efforts. In contrast, the metaphysical notion does not require widespread agreement. Instead, it requires authoritative institutions, which can tell people that if they were to use reason properly, they would all come to agreement on the common good those institutions advocate.

Although the consensual character of social goals and, through them, of human rights appears to fit nicely with our contemporary democratic ethos, it does cause trouble that the metaphysical view of the common good appears to avoid. As discussed above, disagreement exists over all the social goals as well as over the human rights based on them. There are those who defend intolerance, who defend economic growth even when it denies prosperity to large numbers, and who defend limiting the leisure of others in order to ensure their gain. Were a metaphysical view taken, people could pronounce these dissidents mistaken and prohibit further advocacy and pursuit of their goals. On the consensual view, there will be competing goals for society and, hence, competing views of human rights. Each side in the competition will try to win over the other so a consensus can emerge, but neither side can simply declare that it is right and dismiss the other side. That would fly in the face of the consensual approach and lead back to the reliance on authority associated with the metaphysical approach.

Someone might try to resolve differences over what social goals should be adopted by appealing to dignity and respect. What goals would best secure "a life that meets the necessary conditions of dignity and respect"?[19] However, dignity and respect turn out to be variable themselves. Do we deny people their dignity and the respect of others for them when we do not pay them a living wage? Those who pursue the goal of widespread prosperity do so in the belief that a living wage is necessary to have dignity and to receive the respect of others. After all, those without a living wage fail to achieve their basic aim in taking a job, which is to make a living. Those with the goal of an economically growing society will point to employment itself as sufficient to provide dignity and win respect. They would argue that being a part of the grand effort to make the economy grow should add dignity to and earn respect for even the most miserably paid employee. Hence, we cannot resolve conflicts over social goals and human rights by using dignity and respect as criteria. They do not serve as stand-alone principles, since they change their sense with changes in social goals.

However, lack of widespread agreement should not discourage us. The consensual view of social goals and rights does not deny us our convictions.

Those who have suffered from exclusions due to lack of reciprocity along with those in solidarity with them will still seek agreement on a type of society in which those exclusions no longer exist. They will have to compromise with those who benefit from those exclusions and who are convinced that any other type of society would be hell on earth. Making such compromises is, after all, part of respecting the right of others to disagree. However, their initial compromises need not be permanent; continuing to struggle can win back most of what was important about the type of society they wanted.

Consider, for example, the way the United Nations and other bodies have tried to broaden acceptance of the human rights in the Universal Declaration. The United Nations High Commissioner on Human Rights coordinates numerous investigations around the world into alleged human rights abuses. In addition, the ILO, as a specialist agency of the United Nations, investigates alleged abuses of the labor rights of the Universal Declaration as well as additional labor rights.[20] Beyond the efforts of these United Nations bodies, numerous non-governmental organizations—such as Amnesty International, Human Rights Watch, Lawyers Committee for Human Rights (now Human Rights First), and the Center for Gender and Refugee Studies—expose and try to stop human rights abuses. The living wage movement active during the last decade in the United States has made gains toward its modest aim of getting a living wage for employees hired directly or indirectly with municipal funds.[21]

If those involved in any of these human rights efforts have done their work well, they will have recruited others to their vision. Strengthened in this way, they can replace the major compromises they made when they were weaker with agreements closer to their principles. This will eventually reduce, without altogether eliminating, the burdensome exclusions from which many suffer. Furthermore, it will bring a sizeable majority to share their social goals and accept the related human rights.

## Notes

1. See in particular Universal Declaration of Human Rights (1948) and International Covenant on Economic, Social, and Cultural Rights (1976). The United Nations human rights documents referred to in this article are at http://www.un.org/rights.

2. On the goals of the millennium project set out in the 2000 declaration, go to http://www.un.org/millennium/declaration and http://www.millenniumproject.org/goals.

3. See the 2004 International Labor Organization (ILO) document *Global Report on Organizing for Social Justice,* part 1, at http://www.ilo.org.

4. The country-by-country reports of the United Nations Committee on Economic, Social, and Cultural Rights can be found at http://www.un.org/Depts/dhl/resguide/spechr.htm#social.

5. Universal Declaration, Article 23, Section 3.

6. Universal Declaration, Article 24.

7. International Covenant, Part 3, Articles 7 and 11.

8. Consider the case of the United States. ILO data on the ratification of eight "fundamental human rights conventions" ranging over freedom of association and collective bargaining, forced labor, discrimination in employment, and child labor indicates that the United States has ratified only two out of the eight conventions, while most nations have ratified them all (www.ilo.org/ilolex). Mention has already been made of the failure of the United States to ratify the International Covenant on Economic, Social, and Cultural Rights.

9. Both John Rawls and Jürgen Habermas share the prospect of such agreement in their exchange in *The Journal of Philosophy* 92:3 (March 1995), pp. 109–180.

10. Eric Helleiner, *States and the Reemergence of Global Finance: From Bretton Woods to the 1990s* (Ithaca: Cornell University Press, 1994), chapter 1.

11. James Syfers, "Human Rights *versus* Classical Liberalism," in *Not for Sale: In Defense of Public Goods,* edited by A. Anton, M. Fisk, and N. Holmstrom (Boulder, CO: Westview Press, 2000), 145–170.

12. On this topic, see Karl Polanyi, *The Great Transformation: The Political and Economic Origins of Our Time* (Boston: Beacon Press, 1957), chapter 6.

13. Immanuel Kant makes not treating humans merely as a means his second "categorical imperative." See his *Groundwork of the Metaphysic of Morals* (1785), chapter 2.

14. From the 1993 World Congress on Human Rights and Program of Action, found at http://www.un.org/rights.

15. John Rawls, *A Theory of Justice* (Cambridge MA: Harvard University Press, 1971), pp. 15, 102; see also his *Political Liberalism* (New York: Columbia University Press, 1993), pp. 16–17, 50.

16. For a fuller discussion of social goals and their relation to rights and justice, see Milton Fisk, *Toward a Healthy Society: The Morality and Politics of American Health Care Reform* (Lawrence, KS: University Press of Kansas, 2000), chapter 4.

17. The claim that this ideal of prosperity is widely accepted does not

deny the importance of an alternative to it that has no place for a labor market. See, for example, David Schweikart, *Against Capitalism* (New York: Cambridge University Press, 1993), pp. 60–77.

18. ILO, *Global Report on Organizing for Social Justice*, Part 1, sections 31–33.

19. Axel Honneth, "Is Universalism a Moral Trap? The Presuppositions and Limits of a Politics of Human Rights," in *Perpetual Peace: Essays on Kant's Cosmopolitan Ideal*, ed. J. Bohman and M. Lutz-Bachmann (Cambridge, MA: MIT Press, 1997), p. 168.

20. Such as the additional labor rights directly connected with democratic reforms, as emphasized in the ILO's 2004 *Global Report for Social Justice*.

21. Stephanie Luce, *Fighting for a Living Wage* (Ithaca: Cornell University Press, 2004).

# Moral Rights, Moral Responsibility, and the Contemporary Failure of Moral Knowledge
## ⁓ Dallas Willard ⁓

Human rights are in desperate straits around the world. They are widely proclaimed, but brutally violated on a mind-numbing scale. The basic outlook that I wish to represent in this essay is that moral rights depend, for their effective implementation, upon a certain condition in the human community. If the community is not one with a high level of moral substance (that is, not predominantly one of *morally good people*, both in official positions and throughout the population), then moral rights will, at best, degenerate into mere legal rights, and even then, they will be continually subject to failure in the context of need because the individuals involved in such contexts do not act to support them. Those legal rights—where they exist—will also be, at most, honored in the letter, and not in the spirit of human dignity, as Kant and those of similar moral outlook would understand human dignity.

When this is the case, those who have legal rights (such as blacks, women, prisoners of war, or homosexuals) *may* be able to bring governmental processes and forces to bear to secure themselves in certain (obviously important) respects, and that is no small thing. But even that is not a given, and in any case, they will not achieve the type of acceptance and endorsement that persons of genuinely good moral will and character extend to others in a moral community. This will be even truer of people *outside* of ethnic and national groups, and especially when hostilities prevail between such groups.

Clark Butler has written:

> In large impersonal societies, individuals steeped in duty consciousness often lack a sufficient knowledge of others and their claims to guarantee protection of their rights even when they would wish them protected. However conscientious individuals are, they are often unconscious of the secondary consequences of actions. The undercurrent of continuous duty consciousness is compatible with periodic justified eruptions of rights consciousness. Yet a significant difference exists between the rights consciousness of individuals who must arouse a non-existent sense of duty and that of individuals who can call on a pre-established sense of duty in others.[1]

This is a very penetrating observation about the unfortunate human condition. The lack of "a pre-established sense of duty in others" does make "periodic justified eruptions of rights consciousness" inevitable. But I would add that more than such a sense of duty in others is required for a proper functioning of rights in human society. Conscious dutifulness to rights is never enough, and not just for the reasons Butler points out. Rather, such dutifulness can succeed only as a part of a moral character of proactive concern for human goods. Beyond such a sense of duty lies the sense of moral identity that each person carries as a marginal presence in all acts and activities—that is, the sense of what makes *me* a good person, a person *worthy* of approval, inclusion, and support from the human beings around me. This sense of moral worth contains a presumption of the *reality* of moral worth and a presumption of shared *knowledge* of that reality. When the sense of moral reality and knowledge is lacking or mistaken (such as when it takes there to be no such thing as moral reality, or takes moral worth to consist in ethnic identity, or in success at pursuing one's own interest above all, and so forth), then the sense of moral identity of the individual (and the group) will lead to the denial or suppression of the human goods, which it is the primary function of morality to protect and advance.

Among moral human goods, of course, rights themselves stand very high. In fact, they are a kind of meta-good, for their point is always to assure the accessibility of other goods. Their point is never just themselves, never *just* having rights, but a kind of life in which respect and active support for human dignity and well-being is paramount.

Now, what I have called "the sense of moral identity," which each person carries in all of his or her acts and activities, rests upon a presumption of a *shared knowledge* of life and of what makes someone morally acceptable or praiseworthy or not. However fragmentary or misguided the presumed knowledge may be, it is, I think, impossible for a normal human being (I leave out of account sociopathic and extremely traumatized individuals) to conduct his or her life except upon the assumption that there is shared or sharable *knowledge* of who is a morally good person and who is not—and, by extension, of what is right and wrong, of what is morally obligatory or praiseworthy or not, and so forth. Thus, the normal human being accepts the necessity and the possibility of moral guidance and of *learning* about such matters, and the possibility of being wrong with regard to them, that is, of holding false views regarding them.

Throughout the history of ethical theorizing in the Western world, well into the twentieth century, every important thinker has agreed with that. What most strikingly characterizes twentieth-century ethical theorizing is the emergence of *noncognitivism* as a serious contender in the field of moral understanding. Far from being a passing phase, as often seems assumed currently, noncognitivism (now usually in the guise of one "constructionism" or another) has entered the life-blood of Western culture. As a result, there is now no recognized, systematic body of moral teaching that can be presented as *moral knowledge* by the institutions of Western society: chiefly, by the universities, and only slightly less so by the churches or religious institutions—and certainly not by law and government. This fact is the result of what I refer to as "the disappearance of moral knowledge in the twentieth century." If one wishes to see the process through which this came about from the viewpoint of the universities, Julie Reuben's book *The Making of the Modern University* gives the institutional history.[2] It was only during the mid- and late twentieth century that the university became the center of cultural authority and set the societal standard of what counts as knowledge and what does not. Currently, by the standard it sets, moral understanding and judgment do not count as knowledge. This is simply the case, though very few people seem to recognize it.

But the university in the twentieth century was, in this respect, informed and controlled by long-range developments in ethical thought—not by these alone, of course, but essentially by them. Those developments laid the foundation for the emergence and continuing dominance of noncognitivism in our academic culture: indeed, of a noncognitivist culture generally. I want to briefly survey those developments to show, as I take it, how we got where we stand today. I am not going to try to convince anyone that there has been no recovery from noncognitivism, but I believe that a thesis to that effect can be sustained by a careful examination of the work of writers from Hare to Rawls, Williams, MacIntyre and Gibbard.

For purposes of this paper, I shall use the work of G. E. Moore as a dividing line. Although there is an increasing interest today in the immediate predecessors of Moore, such as T. H. Green and F. H. Bradley, it is still true, as it has been for many decades, that discussions of the history of ethics, proceeding backward, stop at Moore and only resume with more distant figures, such as Mill and Kant. This, I think, is because there really was a profound transformation that occurred with Moore, but it was one which had little to do with his famous intuitionism or the other usual topics of ethical theory in the twentieth century. Rather, it had to do with what is to be regarded as the primary subject matter of ethical theorizing.

In the 1880s and 1890s, in the United States and Great Britain at least, a broad consensus about the moral conduct of life prevailed and was regarded as a systematic body of knowledge. It was a consensus that was thought to be rationally grounded in moral theorizing of the sort commonly done in the universities at that time. This consensus was incorporated into a number of widely used textbooks on ethics, prominent among which were John Dewey's *Outlines of a Critical Theory of Ethics*[3] (and, later on, Dewey and James H. Tuft's *Ethics*),[4] John H. Muirhead's *The Elements of Ethics*,[5] and John S. Mackenzie's *A Manual of Ethics*,[6] to mention only three of several textbooks that went through repeated revisions and editions in widespread use.

The main source, by far, for this consensus was the personality and lectures of T. H. Green, forcefully expressed in his short teaching career at Oxford and in his posthumously published *Prolegomena to Ethics*. I shall refer to this body of university teaching simply as "the pre-Moore synthesis" because, on the theoretical side, it was primarily Moore's work that resulted in that consensus evaporating, with nothing *explicitly* replacing it in the academic (and later the cultural) context.

Looking back at the pre-Moore synthesis in ethical theorizing, the first point that stands out is what it took to be the central *subject matter* of ethical inquiry. The favorite term for that subject matter among these writers was "conduct," by which voluntary action, or action with an end in view, was meant. (Sometimes—especially later on in this period—conduct was approached by way of the moral *judgment*. On this approach, someone first identified and examined the characteristically moral judgments and then moved on to an examination of what those judgments are about—which was found to be primarily conduct, or action with an end in view. Then the analysis was turned upon conduct to see what it is and how it divides into "good" and "bad" conduct, and what that means. In other cases someone might speak, not of the judgment, but of the "idea" of obligation, and so forth.)

As for conduct itself, it was regarded as a type of complex and "organic" whole.[7] Dewey, for example, said: "Conduct implies more than something taking place; it implies purpose, motive, intention; that the agent knows what he is about, that he has something which he is aiming at" (*Outlines*, p. 242). And on this broad understanding, conduct is not separable from character. Conduct arises out of the whole person. "Character and conduct are, morally, the same thing, looked at first inwardly and then outwardly" (p. 246). Thus, "To say that a man's conduct is good, unless it is [that is, without it being] the manifestation of a good character, is to pass a judgment that is self-contradictory" (p. 246).

This view of ethical *reality* was widely assumed among pre-Moore teachers and writers. They were, generally, people who believed life to be an organic whole, where the components of conduct were not atomistic units, but thoroughly interpenetrated one another, making the "meaning" or nature of each component dependent upon that of all the others. So the motive and intention, feelings or sentiments, the consequences and the personal character, that go into an action which is *conduct* are not things that can be separately considered in ethical analysis. Considered together, however, they allow us to understand and know—indeed, to teach—what human beings ought to be and to do.

Nevertheless, it is the *will* that stands out in this literature as primary for moral goodness or badness. Mackenzie remarks, "the good will [is] . . . supremely good and [is] . . . the ultimate object approved by the moral judgment" (*Manual*, p. 129). But, of course, "A good will cannot be there without good action," he says, "and there can be no good action without a good will" (p. 129).

T. H. Green had earlier held that the distinction between the good and bad will "must lie at the root of every system of ethics." In his view, "the statement that the distinction between good and bad will must lie at the basis of any system of ethics, and the further statement that this distinction itself must depend on the nature of the objects willed, would in some sense or other be accepted by all recognized 'schools' of moralists, but they would be accepted in very different senses."[8] The good will certainly always be thought of in these writers as a will that is a settled, coherent body of dispositions to act in ways that promote the goods influenced by the action. As James Seth, another luminary in the pre-Moore consensus remarked, "Conduct, therefore, points to character, or settled habit of will. But will is here no mere faculty, it is a man's 'proper self.' The will is the self in action; and in order to act, the self must also feel and know."[9]

The second point that stands out in the pre-Moore synthesis is that it assumed the substance of the moral life, centered on conduct, will, and character, to be an object (subject) of *knowledge*. (Here, let us say that one has knowledge of a certain subject matter if he is capable of—or, in the occurrent sense of "know," if he actually is—representing that subject matter as it is, on an appropriate basis of thought and experience.) Thus, all of the authors concerned, without exception, speak of the *science of ethics* as the field of inquiry in which they are engaged, and on the basis of which they naturally give fairly specific directions concerning what people ought to do and to be. That is a language and a practice that we can hardly imagine anyone in the field of ethical theory using today. But they used it quite confidently, even without a thought. This followed from what they took the subject matter of ethical theorizing to be, plus the assumption that that subject matter is open to examination by observation, abstraction, and theorization. It is the failure of this assumption about the accessibility of will, character, and so forth to *knowledge* that, more than any other single thing, accounts for the current situation with regard to moral knowledge and authority, described above as "the disappearance of moral knowledge."

The third point about the pre-Moore synthesis that must be noted here is that normative, first-level moral judgments were regarded as *a natural part* of moral theory. That is, given the appropriate inquiry into and understanding of the good person or character, and of the good or right action ("conduct"), it was thought that normative judgments of specific application to persons and actions were not only appropriate, but were *required* as a natural part of the work of the ethical theorist. Ethical theorists thought it to be a natural part of their work to say, to *teach*, that certain lines of action were right or wrong, and that certain (types of) people were of good or bad—even "evil"—character. They thought that "moral guidance" through instruction and personal influence was a proper part of their work, for which they were responsible, and that it should be expressed "in class" when appropriate and appropriately. The division between what later came to be known as "meta-ethics" and practical or normative ethics, as that distinction comes into play post-Moore, would have been something inconceivable to them. Contrary to professors of ethics nowadays, they all would have thought that they had moral knowledge that their students did not have and had a "moral authority" based thereon. The rebirth of applied ethics and the flight from meta-ethics beginning in the 1970s failed to reinstate concrete ethical knowledge, since the new applied ethics failed to be the application of any reestablished knowledge of reestablished consensus in ethical theory.

The effect of the pre-Moore consensus was that teachers of ethics expected their teaching to strongly affect the actions of their students, and by many reports, it did. R. G. Collingwood said, in his *Autobiography*:

> The School of Green sent out into public life a stream of ex-pupils who

carried with them the conviction that philosophy and particularly the philosophy they had learned at Oxford was an important thing and that their vocation was to put it into practice.... Through this effect on the minds of its pupils, the philosophy of Green's school might be found, from about 1880 to about 1910, penetrating and fertilizing every part of the national life.[10]

In America, much of the moral drive of the "progressive movement" of the 1890s through the 1930s and later came from the teachings of John Dewey (and like-minded university and professional people) about moral reality, moral knowledge, and the moral life. This was the last time there existed in America a generally shared understanding of moral worth that could publicly serve as the basis of a public program of legal and social reform. (Note how far the work of John Rawls, for example, falls short of any such real effect.)

Dewey at mid-career had this to say about moral worth: "We have reached the conclusion that disposition as manifest in endeavor is the seat of moral worth, and that this worth itself consists in a readiness to regard [to care for] the general happiness—even against contrary promptings of personal comfort and gain" (*Ethics*, p. 364). The words are Dewey's, but he would have been first to tell you that they fairly accurately express the outcome of a remarkably rich period of ethical reflection, running from T. H. Green to Dewey's middle years. They mark the end of that period, however, and the influence of G. E. Moore and "the analysis of ethical concepts" was to change the subject matter of ethical theory away from the moral life itself and would institute the period of ethical nihilism—"noncognitivism" or, at least, agnosticism—that continues up to today in the English-speaking world.

In *After Virtue*, Alasdair MacIntyre, who has long been deeply concerned with the state of affairs I call the disappearance of moral knowledge, perceptively comments:

> We have not yet fully understood the claims of any moral philosophy until we have spelled out what its social embodiment would be.... Since Moore the dominant narrow conception of moral philosophy has ensured that the moral philosophers could ignore this task.[11]

If that is true, we have forgotten what is valid in the claims of the post-Moore moral philosophers.

Now the pre-Moore attitude toward the relevance of moral theory and teaching to responsible moral instruction and guidance, and to the formation of character and society, was the received view from Socrates through the pre-Moore thinkers. It is hard to find any serious exceptions. I know of none. I doubt anyone will seriously question this with respect to classical and medieval thinkers. But the assumed connection between moral theory and moral guidance is strong and vital right up through the pre-Moore period. David Hume in the late 1700s remarks:

> The end of all moral speculations is to teach us our duty; and, by proper representations of the deformity of vice and the beauty of virtue, beget correspondent habits, and engage us to avoid the one, and embrace the other.... What is honourable, what is fair, what is becoming, what is noble, what is generous, takes possession of the heart, and animates us to embrace it and maintain it.[12]

For all the professed admiration of Hume currently, who today would follow him in this? We must keep in mind, however, that it was precisely such a conviction about moral reality and life that animated earlier discussions of rights.

Henry Sidgwick, toward the end of the 1800s, said: "The moralist has a practical aim: We desire knowledge of right conduct in order to act on it."[13] An older contemporary of Sidgwick, Matthew Arnold, in the opening paragraph of his essay "Marcus Aurelius," expressed the view that was the common cultural outlook at the time:

> The object of systems of morality is to take possession of human life, to save it from being abandoned to passion or allowed to drift at hazard, to give it happiness by establishing it in the practice of virtue; and this object they seek to attain by presenting to human life fixed principles of action, fixed rules of conduct. In its uninspired as well as in its inspired moments, in its days of languor or gloom as well as in its days of sunshine and energy, human life has thus always a clue to follow, and may always be making way toward its goal.[14]

The obvious if not pressing question is: What happened? In particular, was it actually *discovered* that there is no possible body of knowledge about moral distinctions and relations upon the basis of which one person might give moral instruction or guidance to another, and moral institutions of right and law be maintained? I cannot believe it was. Of course that whole group of mid-twentieth-century theorists known as noncognitivists ("emotivists") claimed to discover just that. They had a powerful impact upon ethical theory as professionally practiced, and one from which it has not yet recovered to any significant degree. But I suspect that they and the situation they created are more a symptom of deeper-lying causes than a primary cause in their own right.

Certainly the noncognitivists did not *discover* there was no moral knowledge. Even if there is none, *they* did not discover it. Rather, they were engaged in a project (now long-recognized as failing) of redefining knowledge, and redefining knowledge in such a way that moral distinctions could not be "known" in their new sense. A thin triumph at best, from a rational point of view. But they claimed to have *discovered* that knowledge was not what it had long been taken to be, and that, among other astonishing results, there could, in the nature of the case, be no knowledge of the domain which pre-Moore ethical theory had taken as its subject matter. What had passed as moral knowledge (for them, now, "moral language," a not insignificant change of subject) would have to be reinterpreted as something else altogether. In the shadow to the "linguistic turn" in philosophy, such a reinterpretation is exactly what the noncognitivists (such as Ayer, Stevenson, and later R. M. Hare and the "multifunctionalists") offered. It is important to notice that that effort at reinterpretation has continued unabated up to the present, still with nothing in the way of an established or promising result on the horizon. But this failure has not led people to question the fundamental change (the turn to "concepts" and the "logic of moral discourse") which was instituted by Moore. Rather, they just work all the harder in the direction that took its rise from Moore. Surely something deep is driving them.

To understand what actually happened to bring about the shift from a pre- to a post-Moore understanding of moral knowledge and of the practice of moral theory and guidance, we must look, more broadly, to the universities of the late 1800s and early 1900s. The attempt by the noncognitivists to redefine knowledge was part of a much larger social process that can be aptly called the "secularization of the academy." This process marked a shift that certainly was historically necessary, but it also was one that had many unessential and unforeseen consequences.

A part of what was involved comes out in a statement by John Lyons, made in 1998, on how he understands his role as a university teacher to exclude moral instruction: "I do not claim to be morally superior to my students, to have a source of moral knowledge that they do not have, or to convince them of my authority as a teacher of ethics."[15] Now this statement raises a number of questions. Why would anyone think that to give moral guidance is to presume he or she is morally *superior*? And why think that to have moral knowledge would require that someone have a "special source" that others (who do not have the knowledge) do not have, making that person something special—and then, perhaps, morally superior? And why think giving moral guidance involves trying to get people to believe and act on my *authority*?

A part of the irony here is that Lyons, a professor of French, is clearly teaching that it would be morally odious for him or others to do such things as he mentions. There is no doubt that he is prepared to say and to teach this *in class*, and that it is part of the moral guidance he was given by his teachers and cohorts in his socialization as an academic. He is giving moral guidance to one and all in this very statement in which he is explaining why he does not give moral guidance to students. No doubt the things that Lyons here morally reproaches have been done in the past, and in ways deserving of his reproach. Inappropriate and even immoral moralizing by teachers has been done and is now being done, as Lyons acknowledges; and no doubt there is a special danger of this occurring around social institutions, such as universities.[16] But to avoid these dangers it is not necessary (is it even possible?) to deny the existence or possession of moral knowledge, or to deny that it is possible or morally permissible—or even morally required—to pass such knowledge on in appropriate ways when that is suited to the academic situation. Clearly, in making his remarks Lyons presupposes moral knowledge (he *knows*, no doubt, that it is morally wrong to claim to be morally superior to students), and that it is right to pass this knowledge on. And I venture he would feel free, or even obliged, to make his statements here quoted in the classroom, expecting his students to believe them. But what he is doing is all a part of what was involved in the secularization of the academy. The professor had to get out of the business of moral guidance, which had been so closely involved with religion and religious authority. That will be easy if there is no moral knowledge.

Now secularization, with its essential as well as unessential accompaniments, went hand-in-hand with the professionalization of the academic areas. This might be viewed as the positive side of the divorce from religious institutions. The maintenance of standards in a social enterprise such as the university requires appropriate social organizations. Such maintenance is one mark of a profession, and in the past, it has been necessary for the purposes of guaranteeing the expertise of the individual practitioner and the responsibility of the profession to society at large.

But professionalization requires careful identification of a subject matter so that its boundaries may be respected. Philosophy, and especially ethical theory, has long been concerned with the understanding and guidance of life as a whole. But philosophy after 1900 resolutely turns away from that, as one part of secularization, and increasingly does so as its professionalization develops. This requires the identification of a different and unique subject matter for philosophy. That subject matter turns out to be "concepts," and philosophy dutifully turns out to be "logic." A new subject matter and a new method are then in hand—if we can only find out what they are. Verbally at least, "logic, language, and meaning" are the center of focus in what was promised to be a "revolution in philosophy."

Now it should be noted that, in fairly close correspondence with all this, psychology was trying to become *scientific*. (Actually, becoming scientific was high on the agenda for philosophy as well and was the main reason it "became" logic.) In psychology one must forget about the "soul."[17] Becoming scientific meant *experimental* psychology: laboratories and only what could be studied in them, then behaviorism (Watson), deep theory (Freud and others), and most recently brain theory mixed in with computers. What must be noted here for our concerns is that none of these directions of psychology dealt with, or allowed anyone to deal with, the traditional subject matter of ethical theory, though many efforts were made to include that subject matter: "conduct," will, and character.[18]

But it needs to be stated once again with emphasis that, in all of these developments in philosophy and psychology, and in the fields of professionalized learning in general, no one *discovered* that we cannot know, in the ways routinely practiced by pre-Moore ethical theorists, the nature of rational deliberation and choice, of "conduct," will, and character, and of the primary moral distinctions embedded therein. But regardless of that, choice, will, and character *disappear* from the field of acceptable knowledge, especially as they were thought to be known by observation (personal and of others), conceptualization or abstraction, and theoretical organization—the practice of the pre-Moore consensus.

What is the effect of all this on the status of rights and right claims in guiding human behavior, collectively and individually?

Rights claims were always the most resilient segment of moral discourse in the face of noncognitivism. Even in the heyday of emotivism, many never surrendered the view that such claims stand in logical relations to other statements. They simply could not accept the view that rights claims were inherently nonrational. "I have a right to X" was thought of as logically entailing, "You have an obligation not to interfere." And as logical relations were slowly pried loose from truth, in the progression of ethical theorizing in the mid-1900s, rights claims became even more acceptably "cognitive." Overall, however, the reason why rights talk survived the emotivist onslaught to the extent it did was not because of some insight into the objective, truth-bearing status of rights, but because the social and political situation would not tolerate the idea that opposition to the draft, racial segregation, and economic deprivation were simply matters of taste or feeling. In these matters, the objective reality of right and wrong, justice and injustice, good and evil, and the assurance of knowledge thereof were just undeniable to most citizens, including academics. Rights and justice were too vital to life to dismiss to the realm of the noncognitive.

Unfortunately, however, that did not dispel the cloud over moral reality and knowledge which was cast by their exclusion from the domains of science and by the associated noncognitivist offensive, and which could not but affect the force of claims to *moral* rights. *Legal* rights are, of course, another matter—though with problems of their own—except insofar as they are thought to depend upon a moral foundation. Legal rights are the result of political processes and are sanctioned by government action. They may be either moral or immoral. As important as they are, the moral quality of the society in which they exist is what concerns most people.

The legalities of the treatment of the prisoners in Guantanamo may be endlessly discussed, and no doubt will be. But the two sides are really concerned about whether or not the government of the United States should be permitted to treat those prisoners in ways that are regarded by many as immoral. Classifying them as "enemy combatants" to get around provisions of the Geneva Conventions is a typical maneuver to permit treating people in ways not morally acceptable. One side argues legalities to prevent what they regard as immoral—not just illegal—treatment. The other side argues legalities to *permit* treatment that they themselves would recognize as immoral under most circumstances. Here, as in many other scenes of contemporary life, the moral has no effective standing and is replaced with the political and the legal, which then fail to address the deeper issue of "is it right?"

But if there is no moral reality, or no knowledge of it, then the legal and the political are as far as one can go. What more is there to be concerned about? Persons who would respond to "moral" issues beyond that would be foolish, "unrealistic." They would be worrying themselves, perhaps risking their careers or even their lives, for nothing, or at least for something which no one has knowledge of—perhaps for no more that a personal quirk on their part. That is pretty much where the "knowledge" now acceptable as such to the university leaves us. And this explains why sporadic efforts to teach "professional ethics" have no significant impact upon professional behavior and life. They can find no cognitive foundation for the formation of moral character and for becoming a morally responsible person in all the connections of life. And since the university is the arbiter of what counts as knowledge, it rules out any such foundation from other sources and leaves only ethnic identity (ethical relativism) or nonrational personal commitments to go on. These do not provide a satisfactory basis upon which to confront the widespread abuses of human rights that characterize our contemporary world.

I have repeatedly mentioned the reality of moral goodness and of knowledge of moral goodness. Now I would like to briefly state my view of them and point out how that view positions human rights in the broader context of morally acceptable human existence. Here I cannot argue for my view but only state it and offer a few essential clarifications.

The *morally good person*, I would say, is a person who is effectively intent upon advancing the various goods of human life with which they are effectively in contact in a manner that respects their relative degrees of importance and the extent to which the actions of the person in question can actually promote the existence and maintenance of those goods. Thus, moral goodness (as well as badness) is a matter of the organization of human dispositions and will into a system called "character."

"Character" refers to the settled dispositions to act in certain interrelated ways, given relevant circumstances. Character is expressed in what someone does without thinking, as well as to what someone does after acting without thinking. The actions that come from character will usually persist when the individual is unobserved as well as when the consequences of the action are not what the agent would prefer. A person of good moral character is anyone who, from the deeper and more pervasive dimensions of the self, is intent upon advancing the various goods of human life with which he or she is effectively in contact.

The person who is morally bad or evil is someone who is intent upon the destruction of the various goods of human life with which he or she is effectively in contact, or who is indifferent to the existence and maintenance of those goods.

This orientation of the will toward promotion of human good is the fundamental *moral* distinction: the one which is of primary human interest and from which all the others, moving toward the periphery of the moral life and ethical theory, can be clarified. Examples are the moral value of acts (positive and negative); the nature of moral obligation and responsibility; virtues and vices; the nature and limitations of rights, punishment, rewards, justice, and related issues; the morality of laws and institutions; and what is to be made of moral progress and moral education.

A comprehensive and coherent theory of these matters can, I suggest, be developed only if we start from the distinction between the good and bad will or person—which, admittedly, almost no one is currently prepared to discuss. That is one of the outcomes of ethical theorizing through the twentieth century. It is directly opposite to the consensus of the latter decades of the nineteenth century, for which, as we have noted, the fundamental subject of ethical theorizing was the will and its character.[19]

I believe that the orientation of the will provides the fundamental moral distinction because it is what ordinary human beings, not confused or misled by theories of various kinds, naturally and constantly employ in the ordinary contexts of life, both with reference to themselves (a touchstone for moral theory) and with reference to others (where it is employed with much less clarity and assurance). And I also believe that this is the fundamental moral distinction because it seems to me the one most consistently present at the heart of the tradition of moral thought that runs from Socrates to Sidgwick—all of the twists and turns of that tradition notwithstanding.

Just consider the role of "the good" in Plato, Aristotle, and Augustine, for example, stripped, if possible, of all the intellectual campaigns and skirmishes surrounding it. Consider Aquinas's statement:

> [This] is the first precept of law, that *good is to be done and promoted, and evil is to be avoided*. All other precepts of the natural law are based upon this; so that all the things which the practical reason naturally apprehends as man's good belong to the precepts of the natural law under the form of things to be done or avoided.[20]

Or consider how Sidgwick arrives at his "maxim of Benevolence"—"that each one is morally bound to regard the good of any other individual as much as his own, except in so far as he judges it to be less, when impartially viewed, or less certainly knowable or attainable by him."[21] Sidgwick tried hard to incorporate his intuitions of justice and of prudence into this crowning maxim, but with little obvious success.

A few further clarifications must be made. Firstly, I have spoken of the goods of human life in the plural, and have spoken of goods with which we are in *effective* contact (can do something about). The good will is manifested in its active caring for *particular* goods that we can do something about, not primarily in dreaming of "the greatest happiness of the greatest number" or even of my own "happiness" or of "duty for duty's sake." Generally speaking, thinking in high-level abstractions will always defeat moral will in practice. As Bradley and others before him clearly saw, "my station and its duties" is nearly, but not quite, the whole moral scene, and it can never be simply bypassed on the way to "larger" and presumably more important things.

One of the major miscues of ethical theory since the 1960s has been, in my opinion, its almost total absorption in social and political issues. This is for reasons already indicated, and, of course, these issues do also concern vital human goods. They are important, and we should always do what we can for them. But moral theory simply will not coherently and comprehensively come together from their point of view. They do not essentially involve the center of moral reality, the will and character.

Secondly, among human goods (things that are *good for* human beings and enable them to flourish) are human beings and certain relationships to them, and, especially, *good* human beings—that is, human beings that fit the above description. A person's own well-being is a human good, to that person and to others, as is what Kant called the moral "perfection" of oneself. Of course, nontoxic water and food, a clean and safe environment, opportunities to learn and to work, stable family and community relations, and so forth fall on the list of particular human goods. (Most of the stuff for sale in our society probably does not.) Moral rights are primary human goods, and therefore the good person, in my view, will be deeply committed to their recognition and full deployment.

There seems to me no necessity of having a complete list of human goods or a tight definition of what something must be like to be on the list. Marginal issues, "lifeboat" cases, and the finer points of conceptual distinction are interesting exercises and have a point for philosophical training, but it is not empirically confirmable, to say the least, that the chances of having a good will or being a good person improve with philosophical training in ethical theory as that has been recently understood. It is necessary for the purposes of being a good or bad person that he or she has a good general understanding of proximate human goods and of how they are affected by action. And that is also what we need for the understanding of the good will and the goodness of the individual. We do not have to know what individuals would do in a lifeboat situation to know whether or not they have good will, though what they do in such situations may throw light on who they are, or on *how* good (or bad) they are. The appropriate response to actions in extreme situations may not be a moral judgment at all, but one of pity or admiration, of the tragic sense of life or of amazement at what humans are capable of.

Thirdly, the will to advance the goods of human life with which anyone comes into contact is inseparable from the will to find out how to do it and do it appropriately. If someone truly wills the end, that person wills the means, and coming to understand the goods which we effect, and their conditions and interconnections, is inseparable from the objectives of the good person and the good will. Thus, knowledge, understanding, and rationality are themselves human goods, to be appropriately pursued for their own sakes, but also because they are absolutely necessary for moral self-realization as here described. Formal rationality, defined without reference to particular ends or values, is fundamental to the good will, but is not sufficient to it.

Clearly, knowledge of moral distinctions depends upon knowledge of the human self, the subject of those distinctions. What Elizabeth Anscombe said decades ago about the need to quit doing moral theory until we have an adequate "moral psychology" seems very sensible in the light of how knowledge is now understood in the institutions of knowledge.[22] Of course we *cannot* stop theorizing. We have to continue thinking about moral distinctions because we have to act and have to find out how to act. But we can never regain the self (will, character) as a subject of knowledge so long as we insist in forcing the self into a scientistic ("naturalistic") mold. Moral knowledge disappears with authentic self-knowledge, which disappears along with the ascendancy of "naturalism" (scientism). Moral character is not a matter of the physical body at any level of refinement or of its "natural" relations to world and society. As long as the physical realm is regarded as the only subject of knowledge, there will be no moral knowledge and no cognitive foundation of the moral life. This is exactly where we stand today in Western culture and in the university system that presides over it on its epistemic side.

Moral rights have as their primary role resistance against the attitudes and actions of people and arrangements of evil intent. But in order for them to be effective in that role, they must be urged and supported by multitudes of people of good will: people of established benevolence, wisdom, prudence, courage, and temperance. Such people can only support their lives upon their experience of the reality of moral distinctions and values and upon a clear knowledge of their reality and nature. Upon that foundation, when widely shared, moral and then legal rights can frame societies and governments that are not merely *just*, as defined by rights, but are contexts of human flourishing. Pull that foundation away, and justice and rights themselves will not flourish—though we must have them and must always struggle to do the best we can by them. The point is not that we should wait for people to be highly developed or morally perfect to push for the upholding and expansion of rights. We should always do what we can to that end. It is an essential part of individual and corporate moral enculturation and progress. But what we can accomplish thereby depends upon the moral character of multitudes of people nourished and directed by knowledge of the reality and nature of moral values and distinctions. Ironically, the very institutions of knowledge today are turned against that upon which a high level of moral goodness in individuals and society depends.

## Notes

1. Clark Butler, *Human Rights Ethics* (forthcoming), p. 21.
2. (Chicago: University of Chicago Press, 1996).
3. *Outlines of a Critical Theory of Ethics*, 1st ed. (Ann Arbor, MI.: Regis-

ter Publishing Company, 1891). References here are to John Dewey, *The Early Works 1882–1898: Essays and Outlines of a Critical Theory of Ethics* (Carbondale, IL: Southern Illinois University Press, 1969). Hereafter this book will be cited parenthetically as *Outlines* in the text.

4. John Dewey and James H. Tufts, *Ethics* (New York: Henry Holt, 1908). Hereafter this book will be cited parenthetically as *Ethics* in the text.

5. John H. Muirhead, *The Elements of Ethics*, 3rd ed. (London: John Murray, 1928).

6. John S. Mackenzie, *A Manual of Ethics*, 4th ed. (London: W.B. Clive, University Tutorial Press, 1900). Hereafter this book will be cited parenthetically as *Manual* in the text.

7. The metaphysics of "internal relations" dominates the thought of Green and of most of his followers, and certainly that of Dewey.

8. T.H. Green, *Prolegomena to Ethics*, 2nd ed., pp. 154, 155. (Oxford: Clarendon Press, 1884), pp. 160–161. New edition, ed. David O. Brink (Oxford: Clarendon Press, 2003), pp. 174–175.

9. James Seth, *A Study of Ethical Principles*, 12th ed. (New York: Charles Scribner's Sons, 1911), p. 5.

10. R. G. Collingwood, *An Autobiography* (Oxford: Oxford University Press, 1939), p. 17.

11. Alasdair MacIntyre, *After Virtue*, 2nd ed. (Notre Dame, IN.: University of Notre Dame Press, 1984), p. 23.

12. David Hume, *An Enquiry Concerning the Principles of Morals*, ed. L.A. Selby-Bigge (Oxford: Clarendon Press, 2nd ed., 1902), section 1, p. 173.

13. Henry Sidgwick, *The Methods of Ethics*, 7th ed. (New York: Dover Publications, 1966), p. 5. See also Henry Sidgwick, *Practical Ethics: A Collections of Addresses and Essays* (New York and Oxford: Oxford University Press) for many clear statements on the point here at issue.

14. Matthew Arnold, "Marcus Aurelius," *Essays in Criticism: First Series*, vol. 1 (New York: Macmillan, 1930).

15. John D. Lyons, "Upon What Authority Might We Teach Morality?" *Philosophy and Literature*, 22 (1998): 155–160; quotation p. 160. This is one contribution to a "Symposium: Is Morality a Non-Aim of Education?" pp. 136–199 of that volume.

16. Lyons, p. 155.

17. See Edward Reed's marvelous book *From Soul to Mind* (New Haven: Yale University Press, 1997).

18. See how Owen Flanagen tries to accomplish this in his entertaining book *The Problem of the Soul* (New York: Basic Books, 2002). The title misleads.

The problem dealt with is the problem of saving all that matters in human life once it is decided that there is no soul. This book is the current exemplar of a genre that arises in the seventeenth century and runs through works like Ludwig Büchner's *Force and Matter*, the writings of Ernst Haeckel, and Carl Sagan's *Cosmos*. The effort to "save" moral reality and knowledge strictly within the framework of physical reality is noble but hardly successful.

19. See T. H. Green, *Prolegomena to Ethics*; Bradley; Sidgwick, *The Methods of Ethics*; and Dewey, *Outlines*.

20. Saint Thomas Aquinas, *Treatise on Law*, Question XCIV, 2nd Article. Many editions.

21. Sidgwick, *Methods of Ethics*, p. 382.

22. See the opening paragraph of her "Modern Moral Philosophy," *Philosophy*, 33:1–19 (1958), and reprinted in G. E. M. Anscombe, *Ethics, Religion and Politics* (Minneapolis: University of Minnesota Press, 1981), pp. 26–42.

# Contributors

### Clark Butler

Clark Butler is Professor of Philosophy at Purdue University on the Indiana University-Purdue University Fort Wayne Campus and Director of the IPFW Institute for Human Rights. He is the author of five books, including a life in letters on Hegel. His translation of Hegel's *Lectures on Logic* is forthcoming with Indiana University Press. A past Principal Researcher for the National Endowment for the Humanities, he received the Outstanding Research Award at Indiana University-Purdue University Fort Wayne for 2005. His defense of human rights and the ethics of respect for such rights is forthcoming with Editions RODOPI (Amsterdam).

### Jennifer Caseldine-Bracht

Jennifer Caseldine-Bracht holds an M.A. in philosophy from Purdue University, West Lafayette. She received her B.A. from Purdue at Indiana University-Purdue University Fort Wayne, and currently teaches as an Associate Faculty member there. Her primary interests are social and political philosophy, ethics, and logic.

### William Durland

William Durland is an attorney specializing in constitutional and international law cases in Federal courts on human rights and civil liberties. He received his B.A. from Bucknell University, his M.A. from the University of Notre Dame, a J.D. from Georgetown University Law Center with a Ph.D. from the Union Graduate School at Antioch College. He currently teaches part-time at Pikes Peak Community College and is Legal Director of the Center on Law and Human Rights, Colorado Springs, CO. His books include *James Madison and the Historical Crisis in American Federalism* and *Immoral Wars,* and *Illegal Laws: Theology, Law, and Peacemaking in the Palestine-Israeli Conflict*. He is Vice-Chair of the Colorado Springs chapter of the ACLU.

ANISSEH VAN ENGELAND-NOURAI

Anisseh van Engeland-Nourai is a doctoral candidate at the Institut d'Etudes Politiques in Paris, France. She has been a visiting researcher at Harvard Law School. She holds a Masters of Law from the Harvard Law School, a Masters in International Relations (Paris II,), and a Masters in Iranian Studies (Paris III Sorbonne). She is currently employed by the International Committee of the Red Cross to a Protection and Assistance Delegate.

MILTON FISK

Milton Fisk is Professor Emeritus of Philosophy at Indiana University in Bloomington, Indiana. He received his doctorate from Yale University. Prior to coming to Indiana University, he held faculty positions at Notre Dame and Yale. He is author of *Nature and Necessity* (1973), *Ethics and Society* (1980), *The State and Justice* (1989), *Toward a Healthy Society* 2000, and *Bienes Públicos y Justicia Radical* (2004). He served as a board member of the American Philosophical Association—Central Division, and has served on the steering committee of the Radical Philosophical Association.

SABY GHOSHRAY

Saby Ghoshray, Vice-President for Development, World Compliance Company, which specializes is security checks in corporate job searches. He holds an MBA from Cornell University and a Ph.D. from Florida International University. He has published over sixty articles on subjects ranging from the relation of domestic jurisprudence to international law, transnational criminal law, military tribunals, intellectual property in Transnational jurisdictions, and the law of cyberspace.

RICHARD L. JOHNSON

Richard L. Johnson, Professor of German and Peace Studies at Indiana University-Purdue University, Fort Wayne, received his Ph.D. in Germanic Languages and Literatures in 1968 from Harvard University. He has published research on German literature and culture and on nonviolent social movements, including nonviolent alternatives to battery, European peace movements, Aung San Suu Kyi, and Mahatma Gandhi. He wrote *Ich schreibe mir die Seele frei* (I Write my Soul Free), and he edited *Gandhi's Experiments with Truth: Essential Writings by and about Mahatma Gandhi*, which is forthcoming.

## William L. McBride

William L. McBride is Arthur G. Hansen Distinguished Professor of Philosophy at Purdue University—West Lafayette and Secretary General of the International Federation of Philosophical Societies (FISP). He received his B.A. from Georgetown University and his M.A. and Ph.D. from Yale University, where he also taught for several years before moving to Purdue. He is Past President of the North American Society for Social Philosophy. He has authored more than 190 published articles, book chapters, and book reviews and has authored, edited, or co-edited nineteen volumes, among them *Sartre's Political Theory*, *Philosophical Reflections on the Changes in Eastern Europe* and *From Yugoslav Praxis to Global Pathos: Anti-Hegemonic Post-Post-Marxist Essays*.

## David Rudenstine

David Rudenstine is the Dean of the Benjamin N. Cardozo School of Law, Yeshiva University, New York, as well as Sheldon H. Solow Professor of Law. He received a B.A. and a Masters in Art in Teaching from Yale University and a J.D. degree from New York University School of Law. He is the author of the Pulitzer Prize nominated *The Day the Presses Stopped: A History of the Pentagon Papers Case.*, selected by *Publisher's Weekly* as one of the year's best books. He has written or co-authored two other books as well as many scholarly articles in constitutional law, cultural property, freedom of expression, criminal justice, and labor arbitration. In 2000–2001 he was an inaugural Fellow in the Law and Public Affairs Program and Visiting Professor of Public and International Affairs at Princeton University, where he gave the tenth annual Helen Buchanan Seeger lecture at the Center for Hellenic Studies. He has also been a legal services attorney, Director of the Citizens' Inquiry into Parole and Criminal Justice, Counsel to the National News Council, and Acting Director of the New York Civil Liberties Union. Dean Rudenstine has had substantial litigation experience in federal and state courts, and he has served as a labor arbitrator and a court appointed mediator. He has been a member of the Labor and Employment Law Committee of the Association of the Bar of the City of New York, serving as its Chair for three years.

## Dallas Willard

Dallas Willard is Professor of Philosophy at the University of Southern California. Holding his Ph.D. from the University of Wisconsin, he is an award-winning teacher and writes on moral philosophy. He is an internationally recognized authority on the philosophy of Edmund Husserl. Beyond his work in academic philosophy, he is also a nationally acclaimed Christian inspirational author.

# INDEX

*Abrams v. United States*, 20
Abu Graib, 2, 9, 43–44, 50, 144
Afghanistan, 1, 16, 36, 38, 39, 43, 44, 48, 54, 59, 60, 68, 72–73, 85, 86, 87, 89, 90, 93, 94, 97, 103, 104, 105, 108, 110
Al Halabi, Ahmed, 44
Al Odah, Fawzi Khalid Abdullah Fahad, 16
Al Qaeda, 35–36, 38–39, 53–54, 56, 60–61, 88, 91, 95, 96, 103, 110
Algeria, 76, 100?
Alien and Sedition Acts (1798), 48
the alien other, 10, 119–129, 161
aliens, 3, 6–7, 9–10, 11, 16, 18, 22, 25, 34–36, 41, 43–46, 48, 52, 58–59, 82, 98, 115, 119, 123, 125, 137, 145, 151
Alito, Samuel A., 32
American Center on Constitutional Rights, 50
American Friends Service Committee, 47
American Mexican War, 47
Anscombe, Elizabeth, 175
applied ethics, 166
Arnold, Matthew, 168
Ashcroft, John, 57, 57
Augustine, St., 174
Australia, 16, 105
Ayer, A. J., 168

Bakr, Calif Abu, 62

Berg, Thomas S., 60
Bin Laden, Osama, 35, 38, 63, 84
Black, Hugo, 21–22, 25–26
Blackmun, Harry, 24
Bradley, F. H., 163, 174
Brandeis, Louis, 20
Brussels, 5
Burger, Warren, 24
Bush, George, 27–29, 32, 36–38, 43–44, 49, 51, 53, 57, 61–68, 72, 81, 84, 88, 92, 95, 101, 106, 111, 114
Butler, Clark, 162

capitalism, 1, 4, 133, 147
Cato Institute, 59
China, 4, 5, 11, 26
civil rights, 3, 52, 68, 102, 129
Clinton, Bill, 27, 56, 143
closed society, 132–143
Collingwood, R. G., 166
Communist Party, USA, 22–23
Convention Against Torture and Other Cruel, Inhuman, or Degrading Treatment of Prisoners, 52, 55–57, 63
Convention on the Amelioration of the Condition of the Wounded and Sick in Armed Forces, 53
Council of Europe, 2
crimes against humanity, 76, 84, 100
Cuba, 16–17, 37, 82–83, 96, 102, 103–104, 106

democracy, 1, 4, 5, 10, 17, 23, 28, 29–30, 33, 35, 43, 46, 112, 122, 138, 141–142, 149, 154, 156, 157
Dewey, John, 164, 167
Diego Garcia Island, 46
dialogue, 3–8, 10, 12, 72
dignity, 26, 57, 63, 70, 112, 144, 148, 150, 153, 157, 161, 162
diversity, 2, 156
Doctors Without Frontiers, 72, 73
Dunant, Henry, 53
duty consciousness, 162

economic growth, 11, 146, 157
economic refugees, 6, 10
Egypt, 6, 46
enemy combatants, 8–9, 15, 17–19, 172
*Escobedo v. Illinois*, 34
Espionage Act (1917), 19
ethical theory, 163–164
　e.t. and social and political philosophy, 174
European Court of Human Rights, 2
European Union, 2, 4–5

Falluja, 100
farm subsidies, 11
*Federalist Papers*, 29–30
Federalist Party, 48
Fiddler, Ronald, 80
foreign aid, 11
Four Freedoms Speech, 3
France, 4, 9, 11, 68–69
Freud, Sigmund, 171
freedom of speech, 3, 19–20, 22–23
freedom of thought, 3, 7, 10, 12

Gandhi, 119–129
Geneva Conventions, 8–9, 31, 33, 39, 41, 44, 48, 51, 52–63, 66–77, 89, 90–92, 95, 101, 110, 112, 114, 116, 172
Germany, 4–5, 9, 22, 26, 33, 50, 83, 99, 106, 134–135
Gibbard, Alan, 163
Ginsberg, Ruth Bader, 27, 37, 41, 42
global warming, 5
Gonzales, Alberto R., 54–55, 57
good will, 165
Green, T. H., 163
Guantanamo Bay camp, 2, 6–8, 10, 16–17, 36–37, 43–44, 50, 61, 81–82, 98, 102, 103, 104

Habib, Mamdouh, 16
Habibhllah, Mullah, 50
habeas corpus, 16–19, 25, 26, 36, 38, 42, 43, 47, 58–60, 82, 83, 98, 99, 105, 115
Hague Conventions, 33, 48, 56, 95, 110, 116
*Hamdan v. Rumsfield*, 31, 32, 44, 51, 58, 60
Hamdi, Yaser Esam, 25, 28, 36–44, 48, 49, 98, 105
Hamilton, Alexander, 29–30
Hare, R. M., 163, 168
Harlan, John, 24
Hebrews, 6
Hegel, Georg Wilhelm Friedrich, 10, 133
Hicks, David, 16
Hinduism, 62, 120, 122, 124, 127, 129
Hitler, Adolf, 45
Hobbes, Thomas, 35, 133
Holmes, Oliver Wendell, 19–20, 31
human rights, 2–3, 6–12, 15–30, 36–37, 43–46, 49, 42–63, 66–77, 87, 92–93, 102, 11, 113, 128, 136–158, 172, 173
　h.r. education, 2–3, 30
　h.r. ethics, 12
　h.r. and hospitality, 6
　legal h.r., 161
humanitarian law, 8, 61, 66–77, 89, 91, 92–93, 97, 100, 102, 109, 112
humanitarian intervention, 72
humanitarian workers, 72
Hume, David, 16, 168

immigration, 10–11, 36, 43, 132–143
India, 5, 119–130, 148
International Committee of the Red Cross, 53, 56, 66–77, 69, 70, 73, 74, 103
International Criminal Court, 76, 101
International Labor Organization, 146, 149, 158, 159
international law, 8–9, 33, 35, 39, 43–45, 51, 53, 55–57, 60–63, 66, 70, 74, 76, 79, 81–116, 137
Iqbal, Assif, 56, 63
Iraq, 1, 4, 7, 9, 15, 27, 28, 35–36, 39, 43–44, 48, 50, 51, 57, 72–73, 87
Islam, 10, 35

Israel, 35, 44, 46, 48, 50, 76, 138

Japan, 33, 107
Japanese internment, 9, 20–22, 49
Johnson, Lyndon B., 29
*Johnson v. Eisentrager*, 25, 83, 98, 99, 100, 105, 106, 115
Jordan, 46
justice, 9, 26, 35, 52, 61, 84, 85, 87, 101, 107, 112, 120–122, 126, 128, 141, 143, 148, 150, 152, 171, 173, 174, 176
U.S. criminal justice system, 94–97

Kadidal, Shane, 60
Kant, Immanuel, 141, 159, 161, 164, 175
Khandahar, 56
Kennedy, Stephen Breyer, 37, 42, 99
King, Jr., Martin Luther, 52
Korematsu, Fred, 21–22, 41
Kosovo, 1, 73
Kuwait, 16, 105

Lafayette, Marquis de, 9
Lebanon, 44, 46
libertarianism, 3, 8, 153
Lincoln, Abraham, 47, 49
Lindh, Matthew, 36, 48
Locke, John, 35, 139
Lucenti, Martin, 61
Lyons, John, 169–170

majority vote, 7, 56–57
Madison, James, 29–30
Marr, Malanie, 42–43, 59
Mabbs, Michael, 38–39
MacIntyre, Alasdair, 163, 167
MacKenzie, John S., 164
Manu, Code of, 62
Marcuse, Herbert, 10
Marx, Karl, 11, 133, 143
Martens Clause, 56–57
Mayfield, Brandon, 58
McCarthy, Joseph, 22
McCurry, Michael, 27
McNabb-Mallory Rule, 33–34
mercenaries, 6, 9
metaethics, 12, 166
military-humanitarian intervention, 73
*Miranda v. Arizona*, 34
Mohammed, Khalid Sheikh, 36
Montesquieu, Charles Louis, 35

Moore, G.E, 163, 164
moral education, 9, 166–168
the moral good, 162, 173–174
moral judgment, 164
the morally good will, 173
moral knowledge, 162–166
Moussaoui, Zacharias, 36–37, 48
Muirhead, John H., 158
Murphy, Frank, 21–22, 49

Napoleon, 9
Neoconservatism, 5–8, 46
*New York Times*, 23–24, 60
Non-Detention Act, 60
non-cognitivism, 163, 166
non-governmental organizations, 72, 74, 76, 129
normative ethics, 11–12, 166
normative relativism, 12
Northern Alliance, 58
Nuremburg Military Tribunal, 36, 37, 49, 100

Old Europe, 5
O'Connor, Sandra Day, 25, 32, 37
open society, 10, 28, 136

pacifism, 5, 47
Padilla, Jose, 26, 36, 41–44, 58–59
Palestine, 44, 51
Pakistan, 35, 44, 59, 108, 129
Patriot Act, 28, 35–36, 52, 68, 140
peace, 4, 20, 23, 29, 33, 35, 45, 63, 67–68, 70, 90, 119–129, 141, 154
Pearl Harbor, 21–22, 33
Pentagon Papers, 23–25
persons, 45, 59, 173
philosophy, 161–176
    linguistic turn in p., 168
    political p., 46, 141
Plato, 133, 136, 142, 174
political realism, 8
Popper, Karl, 10, 136
poverty, 10–11, 119, 120, 125–127, 146–158
Powell, Colin, 54
preemptive strike, 4–5, 33
prisoners of war, 6, 33, 44, 53–55, 63, 73–74, 81, 89–90, 91, 94, 95, 97, 100, 101, 110, 114, 115, 172
privacy, 36, 61, 68, 71, 80

professional ethics, 172
racism, 50, 119, 122–123
Ramadan, Tariq, 68
Rasul, Shafiq, 15–19, 25–28, 48, 56, 59, 68, 98–101, 115
Rawls, 133–135, 137, 138, 141, 154, 155, 159, 163, 167
Rehnquist, William H., 32, 37, 42
Reuben, Julie, 163
Rice, Condoleeza, 54
rights, 162, 171
  legal r., 172
  moral r., 172, 176
  r. consciousness, 162
Roberts, John, 10, 32
Roman Empire, 133
Roosevelt, Franklin Delano, 3, 20, 49
Rousseau, Jean-Jacques, 7, 35, 140, 142
Russia, 5, 56, 112, 133

Saudi Arabia, 35, 43
Scalia, Antonin, 18, 37, 40, 41, 49, 99, 100, 115
secularization, 168–170
security, 1, 6–8, 10, 16, 19, 23–24, 27–30, 35, 38, 40, 45–47, 51–62, 68–71, 75, 81, 86–88, 93, 97, 107, 108, 113, 136–137, 143
Seth, James, 165
Sheffer, David, 56
Shirer, William, 45
Sidgwick, Henry, 168, 174
Smith Act (1940), 22
socialism, 2–3
social science, 3
social services, 5
Socrates, 124, 142, 167, 174
soft American empire, 1–5, 35
Souter, David, 37, 41, 42
sovereignty, 2–3, 10, 81–83, 99, 100, 102, 106
Soviet Union, 1, 4, 5, 29, 129, 134, 140
Stevens, John Paul, 25, 26, 32, 37, 40, 41, 62, 115
Stevenson, C. L., 168
Strasbourg, 5
Syria, 44, 46, 62
Switzerland, 53

Taliban, 16, 36, 38–39, 48, 53–54, 61, 84–86, 88–91, 99, 103, 105, 108

terrorism, 8, 9, 11, 16, 35, 38, 46, 49, 53, 66–77, 81, 84, 88, 94, 101–102, 109, 110, 111, 112, 114, 126, 146
Thomas, St., 174
Thomas, Clarence, 37, 41
de Tocqueville, Alexis, 15
Alien Tort Claims Act, 83
torture, 6, 26, 33–36, 43, 51, 52, 55, 56, 57, 61, 63, 69, 70, 75, 80,m93, 101, 113–114, 146
Tufts, James H., 164

United Kingdom, 68, 102
  British Empire, 119–129
United Nations, 2–5, 12, 33, 61, 95, 92, 93, 100, 144, 146, 149, 158
  Convention against Torture and Other Cruel, Inhuman, or Degrading Treatment, 52, 55–57, 63
  Human Rights Commission (Council), 158
  International Covenant on Civil and Political Rights, 3, 112
  International Covenant on Economic, Social, and Cultural Rights, 148, 159
  Universal Declaration of Human Rights, 1–3, 12, 68, 69, 92, 112, 137–138, 148–153, 156, 158
United States, 1–6, 9, 10, 15–30, 33, 36–39, 45, 48, 50, 52–53, 63, 66, 70, 72–74, 76, 79, 80–116, 132, 136, 140–141, 147–148, 155, 158, 159, 164, 172
U.S. Central Intelligence Agency, 44, 51, 60
U.S. citizens, 29, 30, 59
U.S. Congress, 1, 16, 19, 20, 22, 26–30, 38–41, 44, 46–49, 51, 60, 62, 68, 97, 98, 110, 132, 148, 153
U.S. Constitution, 2, 8, 19–20, 24, 26, 29, 31, 34, 37, 38, 39, 40, 42–46, 48–50, 52, 58–60, 63, 81, 83, 85, 89, 109, 1l1, 112
1st Amendment, 3, 19–20, 22–23
5th Amendment, 59
6th Amendment, 35
13th Amendment, 19
14th Amendment, 45
U.S. Department of Homeland Security, 52
U.S. Federal Bureau of Investigation, 47

U.S. Justice Department, 43, 44, 47
U.S. Military Tribunals, 8, 9, 26, 31, 32, 36–47, 40, 44, 48, 49, 51, 62, 80–116
U.S. Presidency, 1–2, 15–30, 32, 36, 38, 41–44, 47, 48, 49, 53–55, 57, 60, 67, 81, 84, 87, 105, 109
U.S. Secretary of Defense, 17–18, 38, 42, 84
U.S. Senate Armed Services Committee, 56
U.S. sovereignty, 2–3, 99, 100
U.S. Supreme Court, 7–8, 9, 13, 15–30
U.S. Uniform Code of Military Justice, 44, 51, 84, 85
judicial correction of executive, 8–9, 15, 23, 27–30
U.S. as world policeman, 10
universities, 163–176
unlawful combatants, 74, 79, 88, 90, 95, 96, 111, 114

Uzbekistan, 46

Vietnam, 9, 23

wages, 11, 147–158
war crimes, 26, 57, 76, 90, 100, 107
Walzer, Michael, 141
War on Terror, 35, 36, 43, 49, 80, 81, 88, 89, 91, 94, 95, 100, 101, 102, 105, 106, 115
*Washington Post*, 24, 61
Watson, John B., 171
weapons of mass destruction, 35, 57
Western Civilization, 163
Williams, Bernard, 163
*Wong Wing v. the United States,* 59
World Trade Organization, 11
World War I, 19, 134
World War II, 1, 9, 10, 20–22, 23, 33, 37, 49, 91, 107, 111, 134, 149